RESTORATIVE JUSTICE
101

Styles of Restorative Justice

DR. MAXWELL SHIMBA

Shimba Publishing LLC

Printed in the United States of America

First Printing Edition 2024

SHIMBA
PUBLISHING

Table of Contents

Introduction

Introduction to Restorative Justice Styles

Restorative justice is a powerful approach to addressing harm and fostering healing, rooted in the philosophy that justice should center on repairing harm rather than simply punishing the offender. Unlike traditional justice models, which often prioritize retribution and incarceration, restorative justice focuses on the needs of the victims, the responsibilities of offenders, and the well-being of the broader community. At its core, it seeks to create a sense of balance and restoration, making individuals and communities whole again after harm has occurred.

What is Restorative Justice?

Restorative justice is both a philosophy and a set of practices. Philosophically, it is grounded in values such as empathy, accountability, respect, and communal well-being. It is not merely about assigning blame or administering punishment; rather, it aims to foster healing by involving all parties affected by harm. Victims, offenders, and community members engage in a process where they express their experiences, discuss the impacts of the harm, and determine ways to make amends. This approach allows for personal accountability and meaningful restoration, facilitating healing on multiple levels.

Key Principles of Restorative Justice

1. Accountability: Restorative justice encourages offenders to take responsibility for their actions. Unlike traditional systems where

the focus is on guilt and punishment, restorative justice asks the offender to face the harm they've caused, acknowledge it, and commit to making amends.

2. Repairing Harm: The primary objective of restorative justice is to repair the harm done. This can take the form of apologies, restitution, or actions that serve to restore balance to the affected parties and the community.

3. Involving All Affected Parties: Restorative justice involves all those impacted by harm, including victims, offenders, and community members. Through open dialogue, each party has the opportunity to share their experiences, needs, and perspectives, leading to a collective sense of healing.

4. Transformative Impact on Community: By fostering understanding, empathy, and accountability, restorative justice has the power to transform communities. It builds stronger social bonds, reduces future offenses, and creates a more inclusive approach to justice.

Restorative Justice as a Practice

Restorative justice can take many forms, each tailored to the unique needs and dynamics of the situation. Different styles and practices have emerged globally, each reflecting the cultural, social, and legal contexts in which they were developed. From indigenous practices rooted in communal responsibility to formalized conferencing and mediation, restorative justice has proven adaptable and effective in addressing various types of harm.

Each restorative justice practice falls under a larger restorative framework, such as:

- Community Conferencing: Engages all parties in a structured meeting to discuss the harm and how to make things right.
- Circles and Restorative Circles: Utilize a circle format where participants take turns speaking, guided by a facilitator who ensures respect and focus.
- Victim-Offender Mediation: Provides victims and offenders the opportunity to communicate in a safe, facilitated environment.
- Truth and Reconciliation Processes: Often used in contexts of widespread harm, these processes promote collective healing and historical understanding.

The Importance of Restorative Justice Today

In a world where punitive justice often leads to cycles of harm and alienation, restorative justice offers a hopeful alternative. Its emphasis on empathy and accountability allows individuals to move beyond a mere transaction of punishment and fosters true healing. Restorative justice creates a pathway for a just and compassionate society, one where individuals, families, and communities are empowered to take an active role in addressing harm, preventing future injustices, and restoring peace.

Conclusion

Restorative justice is more than a reaction to wrongdoing; it is a proactive approach to cultivating compassion, responsibility, and healing. This book explores the diverse styles of restorative justice and demonstrates how they can be applied in various settings to transform not only individuals but also entire communities. In the chapters that follow, we will delve into the specifics of each restorative justice style, examining their unique methods, benefits, and the transformative potential they bring to justice systems and communities around the world.

Brief History of Restorative Justice and Its Global Influence

Restorative justice has deep historical roots, with origins traceable to indigenous and traditional societies worldwide. Long before modern legal systems emerged, communities dealt with conflict and harm through collective, restorative methods. Rather than punitive measures, these societies prioritized restoring harmony, focusing on repairing relationships, reintegrating individuals, and ensuring that wrongdoers took responsibility within a communal framework.

Origins in Indigenous and Traditional Societies

Many indigenous groups around the world, including the Māori of New Zealand, Native American tribes in North America, and various First Nations communities in Canada, practiced restorative justice long before it became formalized. For example:

- Māori Justice Practices: In Māori culture, "whānau" (extended family) and "hapū" (sub-tribe) gatherings were commonly used to address wrongdoing. These gatherings allowed all parties involved to discuss harm, its impact on the community, and appropriate ways to repair it. Māori principles like "whanaungatanga" (connectedness) and "manaakitanga" (care for others) are central to restorative practices, fostering a collective approach to justice.

- Native American Peacemaking Circles: In many Native American communities, Peacemaking Circles were a means of resolving disputes and addressing harm. These circles involved community members sitting together in a circle, sharing perspectives, and collaboratively determining solutions. Circles emphasized respect, healing, and restoration rather than punishment.

- Ubuntu and African Justice Systems: In African cultures, the concept of "ubuntu" (which translates to "I am because we are") emphasizes interdependence and community harmony. Traditional justice systems in Africa, such as the "gacaca" courts in Rwanda, prioritize restoring balance and promoting reconciliation among community members rather than merely punishing offenders.

These traditional practices provided the foundation for restorative justice as we know it today, and they continue to influence modern restorative practices globally.

Revival of Restorative Justice in the 20th Century

The modern restorative justice movement began to take shape in the 1970s, largely in response to growing dissatisfaction with traditional criminal justice systems. High recidivism rates, prison overcrowding, and a lack of victim support revealed significant limitations within punitive models. At the same time, criminologists and social justice advocates were exploring alternative approaches to justice that focused on healing and prevention.

- Victim-Offender Reconciliation Programs (VORP): One of the first formalized restorative justice programs was established in Kitchener, Ontario, Canada, in 1974. A local probation officer and a church-based community group developed a program allowing victims and offenders to meet and discuss the impact of the crime. This early victim-offender reconciliation program set the stage for other countries to adopt similar practices.

- Expansion in North America and Europe: By the 1980s and 1990s, restorative justice gained momentum across North America and Europe. Restorative programs, such as victim-offender mediation and family group conferencing, were introduced into juvenile justice systems. Governments and criminal justice agencies recognized the value of restorative practices in reducing recidivism and strengthening community ties.

- Truth and Reconciliation Commissions: The South African Truth and Reconciliation Commission (TRC), established in 1995, marked a pivotal moment for restorative justice on a global scale. The TRC was tasked with addressing the gross human rights violations committed under apartheid, allowing victims and perpetrators to share their experiences publicly. This approach emphasized the importance of national healing and reconciliation, influencing subsequent restorative justice models worldwide.

Influence of Restorative Justice Around the World

Restorative justice has continued to evolve and expand globally, shaping criminal justice systems, educational institutions, and communities. The philosophy of restorative justice has inspired a range of practices, from community-based mediation programs to institutional reforms, with far-reaching impact.

- Europe: Countries such as the United Kingdom, Norway, and Finland have incorporated restorative justice into their criminal justice systems. In the UK, restorative practices are applied in schools, prisons, and community settings, emphasizing prevention and rehabilitation. Norway's prison system, known for its humane and restorative approach, has gained international recognition for its low recidivism rates and focus on reintegration.

- New Zealand: New Zealand has become a leader in restorative justice, especially in its juvenile justice system. Influenced by Māori concepts and practices, the country has integrated restorative practices, such as family group conferencing, as a central component of its youth justice framework. New Zealand's success has encouraged other countries to adapt similar methods for working with young offenders.

- Canada and the United States: Restorative justice has gained traction in both countries across criminal justice, education, and community-based programs. Many American schools have implemented restorative practices to address disciplinary issues, reducing suspensions and fostering a positive school climate. In Canada, Indigenous-led justice initiatives emphasize traditional restorative practices, promoting healing and cultural respect.

- South America, Africa, and Asia: Restorative justice continues to spread to new regions, adapting to the unique needs and cultural traditions of various societies. For example, Colombia has adopted restorative approaches to address the effects of its decades-long civil conflict, while countries like Kenya and India are exploring restorative justice in school and community settings to address social challenges and conflicts.

Modern Applications and Global Collaboration

Today, restorative justice has become a diverse and flexible approach to addressing harm, promoting healing, and restoring trust. It has been applied in criminal justice systems, schools, workplaces, and community organizations worldwide. In addition, international conferences, research networks, and policy initiatives are working to strengthen and standardize restorative practices across countries.

Organizations such as the International Institute for Restorative Practices (IIRP) and the European Forum for Restorative Justice play significant roles in advancing restorative justice education, research, and advocacy globally. These networks foster collaboration among practitioners, researchers, and policymakers, helping to shape restorative justice as a universal and adaptable response to harm.

Conclusion

The history of restorative justice demonstrates its resilience and adaptability, with roots in ancient practices that continue to inspire and guide modern applications. From indigenous traditions to formalized programs, restorative justice has evolved into a globally influential philosophy, proving its relevance across diverse cultural, social, and legal contexts. As it continues to develop and expand, restorative justice offers an inspiring vision for justice systems that prioritize empathy, accountability, and community healing, ultimately contributing to a more just and peaceful world.

In the following chapters, we will explore various styles of restorative justice, examining their unique applications, benefits, and challenges as they contribute to this transformative approach to justice.

How Styles of Restorative Justice Address Community Needs, Justice, and Healing

Restorative justice's core principles emphasize repairing harm, meeting community needs, and fostering healing, making it a compelling approach for building resilience in individuals and communities alike. Each style of restorative justice offers unique methods for addressing different types of harm, while keeping the focus on justice and healing. By involving all affected parties, restorative justice cultivates a sense of shared responsibility, creating pathways for understanding, reintegration, and accountability. This collective effort not only addresses immediate harm but also strengthens communities against future conflicts.

Community Needs: Building Trust and Strengthening Social Bonds

Communities are often left vulnerable when traditional justice systems focus solely on punishment, overlooking the collective trauma and disconnection harm creates. Restorative justice directly addresses these challenges by meeting the psychological, emotional, and practical needs of the community.

1. Community Conferencing: This approach brings together victims, offenders, and community members to discuss the harm and collaborate on solutions. Community conferencing gives a voice to everyone affected and ensures that harm is addressed transparently, building trust among community members.

2. Neighborhood Justice Panels: These panels are typically made up of local volunteers who work together to resolve conflicts or minor offenses. By involving trusted members of the community, these panels reinforce social bonds, create safer neighborhoods, and provide constructive pathways for offenders to make amends.

3. Restorative Circles: Often used in schools, workplaces, and community groups, restorative circles help build a sense of belonging and empathy. These circles encourage participants to share their feelings and perspectives, fostering mutual respect and reducing the risk of future harm by strengthening community relationships.

Justice: Accountability and Fairness in Addressing Harm

Unlike traditional justice systems, which often focus on punitive outcomes, restorative justice emphasizes accountability and fairness by involving the voices of all parties affected by harm. This inclusive approach allows for meaningful restitution and healing, while reinforcing the offender's responsibility toward the affected individuals and the community as a whole.

1. Victim-Offender Mediation: This practice enables direct dialogue between the victim and offender, facilitated by a trained mediator. It allows victims to express how they've been affected, while giving offenders an opportunity to accept responsibility and understand the impact of their actions. This process personalizes justice, making it fairer and more impactful for all parties involved.

2. Restorative Community Service: Unlike conventional community service, which may not directly relate to the offense, restorative community service tasks are often linked to repairing the specific harm done. This approach holds offenders accountable in a constructive manner, encouraging them to make amends in a way that benefits the victim and community.

3. Reparations and Restorative Reparations: Reparative measures focus on compensating victims and addressing their losses, while restorative reparations go beyond financial compensation. They may include apologies, community work, or actions that seek to restore relationships. This form of justice not only holds the offender accountable but also meets the victim's need for recognition and healing.

Healing: Restoring Relationships and Rebuilding Community Well-Being

Healing is an essential aspect of restorative justice, addressing the emotional and relational damage caused by harm. Restorative practices promote healing by allowing victims, offenders, and communities to process emotions, understand the causes of harm, and work together to rebuild relationships and community well-being.

1. Circles of Support and Accountability: In cases of serious harm, restorative circles provide ongoing support for offenders, helping them reintegrate into the community responsibly. These circles also help the community process complex feelings of fear or anger, turning potential resentment into constructive support for the offender's positive change.

2. Family Group Conferencing: Often used in cases involving youth, family group conferencing brings together family members, social workers, and other support figures to address the harm. This approach emphasizes the role of family in supporting both the victim's and offender's healing, fostering an environment where young offenders can grow with the understanding and support of their loved ones.

3. Truth and Reconciliation Processes: Used in contexts of large-scale harm, such as post-conflict societies, truth and reconciliation processes provide a platform for victims and perpetrators to share their experiences. By giving voice to historical trauma and systemic harm, these processes foster collective healing and lay the foundation for rebuilding trust and resilience within communities and nations.

Creating a Ripple Effect: The Broader Impacts of Restorative Justice

The effects of restorative justice extend beyond individuals and individual incidents. When communities adopt restorative approaches, they create cultures of empathy, accountability, and healing. Restorative practices reduce recidivism, prevent future harm, and provide a framework for communities to manage conflicts more constructively. Schools, for instance, have seen improvements in student behavior and reduced suspensions by implementing restorative practices, leading to safer and more inclusive environments.

1. Restorative Schools and Classroom Circles: In educational settings, restorative practices have proven effective at reducing bullying, improving school culture, and promoting positive peer interactions. By giving students a voice in addressing issues and conflicts, restorative practices empower young people to be responsible, compassionate members of their communities.

2. Restorative Cities: Some cities have adopted restorative justice frameworks to address crime, social issues, and community needs holistically. By engaging citizens in restorative practices, restorative cities create a collective sense of purpose, trust, and resilience, reducing the need for punitive measures and enhancing community safety and well-being.

3. Restorative Reentry Programs: For individuals re-entering society after incarceration, restorative reentry programs provide support, accountability, and guidance. These programs, which often involve mentoring and community circles, help former offenders rebuild relationships and secure stable lives, lowering the chances of recidivism and fostering positive contributions to society.

Conclusion

By addressing community needs, fostering a sense of justice, and promoting healing, restorative justice provides a transformative approach to managing harm. Unlike punitive models, which often fail to meet the needs of victims or address root causes, restorative justice empowers communities to address harm collectively, creating safer, more resilient, and more compassionate societies. In the following chapters, we will explore each style of restorative justice in depth, examining how they contribute to justice, healing, and the well-being of all involved. Through these practices, restorative justice continues to demonstrate its profound impact on individuals, communities, and justice systems worldwide.

CHAPTER 1

Community Conferencing

Origins and Principles of Community Conferencing

Community conferencing is a restorative justice approach rooted in the principles of community justice and conflict transformation. This structured, voluntary process allows all individuals affected by a conflict or crime—including victims, offenders, family members, and other community members—to come together to resolve the harm and collaboratively create a plan for moving forward. With its focus on personal accountability, mutual respect, and community healing, community conferencing serves as a powerful tool in the broader restorative justice movement.

This chapter explores the historical origins of community conferencing, its guiding principles, and its applications across various settings. By examining both the theory and practical implementations, this chapter provides a comprehensive understanding of how community conferencing builds safer, more resilient communities.

1.1 Origins of Community Conferencing

Community conferencing emerged from indigenous justice traditions and conflict resolution practices that prioritize communal responsibility and healing over punishment. Early forms of conferencing can be traced back to indigenous societies, such as the Māori of New Zealand, where community members would gather to address harm in a way that maintained social harmony. Influenced by these traditional practices, modern community conferencing began to take shape in the 1980s, particularly within the juvenile justice system in New Zealand, as a response to the limitations of punitive models.

The formal development of community conferencing is credited to New Zealand's adoption of Family Group Conferencing (FGC) for juvenile offenders in 1989. This model emphasized involving not only the youth and their families but also victims and community members in the justice process. According to Braithwaite (2002), family group conferencing was transformative because it highlighted the community's role in both preventing and responding to harm. This idea soon spread to other countries, including Australia, Canada, and the United States, where community conferencing has since become an integral part of both criminal justice and community conflict resolution.

1.2 Principles of Community Conferencing

Community conferencing is founded on several core principles that guide its practice and define its objectives within the restorative justice framework. These principles underscore the philosophy that communities, rather than solely institutions, are best positioned to resolve conflicts and support individual and collective healing.

1. People Can Resolve Conflicts

One of the foundational beliefs of community conferencing is that individuals, when provided with a safe and structured environment, have the inherent capacity to resolve their own conflicts. This principle shifts the locus of conflict resolution from external authorities to the individuals directly affected by the incident. As stated by Zehr (2015), restorative justice "invites people to take responsibility and make things right," underscoring the belief in human agency and the potential for personal growth and transformation.

2. Solutions Are More Effective When People Affected Are Involved

Community conferencing emphasizes the importance of inclusive decision-making. When the individuals impacted by a conflict are actively involved in determining the resolution, the outcomes are more likely to be meaningful, relevant, and adhered to by all parties. Research by Umbreit et al. (2004) suggests that involving victims, offenders, and community members in the decision-making process increases satisfaction and compliance, as individuals feel that their voices and concerns have been heard.

3. Conflicts Are Best Resolved Within the Community

Community conferencing reflects the principle that justice is most effective when situated within the social context of the community where the harm occurred. This approach strengthens communal bonds and ensures that the resolution process is culturally relevant and contextually appropriate. According to McCold and Wachtel (2002), the community itself benefits from being involved, as members gain skills in conflict resolution and develop a deeper sense of shared responsibility for public safety.

4. Accountability Builds Safer Communities

A central tenet of community conferencing is that accountability—encouraging offenders to acknowledge their actions and make amends—builds trust and security within communities. Accountability in a restorative context is constructive, focusing on repairing harm rather than imposing guilt or shame. Zehr (2015) notes that accountability within restorative justice involves "an obligation to make things right," a concept that resonates with community values and fosters a sense of safety and trust.

1.3 The Community Conferencing Process

Community conferencing is a structured process facilitated by a neutral, trained facilitator who guides participants in discussing the incident, expressing their feelings, and working collaboratively to repair the harm. The conferencing process consists of several key stages, each designed to foster open communication, empathy, and cooperative problem-solving:

1. Introduction and Preparation

Before the conference begins, the facilitator meets individually with participants, explaining the purpose and structure of the process, setting guidelines, and addressing any concerns. This preparatory phase is crucial for building trust and ensuring that everyone feels comfortable and safe.

2. Narrative Sharing

During the conference, each participant is given the opportunity to share their perspective on what happened, how they were affected, and what they need to move forward. This narrative-sharing fosters empathy, as individuals hear firsthand how the incident impacted others. According to Gavrielides (2007), the storytelling aspect of restorative practices allows participants to connect on a human level, reducing animosity and increasing mutual understanding.

3. Problem-Solving and Agreement Formation

After all voices have been heard, participants work together to develop a mutually agreed-upon plan to repair the harm. This may include an apology, financial restitution, community service, or other actions tailored to address the needs of both the victim and the offender. Research by Sherman and Strang (2007) shows that restorative agreements, when collaboratively created, are more likely to be meaningful and lasting, as they reflect the shared interests of all parties.

4. Follow-Up and Support

Community conferencing does not end with the creation of an agreement. Many programs include follow-up to ensure that commitments are met and to offer support to all participants. This ongoing support strengthens community relationships and reinforces accountability.

1.4 Applications of Community Conferencing

Community conferencing has broad applications across a variety of settings, each offering unique opportunities to address harm, build relationships, and promote community well-being.

1. Neighborhoods

In community settings, conferencing provides neighbors with a safe and constructive way to address disputes and prevent conflicts from escalating. By involving community members directly, community conferencing fosters a culture of mutual respect and problem-solving, which can be essential for long-term peace and cooperation.

2. Court Diversion Programs

Community conferencing has become a valuable tool in court diversion programs, particularly in cases involving minor offenses. By providing an alternative to formal prosecution, conferencing allows offenders to take responsibility in a constructive way, reducing their likelihood of re-offending. According to a study by Hayes and Daly (2003), participants in restorative justice programs, including community conferencing, report higher levels of satisfaction and lower rates of re-offense than those processed through traditional courts.

3. Juvenile Court Diversion

For young offenders, community conferencing offers a valuable opportunity to learn accountability, empathy, and the impact of their actions on others. This process is particularly effective in juvenile justice, as it emphasizes positive socialization and community support. Studies by McGarrell and Hipple (2007) indicate that restorative practices such as conferencing can have a lasting positive impact on youth by fostering responsibility and reducing recidivism.

1.5 Benefits and Challenges of Community Conferencing (continued)

2. Challenges

- Need for Skilled Facilitators: The success of a community conference largely depends on the skill and neutrality of the facilitator, who must create a safe environment and manage complex emotions. Facilitators require specialized training to navigate power dynamics, encourage honest communication, and ensure balanced participation. According to Wachtel (2016), poorly facilitated conferences can risk re-traumatizing victims or disempowering participants.

- Voluntary Participation: A foundational principle of community conferencing is voluntary participation. However, ensuring genuine willingness to participate can be difficult, especially in cases where individuals feel pressured by social or legal authorities. If participants do not feel truly free to contribute, the authenticity and effectiveness of the process may be compromised.

- Addressing Power Imbalances: In some cases, disparities in power—such as age, socioeconomic status, or previous relationships between participants—can impact the fairness and outcomes of a conference. Effective facilitators work to mitigate these imbalances, yet achieving true equity remains a complex challenge in restorative practices.

1.6 Case Studies of Community Conferencing in Action

To illustrate the impact and versatility of community conferencing, consider the following case studies:

1. Case Study: Community Conferencing in School Settings

In Baltimore, Maryland, community conferencing has been implemented in schools to address conflicts among students and reduce suspensions. When a group of students engaged in a physical fight, rather than resorting to traditional disciplinary measures, school officials facilitated a community conference. Students involved in the incident, their families, and affected staff gathered to discuss the events, express their emotions, and collaboratively create a plan to prevent future altercations. According to Karp and Breslin (2001), such restorative practices in schools not only reduce suspensions but also improve relationships, enhance empathy, and build a positive school culture.

2. Case Study: Juvenile Court Diversion in Australia

Australia's use of community conferencing in juvenile justice has shown positive outcomes for young offenders. A study by Hayes and Daly (2003) on youth offenders who participated in community conferencing found that young people were significantly less likely to reoffend than those processed through the traditional court system. Furthermore, participants reported a heightened sense of responsibility and understanding of the consequences of their actions, underscoring the effectiveness of community conferencing in fostering meaningful accountability among youth.

3. Case Study: Neighborhood Disputes in Northern Ireland

Northern Ireland implemented community conferencing to address longstanding tensions in divided neighborhoods. By engaging in dialogue, community members from differing backgrounds could openly address grievances and collaborate on solutions, reducing hostility and fostering understanding. This approach has been instrumental in building safer, more resilient communities in a region with a history of inter-community conflict (McEvoy and Mika, 2002).

1.7 Conclusion: The Future of Community Conferencing

Community conferencing offers a flexible and transformative approach to conflict resolution. Its foundation in restorative justice principles—accountability, inclusivity, and community empowerment—makes it a valuable model for communities seeking to heal and build safer environments. By involving everyone affected, community conferencing addresses the root causes of conflict, empowering individuals to take responsibility for their actions and work toward meaningful reconciliation. With increasing evidence supporting its effectiveness in diverse contexts, community conferencing is likely to continue expanding as communities around the world seek more inclusive, compassionate ways to resolve disputes.

As interest in restorative justice grows, future research and practice may further refine community conferencing models, exploring new applications and strategies for ensuring equitable participation. Continued investment in training facilitators, addressing challenges like power imbalances, and expanding community awareness will be essential for community conferencing to achieve its full potential as a restorative justice tool.

References

- Braithwaite, J. (2002). Restorative Justice & Responsive Regulation. Oxford University Press.
- Gavrielides, T. (2007). Restorative Justice Theory and Practice: Addressing the Discrepancy. European Institute for Crime Prevention and Control.
- Hayes, H., & Daly, K. (2003). "Youth Justice Conferencing and Reoffending," Justice Quarterly, 20(4), 725-764.
- Karp, D., & Breslin, B. (2001). Restorative Justice in School Communities. Youth & Society.
- McCold, P., & Wachtel, T. (2002). "Restorative Justice Theory Validation," Restorative Justice: Theoretical Foundations. Routledge.
- McEvoy, K., & Mika, H. (2002). "Restorative Justice and the Critique of Informalism in Northern Ireland," British Journal of Criminology, 42(3), 534-562.
- Sherman, L. W., & Strang, H. (2007). Restorative Justice: The Evidence. The Smith Institute.
- Umbreit, M. S., Coates, R. B., & Vos, B. (2004). "Victim Satisfaction with Mediated Offender Dialogue in Restorative Justice," Journal of Interpersonal Violence, 19(2), 150-167.
- Wachtel, T. (2016). Defining Restorative. International Institute for Restorative Practices.
- Zehr, H. (2015). The Little Book of Restorative Justice. Good Books.

This chapter has explored the principles, processes, and applications of community conferencing, emphasizing its role in fostering a sense of community, accountability, and healing. Through practical case studies, research, and theoretical insights, community conferencing emerges as a vital part of the restorative justice landscape, providing individuals and communities with effective tools to transform conflict and build a more just society.

Steps Involved in Conducting a Community Conference

Community conferencing is a structured and inclusive approach to conflict resolution that focuses on restoring relationships, building empathy, and addressing harm in a constructive way. By allowing students and adults to work through disputes, community conferencing can improve relationships and foster a positive environment in settings such as schools, workplaces, and neighborhoods. The following steps provide a framework for facilitators to guide participants, especially in small settings like offices or conference rooms, where trust and open communication are paramount.

Step 1: Explain the Process

A key to engaging participants is clearly explaining the purpose and structure of the community conferencing process. Without understanding the "why," participants may resist the process or misunderstand its goals. It's essential to convey that the purpose of the session is not about proving who is right or wrong but about listening, validating feelings, and working towards a shared resolution.

To clarify the purpose of restorative practices, facilitators can use explanations like:

- "Thank you both for being here. The purpose of this meeting is to allow each person to express their feelings, develop empathy, and ultimately reach a resolution. This is about taking ownership of our actions and repairing any unintentional harm."

- "We're here to create mutual respect. This process helps us express ourselves positively and allows us to hear the other person's feelings, reducing stress or tension when interacting in shared spaces."
- "If we unintentionally hurt someone, it's important to take responsibility and adjust our actions to avoid causing harm in the future."

Facilitators should check for participant understanding by asking questions like, "Can you explain to me why we are using this process?" This encourages them to articulate their understanding, rather than simply nodding along without full comprehension.

Step 2: Build Empathy

Building empathy is a critical component of effective community conferencing. Encouraging participants to consider the emotions and perspectives of others helps shift the focus from winning an argument to understanding the human impact of actions. Empathy serves as a bridge that connects participants' experiences, fostering a sense of shared understanding and compassion.

Facilitators can guide empathy-building through questions and statements such as:

- "Does anyone know what empathy is?" If necessary, define empathy as "the ability to understand and share the feelings of another person."
- "Have you ever felt frustration? How about embarrassment, anger, or sadness? Even if your experience is different, you can relate by connecting to those universal emotions."
- Encourage each participant to express how they felt in specific situations, then ask the other participant to reflect on a similar feeling in their own life, creating a reciprocal understanding.

This step lays the groundwork for the rest of the conversation, as participants begin to view each other with empathy and respect.

Step 3: Grounding Exercise

A grounding exercise helps participants find common ground, creating a foundation for mutual respect. This exercise centers on shared values and goals within the environment where the conflict has occurred.

An effective grounding exercise might include:

- Asking each participant, "What do you want school (or your shared environment) to look, feel, and sound like?"

- If a participant is unsure, prompt them with examples such as, "Would you want school to be a safe place?"

- Repeat this process with each participant to reveal that, despite their differences, they often desire similar things—safety, respect, and a positive atmosphere.

Facilitators then use this exercise to illustrate that while individuals may have unique ways of achieving their goals, the shared values are a uniting factor. This realization can help participants focus on their common objectives rather than their differences.

Step 4: Start the Conversation

Once empathy is established, and common ground is found, the facilitator can guide participants into a direct conversation about the conflict. This step emphasizes using "I" statements to express personal feelings and experiences, rather than placing blame.

The facilitator can start by saying:

- "Okay, [participant], please express your feelings using 'I' statements. This helps us communicate without blaming the other person and allows everyone to feel heard."

- After one participant shares, the facilitator can ask, "Was it your intention to make [participant] feel [emotion]?" If the action was unintentional, this is an opportunity to acknowledge the impact and offer an apology.

In choosing who speaks first:

- For conflicts between two students, the student who feels wronged usually starts.

- In a student-adult conflict, it's often beneficial to allow the student to start, while the adult models empathetic listening and apology.

- In adult conflicts, the person who feels wronged may start, with the other adult practicing empathy.

Step 5: Paraphrasing and Guided Apology

Paraphrasing ensures that participants' statements are clear and empathetic, focusing on feelings rather than accusations. The facilitator can guide participants to use "I" statements and help reframe accusatory statements into expressions of personal experience.

For example:

- If a participant says, "You embarrassed me in front of everyone," the facilitator can rephrase: "You felt embarrassed and upset when you felt singled out in front of others. Is that correct?"

Guided apologies involve taking responsibility and expressing remorse. The facilitator can prompt participants to make apologies meaningful and sincere, fostering a sense of accountability and understanding.

By following these steps, facilitators can guide participants through a restorative process that fosters empathy, open communication, and accountability. When applied in settings like schools, workplaces, or community centers, this approach has the potential to transform relationships, reduce conflict, and build a culture of respect. Over time, individuals who participate in these practices often develop skills that enhance their ability to resolve conflicts independently, promoting a healthier, more cooperative environment.

Case Studies in Community Conferencing for Conflict Resolution

Introduction to Community Conferencing in Restorative Justice

Community conferencing, a foundational element of restorative justice, is a structured process that aims to resolve conflicts, foster accountability, and restore relationships. Rooted in the values of empathy, respect, and open dialogue, community conferencing allows individuals impacted by conflict—whether directly or indirectly—to come together, share their perspectives, and collaboratively find pathways to healing and resolution. This approach moves beyond punitive measures to address underlying causes of conflict and promote sustainable, positive change within communities (Zehr, 2002).

The following case studies illustrate the diverse applications and transformative potential of community conferencing across different settings. From youth-police relations to school-based interventions and victim-offender mediation, these examples highlight how restorative practices can be effective tools in building understanding and reducing recidivism.

1. The Derry, New Hampshire Youth-Police Conflict

One prominent example of community conferencing in action is the "Derry, New Hampshire Youth-Police Conflict" case. Rising tensions and misunderstandings between local youth and law enforcement had escalated, creating a climate of distrust that led to a spike in juvenile offenses. Recognizing the need for an alternative approach, Derry's community leaders initiated a restorative justice program that included community circles to address the conflict and bridge the gap between the youth and police.

Key Elements of the Case Study

- The Problem: Tensions between the youth and law enforcement in Derry, New Hampshire, led to increasing instances of juvenile offenses, partly fueled by a lack of communication and mutual understanding.

- Restorative Justice Approach: To address this issue, trained mediators facilitated community circles where police officers and youth could openly share their experiences and perspectives. These sessions allowed both groups to express their concerns and frustrations, fostering empathy and breaking down misconceptions.

- Positive Outcomes: Over two years, juvenile offenses decreased by 40%. This substantial reduction can be attributed to improved communication and trust between the community's youth and law enforcement. The process demonstrated how community conferencing not only addresses immediate issues but also contributes to building long-term trust and understanding (Braithwaite, 2004).

2. School-Based Conflict Resolution: Balaklava High School, Australia

The educational setting offers a unique environment for implementing restorative practices, as it involves diverse stakeholders—students, teachers, staff, and families—all of whom contribute to and are affected by the school's climate. Balaklava High School in Australia exemplifies the positive impact of integrating community conferencing into schools. The school saw significant reductions in suspensions and incidents of violence after adopting a restorative justice framework, including community conferencing.

Key Elements of the Case Study

- The Problem: High suspension rates and increasing incidents of violence at Balaklava High School indicated a need for alternative disciplinary approaches that could promote healthier student relationships and a safer school environment.

- Restorative Justice Approach: The school implemented restorative practices across its community, involving staff, students, and families in community conferencing sessions. By bringing all parties together, the approach encouraged open communication, accountability, and empathy. These discussions allowed students to better understand the impact of their actions and provided a platform for collective problem-solving.

- Positive Outcomes: The restorative practices approach led to a noticeable decrease in suspensions and violence. Moreover, feedback indicated that students felt more connected to the school community and better equipped to manage conflicts in a constructive manner (Hopkins, 2004).

3. Victim-Offender Mediation: Restoring Trust and Accountability

Victim-offender mediation is another context where community conferencing has proven effective. In cases where young offenders committed property crimes, restorative justice conferences offered a platform for dialogue, accountability, and healing. One such case involved a young offender who had vandalized a local business. Through the mediation, the victim shared the emotional and financial impact of the crime, while the offender took responsibility and made reparative amends.

Key Elements of the Case Study

- The Problem: The offender's actions had left the victim with emotional distress and financial burdens, and traditional justice processes were unlikely to address these needs.

- Restorative Justice Approach: In a mediated setting, both parties discussed the impact of the offense. The victim had the chance to express their feelings, while the offender was encouraged to take responsibility and to acknowledge the harm caused.

- Positive Outcomes: Both the victim and offender reported a sense of closure following the mediation. The offender's willingness to make amends and the victim's openness to forgiveness facilitated healing and restored a sense of community trust (Umbreit, Vos, Coates, & Lightfoot, 2005).

4. Community-Led Initiatives for Crime Prevention

In communities with high crime rates, neighborhood organizations have utilized community conferencing as a proactive measure to address underlying tensions and conflicts. These initiatives provide a space for residents to openly discuss grievances, share ideas for improvements, and take collective responsibility for the well-being of their neighborhood.

Key Elements of the Case Study

- The Problem: Communities experiencing high crime often grapple with a lack of cohesion, where residents feel disconnected from each other and powerless in the face of recurring issues.

- Restorative Justice Approach: Community organizations facilitated conferencing sessions that allowed residents to voice their concerns, discuss solutions, and collaboratively develop action plans for reducing crime and enhancing neighborhood safety. By focusing on empowerment and ownership, community conferencing helped instill a sense of responsibility and collective agency.

- Positive Outcomes: Over time, these neighborhoods experienced lower crime rates and reported stronger community bonds. Community conferencing fostered a sense of ownership among residents, who felt more invested in the well-being of their environment and each other (Bazemore & Schiff, 2001).

Core Elements of Community Conferencing in Restorative Justice

1. Facilitation by a Trained Mediator: A neutral facilitator guides the conversation, ensuring all participants have a voice and the discussion remains constructive and solution-oriented. The facilitator also helps participants manage emotions, enabling a calm and respectful dialogue (Pranis, 2005).

2. Victim Participation: Giving victims a chance to share the impact of the offense helps them feel validated and promotes healing.

This step also enables offenders to recognize the consequences of their actions on others (Zehr, 2002).

3. Accountability and Responsibility: Offenders are encouraged to take responsibility for their actions, which can be transformative, fostering personal growth and accountability that is often missing in punitive justice approaches (Braithwaite, 2004).

4. Focus on Healing and Reconciliation: The goal is to create a safe space for participants to explore solutions together, emphasizing healing and building positive relationships rather than merely assigning blame (Umbreit et al., 2005).

Community conferencing, as demonstrated in these case studies, is an effective method for promoting restorative justice and addressing conflicts across various settings. It allows individuals to experience the benefits of empathy, accountability, and shared responsibility, moving beyond traditional punitive measures to foster sustainable peace and understanding. By incorporating restorative justice principles, communities can create environments where relationships are repaired, trust is rebuilt, and individuals are empowered to contribute positively to their community.

References

- Bazemore, G., & Schiff, M. (2001). Restorative Community Justice: Repairing Harm and Transforming Communities. Routledge.
- Braithwaite, J. (2004). Restorative Justice and Responsive Regulation. Oxford University Press.
- Hopkins, B. (2004). Just Schools: A Whole School Approach to Restorative Justice. Jessica Kingsley Publishers.
- Pranis, K. (2005). The Little Book of Circle Processes: A New/Old Approach to Peacemaking. Good Books.

- Umbreit, M., Vos, B., Coates, R., & Lightfoot, E. (2005). Restorative Justice in the Twenty-first Century: A Social Movement Full of Opportunities and Pitfalls. Journal of Social Work Research and Evaluation, 6(1), 69-85.

- Zehr, H. (2002). The Little Book of Restorative Justice. Good Books.

CHAPTER 02

Circles and Restorative Circles in Restorative Justice

Introduction to Restorative Justice Circles

Circles are a central practice within restorative justice, providing a structured environment for participants to communicate openly, reflect on conflicts, and work toward healing and reconciliation. Rooted in Indigenous practices, circles emphasize equality, collective responsibility, and the transformative power of shared dialogue. By gathering in a literal circle—where each participant sits facing one another, removing hierarchical barriers—these sessions encourage participants to take responsibility, share emotions, and collaboratively address harm (Pranis, Stuart, & Wedge, 2003).

This chapter explores various types of restorative justice circles—Peacemaking Circles, Healing Circles, Sentencing Circles, Accountability Circles, Reintegration Circles, and Support Circles—

each with distinct purposes tailored to different needs within the restorative justice framework. It also examines the core components that make these circles effective in facilitating personal growth and community healing.

Types of Restorative Justice Circles

1. Peacemaking Circles

Peacemaking Circles are focused on conflict resolution, where individuals involved in a dispute come together to discuss their perspectives, express emotions, and identify solutions that address the harm done. The process begins by establishing shared values and ground rules, fostering an environment of respect and empathy. Participants—including the harmed, the responsible, and sometimes community members—are encouraged to share their experiences, ask questions, and collectively work towards a solution that meets everyone's needs.

Key Aspects:

- Purpose: To resolve interpersonal or group conflicts by promoting understanding and mutual accountability.
- Process: Participants express feelings and perspectives, facilitated by guiding questions and active listening.
- Outcome: An agreement on how to repair harm and rebuild trust, often through actions that honor the needs of all involved (Zehr, 2002).

2. Healing Circles

Healing Circles primarily serve those who have experienced trauma, loss, or deep emotional pain. These circles offer a safe and supportive environment for participants to process their experiences, voice their emotions, and receive support from others. In many cases, healing circles are utilized in communities that have faced collective trauma, such as after a natural disaster or act of violence. By creating a space free from judgment, healing circles allow participants to navigate grief and begin the journey toward recovery.

Key Aspects:

- Purpose: To provide emotional support and healing for individuals who have experienced trauma.
- Process: Participants are invited to share their experiences, while others offer empathy, often in silence or with words of encouragement.
- Outcome: Increased emotional resilience, validation of experiences, and a sense of community belonging (Umbreit, Vos, Coates, & Lightfoot, 2005).

3. Sentencing Circles

Sentencing Circles are a restorative practice within the criminal justice system where victims, offenders, community members, and justice professionals collaborate to determine a fair and meaningful sentence for an offender. This type of circle acknowledges the harm caused by a crime and emphasizes accountability, while also aiming to repair relationships. Sentencing circles allow the affected parties to share the impact of the crime and for the offender to take responsibility.

Key Aspects:

- Purpose: To collaboratively determine a sentencing plan that promotes accountability and restoration.
- Process: Victims share how they were affected, and offenders are given the opportunity to express remorse and commit to reparative actions.

- Outcome: A sentencing agreement that emphasizes community safety, accountability, and the offender's reintegration (Johnstone, 2011).

4. Accountability Circles

Accountability Circles are designed to hold individuals responsible for harmful actions by creating a space where they can acknowledge the impact of their behavior and develop a plan to make amends. These circles are often used with young offenders, employees within organizations, or even students in schools to encourage personal responsibility. Participants are asked to listen to how their actions have affected others, fostering empathy and awareness.

Key Aspects:

- Purpose: To help individuals understand the consequences of their actions and encourage meaningful change.
- Process: Participants engage in dialogue that focuses on harm caused, with an emphasis on listening and accepting responsibility.
- Outcome: A commitment to change and a plan for reparative actions that benefit those affected (Hopkins, 2004).

5. Reintegration Circles

Reintegration Circles facilitate the return of an individual into a community after a period of absence or conflict, such as post-incarceration or after a school suspension. The circle helps both the returning individual and the community address any tensions, misunderstandings, or concerns. Reintegration circles are particularly effective for easing transitions, reducing stigma, and fostering a supportive environment for successful reintegration.

Key Aspects:

- Purpose: To support the successful reintegration of individuals back into the community and reduce potential friction.
- Process: Participants discuss any fears or expectations, establishing shared goals for a positive transition.
- Outcome: Improved relationships, reduced recidivism, and a stronger sense of community support (Braithwaite, 2004).

6. Support Circles

Support Circles provide individuals facing personal or communal challenges a supportive network where they can receive encouragement and practical guidance. This type of circle is often employed for people dealing with mental health issues, addiction, or other personal struggles. Support circles help individuals feel less isolated, empowering them to work through difficulties with the backing of a caring community.

Key Aspects:

- Purpose: To offer support and resources for individuals facing challenges.
- Process: Participants share their experiences, while others provide advice, encouragement, and resources.
- Outcome: Increased resilience, empowerment, and a strengthened sense of connection (Pranis, 2005).

Core Components of the Restorative Circle Process

For restorative circles to be effective, several key elements must be maintained throughout the process:

1. Shared Responsibility

All participants in the circle are equally important to the process, with each person holding a unique perspective. Shared responsibility fosters a collective commitment to the outcome, reducing the hierarchical dynamics often seen in conventional justice processes.

2. Active Listening

Participants are encouraged to listen attentively without interruption, respecting each speaker's right to share their story. Active listening creates a space for empathy and understanding, essential elements for healing and reconciliation.

3. Respectful Dialogue

Dialogue in restorative circles focuses on the impact of actions, not blame. Participants are guided to communicate respectfully, emphasizing the importance of honesty and accountability over accusations or defensiveness.

4. Facilitator Guidance

A trained facilitator, sometimes referred to as a circle keeper, ensures the conversation remains focused on healing, reconciliation, and accountability. The facilitator also manages the circle's structure, guiding participants through the discussion while maintaining an atmosphere of respect.

Restorative justice circles, whether used in criminal justice, schools, or communities, provide a structured and supportive environment that promotes healing, accountability, and community cohesion. By fostering open dialogue and shared responsibility, circles allow participants to address harm constructively and work toward meaningful resolutions. Each type of circle—Peacemaking, Healing, Sentencing, Accountability, Reintegration, and Support—offers unique benefits tailored to the specific needs of those involved, making restorative circles an adaptable and impactful approach to conflict resolution and personal growth.

References

- Braithwaite, J. (2004). Restorative Justice and Responsive Regulation. Oxford University Press.
- Hopkins, B. (2004). Just Schools: A Whole School Approach to Restorative Justice. Jessica Kingsley Publishers.
- Johnstone, G. (2011). Restorative Justice: Ideas, Values, Debates. Routledge.
- Pranis, K., Stuart, B., & Wedge, M. (2003). Peacemaking Circles: From Crime to Community. Living Justice Press.
- Umbreit, M., Vos, B., Coates, R., & Lightfoot, E. (2005). Restorative Justice in the Twenty-First Century.

Benefits of Circle Processes and Roles of Participants in Restorative Justice

Circle processes form an essential component of restorative justice, providing a structured yet flexible approach for communities to address conflict, harm, and accountability in an inclusive and compassionate environment. Rooted in Indigenous practices, the circle process centers on equality and shared responsibility, as all participants sit in a literal circle, allowing for a visually and symbolically inclusive structure where everyone's voice matters (Pranis, Stuart, & Wedge, 2003). This chapter examines the various benefits that circle processes offer—such as empowerment, empathy-building, accountability, and collaborative problem-solving—while also detailing the critical roles played by each participant, including the victim, offender, community members, and facilitator, in fostering a transformative and healing experience.

Benefits of Circle Processes in Restorative Justice

Circle processes in restorative justice serve as a foundation for meaningful dialogue and cooperative conflict resolution, offering numerous benefits to individuals and communities alike. These benefits foster an environment conducive to understanding, empathy, accountability, and healing, which are vital for effective restorative justice outcomes.

1. Empowerment and Equal Voice

The circle format, often accompanied by the use of a "talking piece" (an object passed around to designate who has the floor), ensures that each participant has an equal opportunity to speak without interruption. This format diminishes hierarchical barriers, promoting a sense of equality and mutual respect among participants. Empowering individuals with an equal voice encourages active engagement, reduces feelings of marginalization, and enhances each person's agency within the circle (Pranis, 2005).

2. Building Empathy and Understanding

Circle processes facilitate empathy and understanding by creating a space where participants can share their experiences and perspectives openly. When offenders hear directly from victims about the harm caused, they are more likely to understand the emotional impact of their actions, which can be transformative. Similarly, victims gain insight into the offender's circumstances, potentially leading to forgiveness and emotional closure. This mutual exchange fosters empathy, bridging divides and promoting collective understanding (Zehr, 2002).

3. Increased Accountability

One of the core principles of restorative justice is that individuals must take responsibility for their actions. Circle processes encourage offenders to openly acknowledge the harm they have caused and actively participate in the steps required to make amends. This practice of accountability is supported by the presence of the victim, community members, and a facilitator, creating a setting that promotes honest reflection and constructive self-assessment (Johnstone, 2011).

4. Community Healing and Reconciliation

Circle processes allow for collective healing by giving everyone affected by the conflict or harm a voice in the resolution process. Community members, victims, and offenders are all invited to express their emotions, concerns, and needs. This open dialogue is instrumental in building or rebuilding trust, paving the way for reconciliation, and allowing the community to restore relationships that may have been fractured. Such reconciliation processes strengthen social cohesion, reinforcing the community's resilience against future conflicts (Umbreit, Vos, Coates, & Lightfoot, 2005).

5. Collaborative Problem-Solving

By bringing together various perspectives, circle processes foster collaborative problem-solving that addresses the needs of all parties involved. Participants work together to identify solutions that honor the voices of the victim, offender, and community. This inclusive approach to problem-solving promotes creative and sustainable outcomes, as all parties contribute their ideas and insights into how to repair the harm and prevent future conflicts (Hopkins, 2004).

Roles of Participants in Restorative Justice Circles

The success of a restorative justice circle depends heavily on the roles and contributions of each participant. Each individual within the circle plays a specific role, contributing to the dialogue and the overall process in unique ways. This section explores the roles of the victim, offender, community members, and facilitator, examining how each contributes to the circle's objectives of healing, accountability, and restoration.

1. Victim

The victim's role in a restorative justice circle is essential, as they bring a personal perspective on the harm experienced. Victims are given the opportunity to share their emotions, describe the impact of the offender's actions, and express their needs for repair. This process not only allows the victim to be heard but also facilitates their healing by enabling them to participate actively in determining a resolution. In some cases, victims find that sharing their experiences helps them process their trauma and move toward closure (Zehr, 2002).

Key Responsibilities:

- Share their experience and the emotional impact of the harm.
- Communicate needs for reparation and healing.
- Contribute to collaborative solutions by voicing what would promote healing.

2. Offender

The offender in a restorative justice circle plays a crucial role by acknowledging their responsibility for the harm caused. By participating in the circle, the offender is encouraged to reflect on their actions, listen to the victim's account, and take steps toward making amends. This process fosters accountability, as offenders are asked to confront the consequences of their actions in a setting that promotes honesty and openness, without the punitive focus typical of traditional justice systems (Braithwaite, 2004).

Key Responsibilities:
- Acknowledge responsibility for the harm caused.
- Explain their perspective and any underlying circumstances.
- Actively participate in developing a plan to make amends.

3. Community Members

Community members play an invaluable role in providing broader context, support, and guidance within the circle. They represent the community's interests, share insights into how the harm has affected the broader community, and reinforce shared values and expectations. Community members also provide support to both the victim and the offender, emphasizing the community's commitment to healing and reintegration. Their presence underscores that the harm has impacted not just the individuals directly involved, but also the community as a whole (Pranis, 2005).

Key Responsibilities:
- Provide emotional support to both victim and offender.
- Share insights on the harm's impact from the community perspective.
- Assist in maintaining a focus on healing and restoration.

4. Facilitator

The facilitator, sometimes referred to as the circle keeper, is responsible for guiding the process and ensuring that the circle remains a safe and respectful space for all participants. Facilitators maintain the structure and flow of the conversation, ensuring that each person has an opportunity to speak, and that the discussion remains focused on constructive dialogue and healing. They may use specific techniques, such as passing a talking piece, to manage the conversation and encourage active listening. A well-trained facilitator is essential to the circle's success, as they foster an environment conducive to openness, trust, and reconciliation (Umbreit et al., 2005).

Key Responsibilities:

- Guide the circle process and maintain a safe, respectful space.
- Ensure everyone has an opportunity to speak and be heard.
- Facilitate constructive dialogue and focus on shared goals of healing and accountability.

Circle processes in restorative justice are a powerful tool for addressing harm and conflict within communities. By providing an inclusive environment where everyone's voice is valued, circle processes promote empowerment, empathy, accountability, and community healing. Each participant's role—the victim, offender, community members, and facilitator—is integral to the circle's success, as they contribute to a comprehensive and collaborative approach to conflict resolution and healing. Through these roles and benefits, restorative justice circles not only resolve individual conflicts but also foster resilient and connected communities, emphasizing the value of human dignity, respect, and the capacity for transformation.

References

- Braithwaite, J. (2004). Restorative Justice and Responsive Regulation. Oxford University Press.
- Hopkins, B. (2004). Just Schools: A Whole School Approach to Restorative Justice. Jessica Kingsley Publishers.
- Johnstone, G. (2011). Restorative Justice: Ideas, Values, Debates. Routledge.
- Pranis, K., Stuart, B., & Wedge, M. (2003). Peacemaking Circles: From Crime to Community. Living Justice Press.

- Pranis, K. (2005). The Little Book of Circle Processes: A New/Old Approach to Peacemaking. Good Books.

- Umbreit, M. S., Vos, B., Coates, R. B., & Lightfoot, E. (2005). Restorative Justice in the Twenty-First Century: A Social Movement Full of Contradictions. Temple University Press.

- Zehr, H. (2002). The Little Book of Restorative Justice. Good Books.

Techniques and Tools for Effective Circle Facilitation in Restorative Justice

Effective facilitation is critical to the success of restorative justice circles, as it ensures that the circle process is inclusive, respectful, and conducive to meaningful dialogue and healing. Circle facilitation requires both specific techniques and the strategic use of tools that foster a collaborative environment, helping participants share their experiences, reflect deeply, and contribute to finding solutions to address harm. This chapter explores key facilitation techniques—such as establishing community agreements, using a talking piece, asking open-ended questions, and managing group dynamics—as well as tools like circle arrangement, visual aids, and pre-prepared prompts that enhance the effectiveness of the process. Drawing on research and best practices in restorative justice, this chapter aims to provide facilitators with a scholarly guide to leading circles that promote accountability, empathy, and reconciliation within communities.

Key Techniques for Effective Circle Facilitation

Circle facilitators play a unique role as neutral guides, maintaining the structure and focus of the restorative justice process while respecting each participant's voice. Below are essential techniques that help facilitators create a productive environment for restorative dialogue and healing.

1. Establishing Community Agreements

Community agreements, or ground rules, are essential for setting the tone of the circle and promoting a safe and respectful space for participants. Facilitators can engage participants in co-creating these agreements, which typically include principles such as honesty, respect for others' perspectives, confidentiality, and taking turns with the talking piece. Collaborative agreement-setting not only clarifies expectations but also fosters a sense of shared responsibility and trust within the circle (Boyes-Watson & Pranis, 2015).

2. Using a Talking Piece

A talking piece is a central tool in restorative justice circles that signals whose turn it is to speak. By passing the talking piece around the circle, facilitators ensure that every participant has an equal opportunity to share their thoughts without interruption. This technique fosters active listening and allows each person to feel heard and valued. The talking piece can be a culturally meaningful object, symbolizing respect and the collective focus of the circle (Pranis, Stuart, & Wedge, 2003).

3. Active Listening

Active listening is vital for creating an environment where participants feel understood and respected. Facilitators can demonstrate active listening through body language, such as making eye contact and nodding, and by giving verbal affirmations. Reflecting back key points shared by participants also shows empathy and attentiveness, reinforcing a sense of connection and trust (Umbreit, Vos, Coates, & Lightfoot, 2005).

4. Open-Ended Questions

Open-ended questions encourage participants to express themselves more fully and to explore their emotions, experiences, and needs. These types of questions often begin with "how" or "what" and allow participants to go beyond yes-or-no answers, facilitating a more profound and reflective dialogue. Examples include "How did this experience affect you?" or "What do you think could help repair the harm?" Open-ended questions are particularly effective in uncovering underlying issues and fostering a deeper understanding among participants (Hopkins, 2004).

5. Neutral Facilitation

Maintaining neutrality is critical for facilitators, who must refrain from taking sides or offering personal opinions. Instead, facilitators guide the conversation toward constructive outcomes by keeping the focus on the principles of restorative justice, such as accountability, empathy, and healing. Neutral facilitation helps create a safe environment, as participants feel confident that the facilitator is fair and unbiased (Zehr, 2002).

6. Managing Group Dynamics

Circle processes often involve participants with varying levels of power and privilege, which can influence the dynamics within the group. Facilitators must be attentive to power imbalances and ensure that all voices are respected equally. This may involve actively engaging quieter participants, encouraging the use of "I" statements to personalize experiences, and diplomatically intervening if any participant dominates the conversation. Managing group dynamics in this way ensures a balanced and inclusive discussion (Boyes-Watson & Pranis, 2015).

7. Check-Ins and Check-Outs

Starting and ending each circle with check-ins and check-outs allows participants to share their emotional states and reflect on the session. Check-ins at the beginning of the circle can help participants become present and aware of their own emotions, while check-outs at the end provide an opportunity to reflect on the process, share any final thoughts, and clarify any next steps. These practices contribute to a sense of closure and continuity in the circle process (Pranis, Stuart, & Wedge, 2003).

8. Encouraging "I" Statements

"I" statements encourage participants to speak from personal experience, fostering a more empathetic and non-confrontational dialogue. By focusing on their own feelings and perspectives, participants avoid assigning blame and help create a respectful and understanding atmosphere within the circle. This technique is particularly effective in reducing defensiveness and promoting self-reflection, which are essential to the restorative justice process (Hopkins, 2004).

Useful Tools for Circle Facilitation

While techniques form the core of effective facilitation, specific tools can also support the process, making it more structured and accessible to participants.

1. Circle Arrangement

The physical arrangement of participants in a circle is fundamental to the process, symbolizing equality and inclusion. Sitting in a circle allows everyone to see each other and promotes a sense of connectedness, reinforcing the idea that each person's perspective is valued. This arrangement also reduces hierarchical distinctions, as there is no designated "head" or "leader" position (Boyes-Watson & Pranis, 2015).

2. Visual Aids

Visual aids, such as a whiteboard or flip chart, can be helpful for capturing key points, questions, or agreements reached during the circle. Visual aids can serve as reminders of the community agreements, the goals of the circle, or any important reflections shared. They provide a tangible record of the discussion, which can be referred back to in future sessions, reinforcing a sense of continuity and accountability (Umbreit et al., 2005).

3. Prepared Prompts

Facilitators can benefit from having a list of prepared open-ended questions or prompts to guide the conversation, especially when addressing complex or sensitive issues. Prompts can serve as starting points for discussion or help redirect the conversation if it becomes stalled. These questions should align with the principles of restorative justice and encourage reflection, honesty, and empathy (Hopkins, 2004).

4. Role-Playing

In some cases, facilitators may introduce role-playing exercises to help participants gain perspective on each other's experiences. By stepping into another person's role, participants may develop a better understanding of how others feel, which can deepen empathy and encourage mutual respect. Role-playing should be used thoughtfully, as it may not be suitable for all situations (Pranis, Stuart, & Wedge, 2003).

5. Confidentiality Agreements

Confidentiality is crucial for ensuring that participants feel comfortable sharing openly within the circle. Facilitators should emphasize the importance of confidentiality at the beginning of each session and secure a verbal or written commitment from participants to respect it. This agreement builds trust and allows participants to engage fully without fear of repercussions (Boyes-Watson & Pranis, 2015).

Important Considerations for Circle Facilitation

In addition to techniques and tools, facilitators must consider factors such as cultural sensitivity, training, and the setting to create an environment that honors the principles of restorative justice.

1. Cultural Sensitivity

Facilitators must be mindful of cultural differences within the circle, as participants' backgrounds and values may shape their responses to the restorative justice process. This may involve adapting language, rituals, or practices to align with participants' cultural contexts. Demonstrating cultural sensitivity helps facilitators build rapport and respect, fostering a more inclusive atmosphere (Zehr, 2002).

2. Training and Expertise

Facilitators should receive comprehensive training in restorative justice practices to guide circles effectively. Trained facilitators are better equipped to manage complex emotions, mediate conflict, and create a safe space for all participants. Ongoing training also enables facilitators to refine their skills and stay informed about best practices in restorative justice (Umbreit et al., 2005).

3. Appropriate Setting

Choosing an appropriate setting is essential for fostering openness and safety in the circle. Ideally, the space should be private, comfortable, and free from distractions to encourage a calm and reflective atmosphere. Facilitators should ensure that the seating arrangement allows for clear sightlines between participants and promotes physical comfort. The right setting helps participants feel safe and respected, allowing for deeper engagement and a more effective circle process (Boyes-Watson & Pranis, 2015).

Effective circle facilitation in restorative justice requires a blend of practical techniques, supportive tools, and mindful considerations that collectively foster a space for honest dialogue, accountability, and healing. By establishing community agreements, using a talking piece, engaging in active listening, and employing open-ended questions, facilitators can promote a process that respects the voices and experiences of all participants. Tools like circle arrangements, visual aids, and prepared prompts further support this goal by enhancing organization and encouraging active participation.

Additionally, considerations such as cultural sensitivity, facilitator training, and the choice of setting contribute to a process that is both respectful and empowering for all involved. By embracing these practices, restorative justice facilitators help create a transformative space where harm can be acknowledged, relationships can be rebuilt, and communities can move toward healing and reconciliation.

References

- Boyes-Watson, C., & Pranis, K. (2015). Circle Forward: Building a Restorative School Community. Living Justice Press.

- Hopkins, B. (2004). Just Schools: A Whole School Approach to Restorative Justice. Jessica Kingsley Publishers.

- Pranis, K., Stuart, B., & Wedge, M. (2003). Peacemaking Circles: From Crime to Community. Living Justice Press.

- Umbreit, M. S., Vos, B., Coates, R. B., & Lightfoot, E. (2005). Restorative Justice in the Twenty-First Century: A Social Movement Full of Opportunities and Pitfalls. Marquette Law Review, 89(2), 251-304.

- Zehr, H. (2002). The Little Book of Restorative Justice. Good Books.

CHAPTER 03

Victim-Offender Mediation and Dialogue

Victim-Offender Mediation (VOM) is a structured dialogue process within restorative justice that brings together a victim and an offender to communicate openly about the impact of a crime. VOM aims to provide the victim with a platform for expressing their feelings, while allowing the offender to take responsibility and understand the harm caused. Unlike traditional criminal justice processes focused solely on punishment, VOM seeks to address the emotional and relational aspects of the offense, facilitating healing, restitution, and reconciliation. This chapter explores the principles and processes of VOM, its core elements, and the roles of participants, highlighting how this approach can help repair harm and foster accountability.

Key Principles of Victim-Offender Mediation

Victim-Offender Mediation (VOM) is rooted in several guiding principles designed to create a safe, respectful, and productive environment for both parties. These principles include voluntary participation, a victim-centered approach, accountability, and a restorative focus, all of which contribute to the effectiveness of the mediation process in addressing harm and promoting healing.

1. Voluntary Participation

One of the foundational principles of VOM is that both the victim and offender participate voluntarily. This principle ensures that all parties are genuinely willing to engage in the process and contribute to a meaningful dialogue. By entering into mediation of their own free will, participants are more likely to be open to communication, receptive to each other's perspectives, and committed to achieving resolution. Voluntary participation also empowers both parties by allowing them the freedom to withdraw if they feel uncomfortable or unable to continue (Umbreit & Armour, 2011).

2. Victim-Centered Approach

VOM prioritizes the needs and perspectives of the victim, who is often marginalized in traditional justice processes. By centering the victim's experience, the mediation provides a space for the victim to articulate the emotional, psychological, and financial impact of the offense, allowing them to be heard by both the mediator and the offender. This approach helps to validate the victim's feelings, foster healing, and offer closure. A victim-centered approach also empowers the victim to exercise agency by choosing whether to participate, how much to share, and what form of restitution they desire (Zehr, 2002).

3. Offender Accountability

Accountability is a central aspect of VOM, as the process encourages offenders to take full responsibility for their actions. Through direct dialogue with the victim, offenders have the opportunity to understand the harm they caused and the wider impact of their behavior on others. Acknowledging responsibility and actively participating in reparative actions, such as apologies, financial compensation, or community service, allows offenders to demonstrate remorse and work towards making amends. This principle shifts the focus from punitive measures to personal accountability, often leading to genuine change and rehabilitation (Latimer, Dowden, & Muise, 2005).

4. Safe and Supportive Environment

For VOM to be effective, the mediation setting must be safe and supportive. A trained mediator facilitates the conversation, ensuring that both parties feel respected, secure, and free to express themselves without fear of retaliation. A safe environment encourages honest communication and allows participants to process complex emotions, such as anger, guilt, or sadness. The mediator plays a critical role in maintaining boundaries, managing emotions, and guiding the dialogue toward constructive outcomes. Safety protocols, such as separate pre-mediation meetings and clear behavioral guidelines, further protect participants and enhance the effectiveness of the mediation process (Umbreit & Coates, 1993).

5. Restorative Focus

The ultimate goal of VOM is to repair harm, restore relationships, and promote healing for all involved. Rather than focusing solely on retribution, VOM emphasizes restoration through understanding, empathy, and collaboration. By addressing the underlying needs of both the victim and the offender, the mediation process fosters emotional healing and, ideally, helps to rebuild trust between the parties. This restorative focus is aligned with the broader goals of restorative justice, which seeks to create pathways for reconciliation, personal growth, and community reintegration (Braithwaite, 2002).

Key Points in the Victim-Offender Mediation Process

The VOM process comprises several critical steps designed to create an organized and respectful dialogue. Each phase is carefully structured to meet the needs of the victim, promote accountability in the offender, and ensure that the mediation achieves its restorative objectives.

Direct Communication

The core of VOM is direct, face-to-face communication between the victim and offender. This direct interaction allows the victim to ask questions, express feelings, and share their experience of the crime, while the offender has an opportunity to listen, respond, and acknowledge the harm caused. Direct communication humanizes both parties, breaking down barriers that often exist in traditional justice processes and fostering empathy and understanding (Umbreit, Vos, Coates, & Lightfoot, 2005).

Victim Empowerment

A distinguishing feature of VOM is the emphasis on empowering the victim. By providing the victim with an opportunity to speak openly about the offense, VOM gives them a sense of control and agency. Victims often find solace and healing in the knowledge that their voice has been heard and their needs are being considered. Victim empowerment is a crucial factor in the success of VOM, as it fosters emotional healing, reduces feelings of powerlessness, and offers closure (Zehr, 2002).

Offender Accountability

Offenders are encouraged to take full responsibility for their actions and express remorse. By acknowledging their wrongdoing and listening to the victim's perspective, offenders gain a deeper understanding of the consequences of their actions. This accountability is essential to the restorative process, as it reinforces the importance of personal responsibility and encourages the offender to participate in reparative actions (Braithwaite, 2002).

Mediator Role

A trained mediator plays a pivotal role in VOM by guiding the dialogue, managing emotional exchanges, and ensuring a balanced conversation. The mediator creates an environment of respect and neutrality, facilitating communication between the victim and offender and helping both parties reach a mutually beneficial resolution. Skilled mediators use techniques such as active listening, empathy, and open-ended questioning to draw out meaningful insights and encourage constructive dialogue (Umbreit & Coates, 1993).

Restorative Focus

The purpose of VOM is not to assign blame or impose punishment but to restore relationships, repair harm, and promote healing. By focusing on the impact of the crime and the needs of both parties, VOM provides a framework for creating positive outcomes and encouraging personal growth. The restorative focus also supports the reintegration of the offender into the community, reducing the likelihood of reoffending and strengthening community ties (Zehr, 2002).

Important Aspects of the VOM Process

To enhance the effectiveness of VOM, certain procedural elements are incorporated to prepare participants and guide the mediation toward constructive outcomes.

Preparation Meetings

Before the mediation session, the mediator meets separately with the victim and the offender to discuss their expectations, address concerns, and explain the process. These pre-mediation meetings help establish rapport, clarify boundaries, and ensure that both parties feel comfortable and informed. Preparation meetings are essential to building trust, identifying goals, and preparing participants for the emotional intensity of the mediation (Umbreit & Armour, 2011).

Choice and Agency

VOM respects the autonomy of both the victim and offender, allowing them to decide whether to participate and what information they wish to share. This agency is crucial in fostering a sense of ownership and control, which can lead to more authentic and meaningful interactions. By respecting participants' choices, VOM creates a flexible and supportive environment that accommodates individual needs and promotes open communication (Braithwaite, 2002).

Emotional Expression

Emotional expression is encouraged in VOM, as it allows both parties to process their feelings and experiences openly. Victims and offenders are given the opportunity to express a range of emotions, including anger, fear, sadness, and remorse. The mediator provides guidance and support, helping participants navigate these emotions constructively and ensuring that they do not derail the mediation process (Umbreit et al., 2005).

Restitution Plan

In some VOM cases, participants may develop a restitution plan as part of the mediation process. This plan can include various forms of reparation, such as financial compensation, community service, or symbolic gestures like a written or verbal apology. The restitution plan is intended to address the victim's needs and ensure the offender takes responsibility in a tangible way. This step can be crucial in achieving closure for the victim and fostering accountability for the offender. The restitution agreement is often developed collaboratively, giving both parties input into the terms, which enhances the likelihood that the agreement will be honored and respected by both sides (Latimer, Dowden, & Muise, 2005).

The Role of the Mediator in VOM

A skilled and trained mediator is essential to the success of VOM, as they are responsible for creating and maintaining a safe, respectful environment for the dialogue. Mediators are neutral facilitators who guide the conversation, help manage emotions, and ensure that the discussion remains constructive. The mediator's role includes several key tasks:

1. Creating a Safe Environment: The mediator establishes ground rules for respectful dialogue, ensuring that both parties feel secure and comfortable expressing their thoughts and emotions.

2. Managing Emotional Intensity: Given the sensitive nature of VOM, emotions can run high. The mediator is responsible for managing these emotions, encouraging respectful communication, and preventing the conversation from becoming confrontational.

3. Facilitating Constructive Dialogue: The mediator uses active listening, open-ended questions, and empathy to guide the conversation, helping both parties articulate their feelings and understand each other's perspectives.

4. Encouraging Accountability: The mediator fosters an environment where the offender can take responsibility for their actions and express genuine remorse. This aspect is vital to the restorative process and helps the offender move toward rehabilitation.

5. Supporting the Development of a Restitution Plan: If the participants agree to develop a restitution plan, the mediator assists in drafting terms that satisfy both parties. This may involve creative problem-solving and collaboration to find solutions that are meaningful and achievable.

Challenges and Considerations in VOM

While VOM has proven effective in many cases, it is not without challenges. Certain factors must be carefully considered to ensure that the mediation process is safe, fair, and conducive to healing for both parties.

Emotional Readiness

Both the victim and offender must be emotionally ready to participate in VOM. If either party is unable to engage constructively, the process may be counterproductive or even harmful. Pre-mediation meetings help assess readiness and address any unresolved trauma or emotional distress that could hinder the mediation's success (Umbreit & Armour, 2011).

Power Imbalances

Power imbalances between the victim and offender can pose a challenge in VOM. For example, if the offender holds a position of authority over the victim, such as in cases of domestic abuse, this imbalance may affect the victim's ability to speak openly or advocate for their needs. Mediators must be skilled in recognizing and addressing power dynamics to create a fair and equitable environment (Zehr, 2002).

Cultural Sensitivity

Cultural differences between participants can influence communication styles, values, and expectations. Mediators must be culturally competent and sensitive to these differences, adapting their approach to accommodate participants' unique backgrounds and perspectives. This cultural awareness helps to foster trust, inclusivity, and respect in the mediation process (Braithwaite, 2002).

Limitations of Voluntary Participation

While voluntary participation is essential to VOM, it may also limit the program's reach, as some victims or offenders may be unwilling or unable to participate. In cases where participants are reluctant, alternative restorative justice approaches or traditional justice processes may be more appropriate.

The Impact of VOM on Victims and Offenders

VOM has been shown to have a positive impact on both victims and offenders, often leading to increased satisfaction, closure, and personal growth. For victims, VOM provides an opportunity to express their emotions, have their voices heard, and receive answers to lingering questions. Many victims report feeling a sense of relief and closure following VOM, as they gain an understanding of the offender's perspective and witness their remorse.

For offenders, VOM can be a transformative experience that fosters self-awareness, empathy, and a commitment to change. The process encourages offenders to confront the consequences of their actions, fostering a sense of responsibility and motivating them to make amends. Research indicates that offenders who participate in VOM are less likely to reoffend, as the process often leads to personal growth, reflection, and rehabilitation (Latimer, Dowden, & Muise, 2005).

Victim-Offender Mediation is a valuable tool in restorative justice, offering a structured and empathetic process through which victims and offenders can communicate openly, address harm, and work toward healing. Guided by key principles of voluntary participation, victim-centered approaches, offender accountability, and restorative focus, VOM creates a space for genuine dialogue and mutual understanding. With the support of a trained mediator, participants in VOM have the opportunity to move beyond the limitations of the traditional justice system and achieve meaningful resolution, reconciliation, and healing.

The process of VOM reflects the broader goals of restorative justice by prioritizing relationships, addressing emotional harm, and promoting accountability and empathy. As the field of restorative justice continues to grow, VOM represents a powerful example of how dialogue, understanding, and collaboration can foster a more compassionate and effective approach to addressing crime and its consequences.

References

- Braithwaite, J. (2002). Restorative Justice & Responsive Regulation. New York: Oxford University Press.

- Latimer, J., Dowden, C., & Muise, D. (2005). The effectiveness of restorative justice practices: A meta-analysis. The Prison Journal, 85(2), 127-144.

- Umbreit, M. S., & Armour, M. P. (2011). Restorative Justice Dialogue: An Essential Guide for Research and Practice. New York: Springer.

- Umbreit, M. S., Coates, R. B., & Vos, B. (2005). Victim-offender mediation: An evolving evidence-based practice. Handbook of Restorative Justice: A Global Perspective, 52-61.

- Zehr, H. (2002). The Little Book of Restorative Justice. Intercourse, PA: Good Books.

Principles, processes, and challenges of Victim-Offender Mediation, demonstrating its role in fostering empathy, accountability, and healing within restorative justice.

Through well-structured mediation, VOM not only addresses the harm caused by crime but also builds bridges toward a more constructive and humane approach to justice.

Stages of Mediation in Restorative Justice: Preparation, Dialogue, and Resolution

In restorative justice, mediation is structured around three key stages: preparation, dialogue, and resolution. Each stage is essential to fostering an environment where trust can be built, accountability can be acknowledged, and a mutually agreeable solution can be reached. The purpose of restorative mediation is not only to address the harm caused but also to facilitate understanding, empathy, and relationship repair between the parties involved. By focusing on the victim's needs and the offender's accountability, restorative justice mediation aims to create a balanced, healing process that addresses both emotional and material needs.

Preparation Stage: Building Trust and Establishing the Foundation

The preparation stage sets the groundwork for successful mediation by ensuring that each party is prepared and willing to engage in a constructive dialogue. This stage involves separate, individual meetings with each party, during which the mediator gathers information, explains the mediation process, and assesses each participant's readiness for open communication.

Individual Meetings

The mediator begins the preparation stage by meeting separately with the victim and the offender to understand each person's unique perspective, concerns, and expectations. These one-on-one meetings help the mediator establish rapport and trust, allowing each party to openly share their experiences, fears, and motivations without fear of judgment or retaliation (Umbreit, Vos, Coates, & Lightfoot, 2005). Individual meetings are crucial because they provide the mediator with insights into the emotional states and goals of each party, which informs how the mediation should be conducted to meet the specific needs of those involved.

Explaining the Process

The mediator takes time to explain the principles and goals of restorative justice, highlighting its emphasis on healing, accountability, and relationship repair. This explanation is essential, as participants may be unfamiliar with restorative practices and may need reassurance about the goals and procedures of the mediation. During this step, the mediator underscores the importance of active listening, empathy, and a willingness to take responsibility for one's actions. The mediator also clarifies the expectations for the dialogue stage, including how participants should communicate and listen to one another. This clarity helps to alleviate anxieties and misconceptions that may hinder the process (Zehr, 2002).

Assessing Readiness

One of the critical roles of the mediator is to assess the emotional readiness of each participant to engage in a constructive dialogue. This includes evaluating their ability to handle challenging conversations, listen without interruption, and respect the other party's perspective. The mediator uses the preparation meetings to determine whether each participant has the emotional maturity and willingness to participate in the process, and if necessary, they may suggest additional support or delay the mediation until both parties are prepared to engage productively. Readiness is particularly important, as it ensures that both parties can engage respectfully and constructively, increasing the likelihood of a successful mediation outcome (Armour & Umbreit, 2018).

Dialogue Stage: Facilitating Open Communication and Empathy

The dialogue stage is the heart of restorative mediation, where the parties come together in a joint session to discuss their experiences and the impact of the conflict. In this stage, the mediator facilitates structured communication between the victim and the offender, focusing on storytelling, active listening, empathy building, and identifying needs.

Storytelling

A central aspect of the dialogue stage is allowing each participant to tell their story. Storytelling enables individuals to express their experiences, emotions, and the impact of the incident on their lives. For the victim, storytelling can be a cathartic experience, as it provides a platform to share their pain, anger, and fears openly. For the offender, hearing the victim's story firsthand can be a powerful motivator for accountability and change, as it often brings a new awareness of the consequences of their actions (Van Ness & Strong, 2010).

Active Listening

Active listening is a core practice in the dialogue stage, as it fosters understanding and empathy between the parties. The mediator encourages each participant to listen attentively, avoid interrupting, and refrain from judgment while the other person is speaking. Active listening helps to ensure that each party feels heard and respected, promoting a sense of validation and recognition that is often missing in conventional justice processes. For the offender, active listening can be transformative, as it often brings an emotional awareness of the harm they have caused, motivating them to take meaningful steps toward restitution (Umbreit & Armour, 2011).

Empathy Building

Empathy building is essential for transforming negative emotions into understanding and compassion. The mediator guides the participants in recognizing and validating each other's emotions, helping them to see the situation from the other person's perspective. For example, the mediator may ask reflective questions that encourage empathy, such as, "How do you think this experience has affected the other person's life?" or "What would it mean to you if the roles were reversed?" By fostering empathy, the mediator creates a space where both parties can move beyond anger and resentment, paving the way for a genuine willingness to repair the relationship (Braithwaite, 2002).

Identifying Needs

As the dialogue progresses, the mediator helps the participants articulate their needs and concerns arising from the conflict. Identifying needs is crucial, as it provides a foundation for developing a meaningful and restorative resolution. For the victim, this may include a desire for an apology, financial restitution, or assurance that similar harm will not occur in the future. For the offender, identifying needs may involve a desire for forgiveness, understanding, or an opportunity to make amends. By openly expressing their needs, the participants can work together to find solutions that address the harm in a way that satisfies both parties (Latimer, Dowden, & Muise, 2005).

Resolution Stage: Developing and Implementing the Agreement

The resolution stage focuses on creating a concrete plan to address the harm caused, meet the needs of both parties, and promote accountability. This stage involves agreement development, creating a plan of action, ensuring accountability, and, in some cases, follow-up.

Agreement Development

Once the participants have shared their experiences and identified their needs, the mediator facilitates a discussion to develop a mutually acceptable agreement. The goal of this agreement is to outline specific actions that the offender will take to repair the harm caused. This may include financial restitution, community service, or a commitment to participate in rehabilitative programs. Agreement development is collaborative, with both parties contributing to the terms, which enhances the likelihood that the agreement will be meaningful and adhered to by both sides (Umbreit, Vos, Coates, & Lightfoot, 2005).

Plan of Action

The mediator assists the parties in creating a detailed plan for implementing the agreement. This plan outlines the steps each party will take, the timeline for completion, and any resources or support needed to fulfill the agreement. A clear plan of action helps to ensure that the resolution is practical and achievable, increasing the likelihood of compliance and satisfaction for both parties.

Accountability

Accountability is a core principle of restorative justice, and the resolution stage emphasizes the importance of the offender taking responsibility for their actions. The mediator ensures that the offender understands their obligations under the agreement and that they are committed to fulfilling these responsibilities. Accountability fosters a sense of ownership, as the offender's actions become a tangible demonstration of their commitment to change and restitution (Zehr, 2002).

Follow-Up

In some cases, the mediator may schedule follow-up meetings to monitor progress and address any concerns that arise during the implementation of the agreement. Follow-up meetings provide an opportunity for the parties to evaluate the resolution's impact, celebrate progress, and address any unresolved issues. This additional support reinforces the commitment to restorative practices and helps to ensure the long-term success of the mediation.

Key Points about Restorative Justice Mediation

Restorative justice mediation is distinct from conventional dispute resolution, as it prioritizes relationships, accountability, and healing. Key principles that guide this approach include:

1. Focus on Relationships: The primary goal is to repair relationships between those affected by the conflict, not merely to resolve a dispute.

2. Victim-Centered Approach: Significant attention is given to the victim's experience and needs.

3. Taking Responsibility: The offender is encouraged to acknowledge their actions and take responsibility for the harm caused.

4. Voluntary Participation: All parties participate willingly, ensuring a more authentic and impactful process.

The three stages of restorative justice mediation—preparation, dialogue, and resolution—form a structured yet flexible process that fosters healing, accountability, and reconciliation. By focusing on trust-building, empathy, and collaborative problem-solving, restorative mediation offers a compassionate and effective alternative to punitive justice approaches. This chapter has highlighted how each stage contributes to a holistic process that addresses emotional and material needs, strengthens relationships, and promotes a more humane approach to justice.

References

- Armour, M. P., & Umbreit, M. S. (2018). Restorative Justice Dialogue: An Essential Guide for Research and Practice. New York: Springer.

- Braithwaite, J. (2002). Restorative Justice & Responsive Regulation. New York: Oxford University Press.

- Latimer, J., Dowden, C., & Muise, D. (2005). The effectiveness of restorative justice practices: A meta-analysis. The Prison Journal, 85(2), 127-144.

- Umbreit, M. S., Vos, B., Coates, R. B., & Lightfoot, E. (2005). Victim-offender mediation: An evolving evidence-based practice. Handbook of Restorative Justice: A Global Perspective, 52-61.

- Zehr, H. (2002). The Little Book of Restorative Justice. Intercourse, PA: Good Books.

Examples and Impact of Victim-Offender Mediation on Victims, Offenders, and Communities

Victim-Offender Mediation (VOM) is a unique approach in restorative justice that brings victims and offenders together in a facilitated setting to discuss the crime and its impact. VOM is designed to promote healing, accountability, and understanding, with positive outcomes observed for victims, offenders, and communities. Through direct communication, VOM allows both parties to address the emotional, psychological, and practical effects of the crime. This chapter explores real-life examples of VOM and examines its impacts on victims, offenders, and the broader community, illustrating its potential for transformation and repair.

Examples of Victim-Offender Mediation

VOM is applied across a wide range of criminal cases, from property-related offenses to interpersonal crimes. Each case demonstrates how VOM can address the unique needs of the individuals involved and create opportunities for reconciliation, understanding, and resolution.

Example 1: Shoplifting Incident

In cases of minor theft or shoplifting, VOM can be instrumental in addressing the harm caused and preventing future offenses. For example, a shop owner who has experienced a series of thefts may feel frustrated, violated, and financially harmed. Through VOM, the shop owner is given a platform to communicate these feelings to the offender, who may not have fully grasped the consequences of their actions. In one instance, a teenage offender participated in VOM with a small business owner. Through dialogue, the shop owner was able to express the financial impact and sense of betrayal, while the offender, seeing the human cost of their actions, committed to a restitution plan that included community service and an apology. This engagement not only empowered the victim but also fostered a sense of accountability in the offender, reducing the likelihood of future shoplifting incidents (Umbreit, Vos, Coates, & Lightfoot, 2005).

Example 2: Domestic Violence Survivor and Abuser

In more serious cases, such as domestic violence, VOM can serve as a healing space for victims to express their trauma and for offenders to confront the impact of their actions. Domestic violence cases require careful screening and skilled facilitation, ensuring the safety and comfort of the survivor. In one documented case, a survivor of domestic violence met with her former partner through VOM. Guided by a trained mediator, she was able to articulate the lasting emotional and psychological trauma inflicted by the abuse, which prompted the offender to acknowledge the harm and take responsibility. Although VOM does not replace the criminal justice process in such cases, it provided the victim with a unique space for empowerment and closure (Daly, 2006).

Example 3: Property Damage and Restitution Plan

In cases involving property damage, VOM offers a practical framework for offenders to make amends. For instance, in a case involving vandalism of a community park, a group of teenage offenders met with community representatives and residents affected by the crime. This facilitated meeting allowed community members to convey the personal and communal impact of the vandalism. Through dialogue, the teenagers recognized the broader consequences of their actions and collaborated with the community to develop a restitution plan, which included volunteer work and a formal apology to residents. This example highlights how VOM can repair fractured relationships within a community and promote mutual understanding.

Impact on Victims

For victims, the benefits of participating in VOM are numerous, as the process addresses both the emotional and psychological effects of the crime.

Empowerment

One of the most significant impacts of VOM on victims is the sense of empowerment it fosters. Traditional criminal justice processes often overlook the victim's voice, leaving them feeling unheard and marginalized. In contrast, VOM gives victims the opportunity to share their story, express their emotions, and influence the resolution process. By directly confronting the offender, victims can regain a sense of agency and control, which is particularly important in cases where they may have felt helpless or vulnerable (Umbreit, 2000).

Reduced Anger and Fear

Meeting the offender in a controlled, facilitated environment can help reduce feelings of anger and fear. Studies have shown that victims who participate in VOM often report feeling less fearful and more secure after confronting the offender and understanding their motivations. This reduction in fear and anger can be transformative, allowing victims to move forward without the psychological burden that the crime may have imposed (Strang, 2002).

Improved Sense of Justice

VOM provides victims with a sense of justice that may be absent in traditional legal proceedings. Rather than being passive participants, victims are actively involved in shaping the outcome and can directly influence the restitution terms. This involvement can enhance their perception of justice being served, as the process is more responsive to their needs and concerns (Van Ness & Strong, 2010).

Potential for Healing and Forgiveness

VOM creates an environment where victims can begin to process their emotions and potentially move towards forgiveness. While forgiveness is not an expected outcome, it is possible within the VOM framework, as direct communication and accountability foster understanding and healing. This process can be particularly meaningful in cases involving individuals who share community ties, as forgiveness can pave the way for restored relationships and trust.

Impact on Offenders

For offenders, VOM offers a path to accountability, empathy development, and behavioral change, all of which contribute to a reduced risk of recidivism.

Increased Accountability

Facing the victim and hearing firsthand about the consequences of their actions can compel offenders to take greater responsibility. Unlike traditional punishments, which may breed resentment, VOM emphasizes personal accountability by requiring offenders to confront the human impact of their actions. This accountability is a key factor in promoting genuine remorse and a desire to make amends (Braithwaite, 2002).

Empathy Development

Hearing the victim's perspective can foster empathy and a deeper understanding of the harm caused by their actions. Many offenders lack insight into the emotional and psychological impact of their behavior, but VOM provides them with a direct, personal encounter with the consequences of their actions. This empathy-building experience can motivate offenders to change their behavior, as they come to understand the importance of respecting others' rights and well-being (Sherman & Strang, 2007).

Motivation to Make Amends

VOM often instills a desire in offenders to make meaningful reparations, as they recognize the harm caused and wish to contribute positively to the victim's healing. Restitution agreements provide offenders with a tangible way to take responsibility, which may include apologies, community service, or financial compensation. This active involvement in the resolution process reinforces accountability and provides a structured path to redemption.

Reduced Recidivism

Research suggests that VOM participation is associated with lower recidivism rates, as offenders who engage in restorative practices are less likely to reoffend. The development of empathy, accountability, and an understanding of the impact of their actions are key factors that contribute to this behavioral change. Reduced recidivism not only benefits the offender but also contributes to community safety and well-being.

Impact on Communities

The effects of VOM extend beyond the individuals involved, as it promotes community cohesion, reduces crime rates, and enhances public perceptions of justice.

Community Cohesion

By bringing victims and offenders together to address harm, VOM can help restore fractured relationships within the community. It encourages open dialogue and fosters mutual respect, contributing to a more cohesive, understanding, and supportive community environment. In cases where offenders and victims share community ties, VOM can be particularly impactful, as it allows community members to address conflicts directly and collaboratively (Zehr, 2002).

Reduced Crime Rates

The lower recidivism rates associated with VOM contribute to reduced crime rates in communities. As offenders develop accountability and empathy, they are less likely to engage in future criminal behavior. This reduction in crime not only enhances community safety but also reduces the social and financial costs associated with repeat offenses.

Positive Perception of the Justice System

Communities that witness VOM in action often develop a more positive perception of the justice system. By observing that victims are heard, offenders are held accountable, and harm is addressed constructively, community members may view the justice system as more humane, effective, and responsive to their needs. This improved perception can foster greater trust in legal and social institutions, contributing to stronger social bonds and greater public cooperation with justice initiatives.

Important Considerations for VOM

Despite its benefits, VOM is not universally suitable and must be approached with care.

1. Victim Choice: Participation in VOM should always be voluntary for victims, with appropriate support systems available to

ensure their safety and well-being. Victims should feel free to decline participation without consequence.

2. Case Suitability: Not all crimes or offenders are suitable for VOM. Careful screening is necessary to determine whether a case is appropriate, particularly in serious cases where power imbalances or safety risks exist.

3. Trained Facilitators: Skilled mediators are crucial to guide the VOM process effectively, as they ensure respectful dialogue, manage emotions, and facilitate productive outcomes.

Victim-Offender Mediation represents a transformative approach within restorative justice, offering victims a sense of empowerment, giving offenders a path to accountability, and fostering a safer, more cohesive community. Through examples and documented impacts, it is clear that VOM can significantly benefit those directly and indirectly affected by crime, contributing to the broader goals of healing, relationship repair, and societal well-being. With careful implementation, VOM has the potential to enhance the justice system, addressing the root causes of harm and creating a more compassionate and effective framework for conflict resolution.

CHAPTER 04

Restorative Community Service

Restorative community service represents a transformative approach within the restorative justice framework. While traditional community service typically focuses on fulfilling a court-ordered requirement through the performance of specific tasks, restorative community service emphasizes repair, accountability, and active engagement with the victim, community, and other stakeholders. By promoting dialogue and a deeper understanding of the harm caused, restorative community service encourages offenders to take meaningful actions to repair relationships and contribute positively to the community. This chapter explores the core differences between traditional and restorative community service and highlights the impact of restorative approaches through examples and scholarly perspectives.

Differences Between Traditional and Restorative Community Service

The goals, structure, and outcomes of traditional and restorative community service differ significantly. In traditional community service, offenders are often required to complete hours of service as a penalty, focusing primarily on performing tasks without addressing the root causes or impacts of their actions. Restorative community service, on the other hand, is designed to directly address the harm caused and encourage a sense of responsibility in the offender, emphasizing dialogue, accountability, and the engagement of the broader community.

Focus on Harm Repair

In traditional community service, the primary focus is on fulfilling a sentence requirement rather than addressing the specific harm caused. Tasks such as cleaning public areas, sorting donations, or assisting in community projects are commonly assigned. While these tasks contribute to the community, they do not necessarily address the underlying issues or the harm experienced by the victim or the community directly affected by the offense.

Restorative community service, however, is oriented towards meaningful harm repair. Rather than generic tasks, restorative service involves actions directly related to the offense, often chosen in collaboration with victims and community representatives. For example, if a young offender vandalizes a public park, a restorative approach would involve working closely with community members to repair the damage, such as repainting and restoring park structures, planting trees, or organizing a community event to restore trust. This method emphasizes taking active steps to amend the harm done, providing a tangible sense of restoration for both the offender and the community (Bazemore & Umbreit, 1995).

Victim Involvement

Traditional community service typically excludes the victim from the process. It is focused on the offender fulfilling service hours and meeting court-mandated requirements, with minimal or no interaction with the victim. As a result, victims may feel excluded from the justice process and may not experience a sense of resolution or acknowledgment of the harm caused.

Restorative community service, in contrast, prioritizes victim involvement. By including victims in the process, restorative service creates a space for them to share their experiences and participate in deciding how the offender can make amends. This approach not only validates the victim's experiences but also fosters a sense of empowerment and closure. For example, in cases of property damage, victims may engage in discussions with the offender to determine specific ways to repair or compensate for the harm. This inclusive approach allows for a more meaningful form of accountability, as the offender is directly confronted with the real impact of their actions on others (Johnstone, 2011).

Accountability and Dialogue

One of the central tenets of restorative justice is accountability, which involves taking responsibility for one's actions and understanding the broader consequences. Traditional community service often lacks this element, as offenders may view the service as a mere obligation to fulfill without truly understanding or addressing the harm caused. This approach can reduce accountability to a checklist, rather than fostering a sense of personal responsibility or growth.

In restorative community service, accountability is achieved through dialogue and active participation. Offenders engage in facilitated discussions with victims, community members, and mediators, which allows them to listen to the perspectives of those affected by their actions and express their own remorse or regret. This dialogue fosters a sense of empathy, as offenders are encouraged to acknowledge the harm they caused and work collaboratively toward solutions that restore balance. Studies suggest that restorative approaches enhance an offender's willingness to take responsibility and contribute to reduced rates of recidivism, as offenders internalize the importance of making amends (Sherman & Strang, 2007).

Community Engagement

While traditional community service may contribute to the community in a general sense, it rarely engages the community in meaningful ways. Offenders often perform tasks in isolation or under the supervision of community service supervisors, without interaction with community members who may have been affected by the offense. This approach limits opportunities for offenders to understand the social impact of their actions or to develop positive connections with the community.

Restorative community service, however, encourages active community engagement. Community members, including victims and local stakeholders, participate in the planning and implementation of the service tasks, promoting a sense of collective responsibility and cohesion. By involving the broader community, restorative service provides an opportunity for community members to witness the offender's commitment to repair and for the offender to reintegrate into the community with renewed support and trust. Community engagement has been shown to strengthen the effectiveness of restorative practices, as it encourages healing on a collective level and builds a more cohesive social fabric (Zehr, 2002).

Example Scenarios

The differences between traditional and restorative community service can be illustrated through concrete examples that highlight the varied approaches and outcomes of each method.

Traditional Community Service Example

In a traditional community service setting, a high school student who has vandalized school property might be assigned to clean graffiti in the schoolyard or assist with maintenance tasks after school. While this form of service holds the student accountable to a certain extent, it is largely focused on fulfilling a requirement, with little attention given to repairing relationships with the affected students or school community. The student may complete the assigned hours without fully understanding the impact of their actions on others or taking responsibility in a meaningful way.

Restorative Community Service Example

In contrast, in a restorative community service model, the same student would participate in a mediated session with other students, school staff, and potentially parents. This dialogue session would provide an opportunity for the affected students to share how the vandalism impacted their sense of pride and safety within the school. The student who committed the offense would then apologize directly and work with the school community to decide on actions to repair the harm, such as organizing a school beautification project, leading an assembly on respect for shared spaces, or creating art to cover the area impacted by the vandalism. By participating in these efforts, the student not only repairs physical damage but also contributes to restoring trust within the school community.

Scholarly Perspectives on Restorative Community Service

Research has demonstrated that restorative community service can have positive impacts on both offenders and communities. Studies indicate that restorative practices, by emphasizing empathy, responsibility, and community engagement, contribute to positive behavioral changes in offenders, including a reduced likelihood of reoffending. According to Bazemore and Umbreit (1995), restorative service allows offenders to confront the consequences of their actions in a direct and meaningful way, which fosters a deeper understanding of accountability and empathy.

Similarly, Sherman and Strang (2007) found that restorative community service often enhances community trust in the justice process, as it actively involves victims and local stakeholders, giving them a sense of voice and influence. This participatory approach can also improve victims' satisfaction with the outcome, as they witness tangible efforts toward restoration and healing.

Zehr (2002) emphasizes that restorative practices benefit communities by promoting cohesion and reducing stigmatization. When offenders are given the chance to make amends in meaningful ways, they are more likely to be accepted back into the community and less likely to reoffend, contributing to long-term reductions in community crime rates.

Restorative community service redefines traditional notions of punishment and accountability by placing harm repair, accountability, and dialogue at its center. Unlike traditional community service, which often emphasizes fulfilling a requirement, restorative service focuses on the offender's active engagement in repairing harm, both tangible and intangible. By involving victims and communities in this process, restorative service fosters empathy, builds trust, and contributes to the healing of individuals and communities alike. Through its emphasis on meaningful accountability and community engagement, restorative community service has emerged as an effective tool for promoting behavioral change and strengthening social bonds, aligning with the broader goals of restorative justice.

Benefits of Restorative Community Service

Restorative community service offers a transformative approach to addressing crime by prioritizing healing, accountability, and active community engagement. Unlike traditional community service, which often involves fulfilling set hours of service as a punishment, restorative community service encourages offenders to make meaningful contributions that directly address the harm caused. This approach benefits not only the community but also the offender by fostering skill development, enhancing self-worth, and reducing the likelihood of reoffending. This chapter examines the benefits of restorative community service for both the community and the offender, along with key aspects that make it effective within restorative justice frameworks.

Benefits for the Community

Restorative community service provides tangible and intangible benefits to the community, promoting a safer, more cohesive society while fostering a sense of justice and closure for victims and community members.

Direct Positive Impact

Restorative community service allows offenders to participate in projects that address specific needs within the community. These projects can range from cleaning parks and assisting in shelters to supporting local charities and public initiatives. By directly engaging with the community, offenders make contributions that improve the quality of life for residents, create safer environments, and foster communal pride. This direct impact is significant as it helps transform neighborhoods and builds a supportive environment for all members (Bazemore & Maloney, 1994).

Sense of Justice

A unique aspect of restorative community service is its ability to create a sense of justice for victims and community members. Observing offenders actively contribute to community welfare can provide a sense of closure, as offenders visibly work to repair the harm they caused. When offenders make meaningful contributions, the community witnesses justice in action, leading to a greater sense of fairness and satisfaction with the justice system. This approach contrasts with traditional punishment, which may leave victims feeling that justice is incomplete (Umbreit, Vos, & Coates, 2006).

Community Engagement

Restorative community service promotes community involvement in the justice process, strengthening social cohesion. Involving community members in selecting service projects fosters a sense of ownership and engagement, empowering them to take part in the healing process. When communities collaborate in shaping service projects, they feel more connected and valued, leading to stronger bonds between residents and creating an environment of collective responsibility (Johnstone & Van Ness, 2007).

Reduced Crime

Research suggests that restorative community service can help reduce crime by addressing the underlying factors that contribute to criminal behavior. By providing offenders with opportunities for personal growth, skill development, and positive social interactions, restorative service may reduce recidivism rates, fostering a safer community. In a 2015 study, offenders participating in restorative justice programs were found to have lower reoffending rates, as these programs encouraged accountability and social reintegration, decreasing the likelihood of future offenses (Sherman, Strang, & Woods, 2015).

Benefits for the Offender

Restorative community service offers several rehabilitative benefits for offenders, including increased accountability, skill development, and improved self-image. Through active engagement in positive contributions, offenders can transform their lives, restoring their sense of purpose and identity within society.

Accountability and Responsibility

One of the primary benefits of restorative community service is that it encourages offenders to take responsibility for their actions. Rather than passively serving time or paying fines, offenders actively work to repair the harm they caused, fostering a sense of accountability. This process often leads offenders to acknowledge the impact of their actions on victims and the community, prompting reflection and a genuine desire to make amends. The restorative approach's emphasis on responsibility has been linked to personal growth and a reduced likelihood of future offenses (Zehr, 2002).

Skill Development

Restorative community service provides offenders with valuable opportunities to develop practical skills. By participating in projects that require teamwork, communication, and problem-solving, offenders gain experience that can enhance their employability and contribute to future success. Skills such as time management, conflict resolution, and leadership are often cultivated in community service settings, helping offenders prepare for positive reintegration into the workforce (Bazemore & Maloney, 1994).

Positive Self-Image

Contributing positively to the community can significantly impact an offender's self-esteem and sense of self-worth. Restorative community service allows offenders to see themselves as capable of making positive changes, countering feelings of guilt, shame, or low self-regard that may accompany criminal behavior. Studies have shown that when offenders engage in restorative practices, they often experience increased self-esteem and a more positive self-concept, which contributes to long-term behavioral changes (Braithwaite, 1989).

Reintegration into Society

Restorative community service serves as a bridge for offenders to reconnect with society. Through active participation in community projects, offenders build new social networks and foster a sense of belonging. By working alongside community members, they demonstrate their commitment to positive change, which can help rebuild trust and support their reintegration. This process of social reintegration is vital for reducing stigma, allowing offenders to redefine their role within the community (Maruna, 2001).

Reduced Stigma

Offenders who engage in restorative community service may experience a reduction in the stigma associated with their criminal record. By making amends and contributing to the well-being of others, they challenge stereotypes of criminality and show that they are committed to change. Restorative practices allow offenders to reintegrate into society with a positive reputation, reducing the social barriers they face after serving their sentence (Braithwaite, 1989).

Key Aspects of Effective Restorative Community Service

For restorative community service to be truly effective, certain key aspects should be considered. These components ensure that the process aligns with restorative justice principles and maximizes the benefits for victims, offenders, and the community.

Victim Involvement

The active involvement of victims is a cornerstone of restorative justice. Ideally, victims should have a voice in determining the type of community service an offender performs. By including victims in this process, restorative community service provides them with an opportunity for empowerment, as they can suggest ways the offender can repair the harm. Victim involvement helps build a sense of justice, as it enables victims to have a say in how their needs are addressed (Umbreit, Vos, & Coates, 2006).

Meaningful Work

Restorative community service is most impactful when it directly relates to the offense and provides a tangible benefit to the community. For instance, if an offender is responsible for vandalism, a restorative service could involve assisting in community beautification efforts. This relevance makes the service more meaningful, allowing the offender to directly address the harm they caused while contributing to a positive outcome (Zehr, 2002).

Supervision and Support

For restorative community service to succeed, offenders need adequate support and supervision throughout the process. Trained supervisors or facilitators can guide offenders, helping them develop the skills necessary for successful completion. Support systems, such as counseling and mentorship, may also be beneficial, as they encourage offenders to reflect on their progress and reinforce positive behaviors (Bazemore & Maloney, 1994).

Restorative community service is a powerful tool within restorative justice that benefits both communities and offenders by promoting active accountability, skill development, and social reintegration. Unlike traditional community service, which often lacks engagement and relevance, restorative service directly addresses harm, creating a space for healing and transformation. By actively contributing to the community, offenders experience personal growth, while communities benefit from enhanced cohesion, reduced crime, and an increased sense of justice. With victim involvement, meaningful work, and adequate support, restorative community service can foster lasting change, helping to rebuild trust and strengthen social ties within society. Through these efforts, restorative community service redefines justice as a process of healing, one that restores individuals, relationships, and communities.

References

- Bazemore, G., & Maloney, D. (1994). Rehabilitating Community Service: Toward Restorative Service Sanctions in a Balanced Juvenile Justice System. Federal Probation.

- Braithwaite, J. (1989). Crime, Shame, and Reintegration. Cambridge University Press.

- Johnstone, G., & Van Ness, D. W. (2007). Handbook of Restorative Justice. Willan Publishing.

- Maruna, S. (2001). Making Good: How Ex-Convicts Reform and Rebuild Their Lives. American Psychological Association.

- Sherman, L. W., Strang, H., & Woods, D. J. (2015). Restorative Justice and Recidivism: A Systematic Review of the Research. Cambridge University Press.

- Umbreit, M., Vos, B., & Coates, R. (2006). Restorative Justice Dialogue: An Essential Guide for Research and Practice. Springer Publishing.

- Zehr, H. (2002). The Little Book of Restorative Justice. Good Books.

Best Practices for Implementing Restorative Community Service Programs

Implementing restorative community service programs requires careful planning, empathy-building, and collaboration among all parties involved to ensure the program's success and sustainability. Unlike traditional community service, which may focus solely on fulfilling punitive requirements, restorative community service emphasizes repairing harm, meeting the needs of those affected, and fostering meaningful skill development for offenders. This chapter provides best practices for effectively implementing restorative community service programs, offering guidance on process explanations, empathy-building, plan development, and monitoring. It also discusses restorative practices like community-building circles, restorative conferences, and restorative chats, all of which foster connection and accountability.

Best Practices for Implementing Restorative Community Service Programs

Successful implementation of restorative community service programs hinges on establishing clear expectations, nurturing empathy, identifying needs, and providing meaningful skills. The following best practices outline strategies to enhance the restorative process for all participants.

1. Explain the Process

One of the foundational steps in implementing a restorative community service program is to ensure that participants—offenders, victims, and facilitators—clearly understand the process. Participants should be aware of the objectives, responsibilities, and expected outcomes, creating a shared understanding and transparency in the program. By explaining each step, facilitators can reduce any confusion or apprehension and build a sense of commitment to the restorative journey (Zehr, 2002). Clear communication builds trust and ensures that everyone involved is aligned with the program's purpose.

2. Build Empathy

Empathy is a core element of restorative justice, as it allows offenders to recognize the impact of their actions on victims and the community. Facilitators can encourage empathy-building through activities like sharing personal stories, participating in dialogue circles, and discussing the emotional, social, and financial consequences of the offense. Empathy-building helps offenders develop a deeper understanding of the harm they have caused, which can lead to genuine remorse and a desire to make amends (Umbreit, Vos, & Coates, 2006). Additionally, victims feel acknowledged and validated, fostering healing on both sides.

3. Identify Needs

An effective restorative program addresses the needs of all parties involved: victims, offenders, and the community. Facilitators should work closely with victims to understand their perspectives and any specific needs for reparation. Offenders' needs should also be considered, as they may require support, guidance, and opportunities for personal growth throughout the process. By identifying and addressing the needs of each party, restorative community service can offer a holistic approach that promotes healing, accountability, and reparation (Bazemore & Maloney, 1994).

4. Develop a Restorative Plan

Creating a restorative plan tailored to the incident and its impact is essential for achieving meaningful outcomes. The plan should address the root causes of the harm, propose actions to repair the damage, and provide support for offenders as they work toward reconciliation. This plan could include specific community service projects, skill-building opportunities, and support resources to help offenders learn from their mistakes. A well-developed plan also allows for collaborative input, which enhances ownership and commitment to the restorative process (Braithwaite, 1989).

5. Monitor the Plan

Ongoing monitoring and support are crucial for the successful completion of the restorative plan. Facilitators should regularly check in with offenders to provide guidance, encouragement, and any necessary adjustments to the plan. Monitoring helps ensure accountability and helps offenders stay on track. Support systems, such as counseling or mentorship, can be valuable in addressing any obstacles offenders may encounter, ultimately enhancing their success and the program's effectiveness (Johnstone & Van Ness, 2007).

6. Give Participants Time

Restorative processes are complex and often require time for participants to fully process and engage with the experience. Allowing adequate time for reflection, remorse, and meaningful engagement ensures that offenders are not simply rushing through a checklist but are genuinely learning from the process. This time can facilitate genuine change in offenders' attitudes and behavior, making the experience more impactful and enduring (Maruna, 2001).

7. Use Meaningful Skills

To maximize the impact of restorative community service, it's essential to provide offenders with work that not only benefits the community but also equips them with valuable, transferable skills. Engaging offenders in meaningful work experiences—such as teamwork, leadership, or practical skills—enhances their employability and sense of personal growth. When offenders learn valuable skills through community service, they are better prepared to reintegrate into society, reducing their likelihood of reoffending (Bazemore & Maloney, 1994).

8. Focus on Connection

Restorative community service should prioritize fostering connections among participants and the broader community. When offenders feel connected to their peers and community members, they are more likely to feel a sense of belonging and responsibility. Building these connections can help to mitigate social isolation, reinforce positive behavior, and support the reintegration process, creating a more cohesive and supportive community environment (Zehr, 2002).

Restorative Practices in Community Service

Implementing restorative community service often involves specific practices designed to facilitate dialogue, accountability, and relationship-building. Below are some common restorative practices used in community service programs.

Community Building Circles

Community building circles are versatile tools that bring together community members, offenders, and victims to share experiences, express feelings, and build relationships. These circles encourage open communication, empathy, and mutual understanding, helping participants form a shared commitment to community well-being. Community building circles can be used at various stages of the restorative process, from initial discussions to the completion of community service projects, promoting a collaborative environment (Pranis, 2005).

Restorative Conferences

Restorative conferences are structured meetings between offenders and those impacted by their actions, including victims, family members, and community representatives. These conferences provide an opportunity for offenders to hear directly from those affected, fostering a deeper understanding of the consequences of their behavior. Through structured dialogue, participants can discuss the offense, its impact, and possible ways to repair the harm. Restorative conferences have been shown to increase offender accountability and promote healing for victims (Umbreit, Vos, & Coates, 2006).

Norm Setting

Norm setting is a proactive restorative practice that involves establishing shared expectations and norms within a group setting, such as a classroom or community program. By collaboratively defining acceptable behaviors and values, participants feel more ownership over the community's standards and are more likely to adhere to them. Norm setting can be especially effective in educational environments, where students learn to respect each other and work together to maintain a positive and inclusive atmosphere (Stinchcomb, Bazemore, & Riestenberg, 2006).

Restorative Chats

Restorative chats are informal, one-on-one conversations between facilitators and participants, often used in classrooms or community programs. These chats can help address minor issues before they escalate, providing an opportunity for reflection and redirection. Restorative chats promote a sense of care and attentiveness, allowing participants to feel heard and understood. When used consistently, restorative chats can foster a supportive environment that reinforces positive behavior (Johnstone & Van Ness, 2007).

Implementing restorative community service programs requires thoughtful planning, empathy-building, and collaborative engagement to foster healing and accountability. By incorporating best practices like explaining the process, building empathy, identifying needs, developing restorative plans, and using meaningful skills, facilitators can create impactful and transformative programs. Additionally, restorative practices like community-building circles, restorative conferences, norm setting, and restorative chats encourage open dialogue, mutual understanding, and a sense of responsibility. These practices provide a foundation for a restorative approach that not only repairs harm but also builds stronger, more resilient communities.

Restorative community service emphasizes positive change and growth, offering offenders an opportunity to rebuild trust and relationships while making a meaningful contribution to society. Through these best practices and restorative practices, community service becomes more than just a punishment—it becomes a journey of personal development, social reintegration, and community healing.

References

- Bazemore, G., & Maloney, D. (1994). Rehabilitating Community Service: Toward Restorative Service Sanctions in a Balanced Juvenile Justice System. Federal Probation.
- Braithwaite, J. (1989). Crime, Shame, and Reintegration. Cambridge University Press.
- Johnstone, G., & Van Ness, D. (2007). Handbook of Restorative Justice. Willan Publishing.
- Maruna, S. (2001). Making Good: How Ex-Convicts Reform and Rebuild Their Lives. American Psychological Association.
- Pranis, K. (2005). The Little Book of Circle Processes: A New/Old Approach to Peacemaking. Good Books.
- Sherman, L., Strang, H., & Woods, D. J. (2015). Restorative Justice and Recidivism: Promises Made, Promises Kept? Restorative Justice International.
- Stinchcomb, J. B., Bazemore, G., & Riestenberg, N. (2006). Beyond Zero Tolerance: Restoring Justice in Secondary Schools. Youth Violence and Juvenile Justice.
- Umbreit, M. S., Vos, B., & Coates, R. B. (2006). Restorative Justice Dialogue: An Essential Guide for Research and Practice. Springer.

CHAPTER 05

Reparations and Restorative Reparations

In the context of justice, the terms "reparations" and "restorative justice" signify approaches that focus on healing rather than punishment. While reparations specifically involve compensating for harm caused, often through financial or symbolic means, restorative justice encompasses a broader range of actions aimed at repairing relationships, fostering dialogue, and rebuilding trust among victims, offenders, and communities. Reparative justice, therefore, is an integral aspect of restorative justice that emphasizes directly addressing harm suffered by victims through reparations, apologies, and community engagement. This chapter examines the relationship between reparations and restorative justice, the importance of a victim-centered approach, and the various forms and challenges associated with reparative practices.

Understanding Reparative Justice and Its Role in Restorative Justice

Reparative justice is a subset of restorative justice that prioritizes tangible actions to address the harm caused by offenses. It seeks to move beyond conventional punitive measures by focusing on redress and healing. According to Zehr (2002), restorative justice aims to "address the needs of those impacted by crime or injustice and engage those responsible in taking steps to repair the harm." Reparations play a crucial role in this process, providing a structured means of acknowledging harm and making amends, whether through financial compensation, apologies, or community-based initiatives.

Key Aspects of the Relationship Between Reparations and Restorative Justice

Several key principles underscore the relationship between reparations and restorative justice, highlighting how these concepts complement each other in fostering healing and accountability.

1. Focus on Repairing Harm

Both reparations and restorative justice prioritize repairing harm over simply punishing the offender. Instead of focusing on retribution, these approaches seek to address the root causes and consequences of harm. By emphasizing repair, restorative justice provides a holistic response that values the well-being of victims, the rehabilitation of offenders, and the health of communities (Bazemore & Maloney, 1994). In cases of severe or historical injustice, reparations may also extend beyond the immediate victim to address long-standing harm to entire communities.

2. Beyond Financial Compensation

While financial compensation is a common form of reparation, restorative justice embraces a broader set of reparative actions that may not always be monetary. Restorative approaches recognize that financial compensation alone may not fully address the emotional and social consequences of harm. Non-financial reparations—such as apologies, community service, and efforts to prevent future harm—offer symbolic and practical avenues for offenders to make amends, enhancing the healing process for victims (Daly, 2002). This broader perspective allows for a more meaningful engagement in the reparative process, as it acknowledges the complexities of harm and the need for comprehensive redress.

3. Victim-Centered Approach

Restorative justice and reparations are fundamentally victim-centered, prioritizing the needs, perspectives, and participation of the harmed party. Giving victims a voice in the process empowers them to share their experiences, articulate their needs, and shape the reparative actions that offenders undertake. This victim-centered approach provides a sense of agency to those who may have felt disempowered by the harm, facilitating emotional and psychological healing (Umbreit & Armour, 2011). The focus on the victim's needs also reinforces the accountability of the offender, as they are directly confronted with the impact of their actions and the expectations for making amends.

4. Community Involvement

Community involvement is a hallmark of restorative justice that distinguishes it from traditional justice approaches. By incorporating community members into the process, restorative justice seeks to foster a sense of collective responsibility and repair. Community reparations—such as investments in education, healthcare, or infrastructure—recognize the broader societal context in which harm occurs, addressing structural issues that may have contributed to the offense (Johnstone & Van Ness, 2007). Community involvement also enables a more supportive and inclusive process, where all parties can engage in dialogue and work together to create lasting change.

Examples of Reparations within Restorative Justice

Reparations within restorative justice can take various forms, depending on the context and the specific needs of victims, offenders, and communities. Below are some common examples of reparative actions that are integrated within restorative justice processes.

Victim-Offender Mediation

Victim-offender mediation provides a structured setting for victims and offenders to engage in direct dialogue. In cases where financial or symbolic reparations are appropriate, victims may request compensation as part of the offender's restorative plan. This direct engagement allows victims to express their needs and for offenders to understand and address the harm they have caused. Research shows that victim-offender mediation can lead to higher satisfaction rates among victims, as it provides a platform for accountability and healing (Umbreit & Vos, 2000).

Community Reparations

Community reparations recognize the harm caused not only to individual victims but also to entire communities. For example, communities affected by historical injustices—such as racial discrimination, land dispossession, or economic inequality—may advocate for reparations in the form of investments in local infrastructure, education, or healthcare services. These community-level reparations serve as a tangible acknowledgment of systemic harm and provide long-term benefits to those impacted. Restorative justice advocates view these measures as essential for addressing historical grievances and fostering social equity (Walker, 2010).

Criticisms and Considerations in Implementing Reparative Justice

While the principles of reparative justice offer numerous benefits, the implementation of these practices is not without challenges. Some of the primary criticisms and considerations include complexities in determining reparations, power dynamics, and the risk of further victimization.

1. Implementation Challenges

One of the significant challenges in reparative justice lies in determining the appropriate form and amount of reparations. For individual cases, calculating financial compensation or identifying relevant symbolic actions may be relatively straightforward. However, when addressing large-scale harm—such as historical injustices or mass victimization—determining fair reparations becomes complex and may involve political, social, and economic factors. This complexity can lead to debates over what constitutes adequate reparations and who should be eligible to receive them (Daly & Stubbs, 2006).

2. Power Dynamics

Restorative justice processes must be carefully designed to ensure equitable participation and avoid reinforcing existing power imbalances. In some cases, victims may feel pressured to accept reparations or forgive offenders, especially if they are economically or socially disadvantaged. Facilitators play a critical role in managing these dynamics, ensuring that victims' needs and voices remain central and that offenders' accountability is not compromised. Power dynamics must be addressed transparently to maintain the integrity of the reparative process (Zehr, 2002).

3. Risk of Further Victimization

If not managed sensitively, restorative justice processes can inadvertently lead to further victimization. For example, forcing a victim to face an unrepentant offender or pushing them to accept insufficient reparations can exacerbate their trauma. Careful attention to the readiness and willingness of both parties, as well as thorough preparation and support, is essential to minimize the risk of re-traumatization and ensure that the reparative process remains genuinely restorative (Umbreit & Armour, 2011).

Reparations and restorative justice are interconnected approaches that place healing and accountability at the forefront of the justice process. Reparative justice, as a component of restorative justice, seeks to provide direct redress to victims through financial compensation, symbolic actions, and community-focused initiatives. By focusing on repairing harm, empowering victims, and involving the community, reparative justice offers a comprehensive approach to addressing wrongdoing and promoting reconciliation.

While implementing reparative justice presents challenges—such as determining fair reparations, managing power dynamics, and preventing re-victimization—these practices have the potential to transform justice systems and promote a more inclusive and humane approach to conflict resolution. Through the examples of victim-offender mediation and community reparations, this chapter highlights the ways in which reparative justice can contribute to both individual healing and social equity, ultimately fostering stronger, more resilient communities.

References

- Bazemore, G., & Maloney, D. (1994). Rehabilitating Community Service Toward Restorative Service Sanctions in a Balanced Justice System. Federal Probation, 58, 24–35.

- Daly, K. (2002). Restorative Justice: The Real Story. Punishment & Society, 4(1), 55–79.

- Daly, K., & Stubbs, J. (2006). Feminist Engagement with Restorative Justice. Theoretical Criminology, 10(1), 9–28.

- Johnstone, G., & Van Ness, D. (2007). Handbook of Restorative Justice. Willan Publishing.

- Pranis, K. (2005). The Little Book of Circle Processes: A New/Old Approach to Peacemaking. Good Books.

- Umbreit, M. S., & Armour, M. P. (2011). Restorative Justice Dialogue: An Essential Guide for Research and Practice. Springer.

- Umbreit, M. S., & Vos, B. (2000). Restorative Justice in the Twenty-First Century: A Social Movement Full of Opportunities and Pitfalls. Marquette Law Review, 89, 251–304.

- Walker, M. (2010). What is Reparative Justice?. University of Virginia Press.

- Zehr, H. (2002). The Little Book of Restorative Justice. Good Books.

Here are some scholarly articles and sources that discuss reparations in response to both historical and contemporary injustices, including reparations for slavery and other forms of structural injustice. These articles cover various perspectives, case studies, and frameworks for understanding reparative justice:

1. "The Case for Reparations" by Ta-Nehisi Coates
   The Atlantic (2014)

   While not a peer-reviewed article, this essay provides an influential and thorough analysis of the historical and economic context of reparations for African Americans in the United States. Coates explores systemic racism, the legacy of slavery, and discriminatory policies, arguing for reparations as a necessary step to address structural injustices. This piece is often referenced in scholarly discussions for its compelling narrative and extensive historical grounding.

2. "Reparations for Slavery and the Slave Trade: A Transnational and Comparative History" by Ana Lucia Araujo

European Review (2017), 25(4), pp. 507-519

This article takes a transnational approach to reparations for slavery, comparing how different countries and groups have addressed demands for reparative justice. Araujo reviews the historical demands for reparations, the challenges in implementation, and the ongoing struggles for acknowledgment and redress, particularly in the United States and the Caribbean.

3. "The Case for Reparations in the United States" by William A. Darity Jr. and A. Kirsten Mullen

The Journal of Economic Perspectives (2020), 34(1), pp. 1-27

This paper provides an economic analysis of reparations for African Americans, exploring the financial feasibility, moral justification, and possible frameworks for delivering reparations. Darity and Mullen highlight the wealth gap as a direct outcome of slavery and discrimination, advocating for reparations as a means to address the legacy of these injustices.

4. "Restorative Justice for Indigenous Peoples: Restoring Land and Culture" by Jeff Corntassel and Cindy Holder

In Restoring Indigenous Self-Determination: Theorizing Indigenous Rights and Restorative Justice (2021)

This book chapter addresses reparations and restorative justice as they pertain to Indigenous rights, focusing on land restoration and cultural revitalization. Corntassel and Holder argue that reparations for Indigenous peoples must go beyond financial compensation to include cultural and territorial restoration, respecting Indigenous self-determination and sovereignty.

5. "Backward-Looking Reparations and Structural Injustice" by Bernard R. Boxill

Ethics (2003), 113(4), pp. 707-730

Boxill examines the moral and philosophical arguments surrounding backward-looking reparations, especially in the context of structural injustice. This article focuses on the ethics of reparations, analyzing the extent to which reparations can address historical wrongs, and whether they can rectify inequalities embedded within social structures.

6. "Reparations as a Means for Addressing Past Injustices: The American Indian and African American Experience" by Robert J. Miller

Boston University Law Review (2008), 89(3), pp. 667-698

Miller examines both the American Indian and African American experiences with reparations in the U.S., focusing on the legal and policy challenges to implementing reparative measures. The article provides case studies on reparative initiatives for Native American land rights and African American slavery reparations, discussing successes and limitations in both contexts.

7. "Reparations as Restorative Justice: Rethinking the Black Reparations Movement" by Jovan Scott Lewis

Cultural Anthropology (2020), 35(3), pp. 470-488

This article explores reparations through a restorative justice framework, arguing for reparations not only as financial compensation but as a transformative process that addresses identity, dignity, and historical trauma. Lewis examines how reparations movements worldwide intersect with restorative justice principles, focusing on African American reparations.

8. "Racial Reparation: Beyond Righting the Past" by Andrew Valls

Political Theory (2003), 32(1), pp. 28-47

Valls offers a philosophical exploration of reparations for slavery and racial discrimination, emphasizing the potential of reparations to create a more equitable future. He examines arguments for reparations that go beyond historical redress, discussing how reparations can contribute to structural change and long-term social justice.

To overcome this, practitioners must work closely with Indigenous leaders and incorporate culturally relevant practices, such as traditional storytelling, healing circles, and ceremonies.

3. Resource Constraints and Sustainability

Effective restorative justice programs require adequate resources to support long-term reconciliation, reparation, and community development. Many Indigenous communities face funding shortfalls, limiting their ability to sustain programs or expand their reach. Governments and institutions must commit to ongoing financial support to ensure restorative justice efforts are not one-time events but lead to lasting change.

4. Balancing Individual and Collective Reparations

While restorative justice often focuses on individuals directly harmed, Indigenous injustices frequently involve whole communities. A key challenge is to create reparations that acknowledge both personal and collective harm. Addressing systemic issues, such as poverty, land loss, and cultural erasure, requires reparations that go beyond individual compensation to include broader community support and development.

Recommendations for Effective Restorative Justice Programs

1. Develop Community-Driven Initiatives

Programs should be developed in partnership with Indigenous communities, respecting their autonomy and empowering them to design solutions that align with their values and needs. This could include advisory councils composed of Indigenous representatives to guide restorative justice initiatives and ensure accountability.

2. Incorporate Traditional Practices and Knowledge

Restorative justice initiatives should draw from Indigenous cultural practices, such as peacemaking circles, ceremonies, and community gatherings. This approach allows for healing that aligns with Indigenous spiritual and cultural beliefs and acknowledges their traditional systems of justice.

3. Commit to Long-Term Support and Monitoring

For restorative justice programs to be effective, they must be sustainable and continuously evaluated. Governments and institutions should commit to long-term funding, regular progress assessments, and adjustments to ensure that the programs are meeting the needs of Indigenous communities.

4. Education and Public Awareness

Educating the wider public about historical injustices against Indigenous peoples and the purpose of restorative justice can build support and understanding. Public awareness campaigns can help to reduce prejudice, foster empathy, and promote solidarity between Indigenous and non-Indigenous communities.

Conclusion: The Transformative Potential of Restorative Justice

Restorative justice provides a powerful framework for addressing historical injustices against Indigenous peoples, focusing on healing, community involvement, and cultural respect. While financial reparations are often critical, restorative justice emphasizes a more profound form of repair, involving recognition, acknowledgment, and communal healing. The approach has proven effective in various national contexts, from Canada to New Zealand, demonstrating that restorative practices can bridge divides, foster healing, and establish pathways toward justice and reconciliation.

However, for restorative justice to reach its full potential, it must overcome significant challenges, including institutional resistance, cultural sensitivity, resource constraints, and the need for both individual and collective reparations. With thoughtful implementation, long-term commitment, and genuine collaboration with Indigenous communities, restorative justice can lay the foundation for a future in which historical injustices are acknowledged, relationships are mended, and Indigenous peoples are empowered to thrive on their own terms.

References

- Alfred, T., & Corntassel, J. (2005). Being Indigenous: Resurgences against contemporary colonialism. Government and Opposition, 40(4), 597-614.
- Borrows, J. (2002). Recovering Canada: The Resurgence of Indigenous Law. University of Toronto Press.

- Truth and Reconciliation Commission of Canada. (2015). Final Report of the Truth and Reconciliation Commission of Canada: Volume One, Summary. James Lorimer & Company.

- Zehr, H. (2002). The Little Book of Restorative Justice. Good Books.

- Cunneen, C. (2018). Indigenous Peoples and Justice: Law and Society. Routledge.

Methods for Designing Reparative Processes that Focus on Healing and Restoration

Designing reparative processes centered on healing and restoration involves creating justice frameworks that prioritize the needs and voices of victims, engage offenders in meaningful accountability, and foster community participation. Effective restorative justice approaches go beyond punitive measures to repair harm, rebuild trust, and promote long-term reconciliation. This chapter outlines core methods for establishing reparative processes that emphasize healing, including victim-offender dialogues, community involvement, reintegration programs, and culturally sensitive practices.

1. Victim-Centered Engagement

A successful reparative process must start with a victim-centered approach, focusing on understanding the harm caused and addressing the needs of those directly affected. Key components of victim-centered engagement include:

- Providing Safe Spaces for Expression: Victims need secure and respectful environments to share their experiences, express emotions, and articulate their needs. Creating spaces where victims feel heard can help them regain a sense of agency and control in their healing process.

- Individualized Reparation Plans: Not all victims require the same reparative measures. Facilitators should work with each victim to develop individualized plans that address their unique needs, whether they involve emotional support, financial restitution, or symbolic gestures such as apologies or community service.

- Supporting Emotional Healing: Integrating support services, such as counseling or mental health resources, can help victims process trauma and contribute to their healing journey.

2. Dialogue-Based Accountability

Dialogue between victims and offenders is at the core of restorative justice. A structured, facilitated conversation allows offenders to understand the impact of their actions, take responsibility, and engage directly in making amends. Techniques for effective dialogue-based accountability include:

- Victim-Offender Mediation: This formal process involves a trained mediator who facilitates a discussion between the victim and the offender. The goal is for offenders to understand the harm they caused and agree on actions to make amends. Studies indicate that victim-offender mediation can lead to increased satisfaction for victims and a higher sense of accountability for offenders.

- Circles and Peacemaking Circles: Circles, or peacemaking circles, provide a collective space where victims, offenders, family members, and community representatives can discuss the offense and its impact. Guided by a trained facilitator, each participant has an equal opportunity to share their perspectives, listen to others, and collaboratively decide on reparative actions. This approach is often used in Indigenous communities and offers a holistic path toward reconciliation.

- Restorative Conferencing: This method, similar to mediation, involves structured meetings between victims, offenders, and other stakeholders. By focusing on accountability and collaborative decision-making, restorative conferencing can lead to consensus on actions for reparation and foster a mutual understanding of the harm caused.

3. Community Involvement and Reintegration

Healing and restoration often require the involvement of the community, as crimes and conflicts can have ripple effects that impact the broader social fabric. Community involvement helps ensure that reparative processes are meaningful and contextually relevant. Methods include:

- Community Service as Reparation: Offenders can engage in community service projects that directly benefit the community or address the harm caused by their actions. Community service provides a visible demonstration of accountability and can help rebuild trust between the offender and the community.

- Community-Based Reparative Boards: Reparative boards consist of community members who meet with offenders to discuss the harm caused and agree on appropriate reparative actions. The process allows offenders to take accountability in a supportive environment and connects them with community mentors who guide them in making amends.

- Public Apologies and Educational Initiatives: For historical or systemic injustices, public apologies, memorials, or educational programs can acknowledge harm and promote understanding. These actions can also serve to educate community members on the impact of past wrongs, fostering a more inclusive, empathetic society.

4. Culturally Sensitive and Inclusive Approaches

A successful reparative process must respect the cultural backgrounds and values of those involved, particularly for Indigenous communities, whose approaches to justice often emphasize restoration over punishment. Culturally sensitive methods include:

- Integrating Traditional Practices: Indigenous communities may have traditional approaches to justice, such as talking circles or elder-led reconciliation ceremonies. Integrating these practices into the restorative justice process ensures cultural respect and makes the process more meaningful for Indigenous participants.

- Tailoring Programs to Community Needs: Restorative programs should be designed in collaboration with community leaders, elders, and cultural advisors. This ensures that processes are appropriate to the cultural, spiritual, and social values of the community.

- Language and Accessibility Considerations: For processes to be inclusive, facilitators should consider language barriers and provide translation services or accessible materials where necessary, enabling all participants to engage fully.

5. Long-Term Monitoring and Follow-Up

Healing and restoration are often long-term processes. Follow-up measures help ensure that reparative actions are sustained over time and provide continued support for both victims and offenders.

- Regular Check-Ins: Facilitators or community mentors can conduct regular follow-ups with offenders to monitor progress, provide support, and ensure compliance with agreed reparative actions. This ongoing support helps offenders stay accountable and reinforces their commitment to making amends.

- Ongoing Victim Support: Victims may need continued support long after the initial reparative actions are completed. Providing resources such as counseling, community support groups, or legal assistance ensures that victims feel supported throughout their healing journey.

- Community Accountability and Feedback: Community members can be encouraged to provide feedback on the reparative process, helping facilitators adjust and improve programs based on the community's evolving needs. This also reinforces a community-wide commitment to restorative justice and fosters transparency and trust.

Toward a Holistic Reparative Justice Model

Designing reparative processes that focus on healing and restoration requires a multifaceted approach centered on victim engagement, dialogue, community involvement, cultural sensitivity, and ongoing support. By prioritizing these elements, restorative justice can transform the experience of justice from one of punishment to one of healing and community empowerment. Such processes not only address individual harm but also build stronger, more resilient communities that are better equipped to prevent and respond to harm in the future.

In embracing these methods, restorative justice can move beyond merely addressing the aftermath of harm and contribute to systemic change that promotes social equity, reconciliation, and a deeper understanding of justice as a process of healing for all involved.

Scholarly Methods for Designing Reparative Processes Focused on Healing and Restoration

Designing reparative processes that emphasize healing and restoration requires an approach rooted in both theoretical frameworks and evidence-based practices. These processes go beyond punishment by incorporating the needs of victims, engaging offenders in meaningful accountability, and facilitating community involvement. Scholars in restorative justice emphasize that reparative processes should be guided by empathy, dialogue, and culturally sensitive practices that promote long-term healing for individuals and communities impacted by harm. This chapter outlines core methods for developing reparative processes with a focus on healing, grounded in key principles of restorative justice and supported by scholarly research.

1. Victim-Centered Engagement

The cornerstone of any effective reparative process is a victim-centered approach. Scholarly work highlights that reparative processes should prioritize victims' voices, experiences, and needs to support emotional and psychological healing. Key methods for victim-centered engagement include:

- Trauma-Informed Practices: According to Zehr (2002), designing reparative processes with an understanding of trauma ensures that victims are not re-victimized. Trauma-informed practices prioritize creating safe, supportive spaces where victims can share their stories without fear of judgment or retaliation.

- Empowerment Through Participation: Engaging victims in the design and implementation of reparative measures is essential. Research shows that involving victims in decision-making can provide them with a sense of agency and control, aiding in their healing (Umbreit, 2001). This can include opportunities to participate in restorative dialogues, suggest forms of reparation, or even decline participation if they are not ready.

- Customized Reparation Plans: Customizing reparative plans based on the unique needs of each victim is critical. Bazemore and Maloney (1994) emphasize that while some victims may benefit from financial restitution, others may seek symbolic gestures, community service, or formal apologies. Tailoring reparations to individual needs ensures that they are meaningful and responsive to the victim's emotional and material well-being.

2. Dialogue-Based Accountability and Empathy Building

Dialogue is a foundational method in restorative justice, fostering understanding, empathy, and accountability. Scholarly methods for implementing dialogue-based accountability include:

- Victim-Offender Mediation (VOM): VOM is widely recognized as an effective method for facilitating direct communication between victims and offenders. Research by Umbreit and Armour (2011) indicates that VOM can lead to increased empathy, as offenders hear firsthand accounts of the harm they caused, and victims gain insight into the offender's perspective. Trained mediators ensure a safe, structured conversation that helps both parties move toward resolution.

- Peacemaking Circles: Drawing on Indigenous practices, peacemaking circles bring victims, offenders, community members, and facilitators together in a circle format that encourages equal participation and mutual respect. Studies by Pranis (2005) show that circles provide a sense of equality and shared responsibility, allowing participants to build empathy and work collaboratively toward healing. Peacemaking circles can be especially effective for community-wide harm or historical injustices, as they involve collective dialogue.

- Empathy-Building Exercises: Integrating specific empathy-building exercises within reparative processes, such as reflective listening and role reversal, can help offenders fully comprehend the impact of their actions. Empathy-building exercises are associated with a reduction in reoffending, as they foster emotional understanding and remorse, which motivates offenders to make amends (Braithwaite, 1989).

3. Community Involvement and Collective Responsibility

Involving the community in reparative processes acknowledges that harm often affects a wider circle beyond the immediate victim. Scholarly research supports the inclusion of community members as a means to enhance collective responsibility and social cohesion. Methods include:

- Community Restorative Boards: Community boards consist of community members who meet with offenders to discuss the impact of the offense and agree on appropriate reparative actions. Bazemore and Schiff (2005) highlight that these boards serve as a form of communal accountability, as they connect offenders with local mentors and promote a sense of obligation to repair harm within the community.

- Service-Oriented Reparations: Offenders can be assigned reparative tasks that benefit the community, such as environmental cleanup or volunteering with local organizations. Research by Stinchcomb et al. (2006) demonstrates that service-oriented reparations provide offenders with an opportunity to give back, while also addressing the community's needs. Service projects are most effective when they are directly related to the harm caused, creating a tangible sense of restitution.

- Public Apologies and Educational Programs: In cases of systemic or historical harm, public apologies and educational initiatives acknowledge the collective impact and serve as reparative actions for entire communities. Educational programs also promote awareness and empathy within the broader community, fostering a supportive environment for victims and offenders alike.

4. Cultural Sensitivity and Inclusivity

Effective reparative processes must be culturally sensitive, respecting the diverse backgrounds and values of participants. Scholarly research suggests that cultural sensitivity is crucial for achieving authenticity in the restorative justice process. Methods for promoting cultural sensitivity include:

- Integration of Traditional Practices: Scholars like Jeff Corntassel and Cindy Holder (2010) argue that incorporating traditional Indigenous justice practices, such as talking circles and elder-led reconciliation ceremonies, can make reparative processes more culturally respectful and meaningful for Indigenous participants. Recognizing and honoring these traditional practices fosters healing that aligns with cultural beliefs.

- Involvement of Cultural Advisors: Including cultural advisors or community elders in the reparative process can help bridge cultural divides and ensure that the methods used are appropriate for the community involved. This approach promotes a more inclusive process and prevents misunderstandings that might hinder the restorative journey.

- Language Accessibility and Representation: Ensuring that all materials, discussions, and reparative processes are accessible in the participants' preferred languages is critical for inclusivity. Scholars suggest that language accessibility enhances engagement and respect for diverse communities, helping all participants feel valued and understood (Cunneen, 2018).

5. Long-Term Support and Monitoring for Sustainable Healing

Long-term support is essential to ensure that reparative processes are not merely symbolic but lead to sustained healing and restoration. Scholarly recommendations for achieving long-term impact include:

- Follow-Up Meetings: Umbreit et al. (2006) recommend scheduling regular follow-up meetings with offenders and victims to assess the effectiveness of reparative actions, address any unresolved issues, and provide continued support. These meetings can help reinforce accountability and strengthen the relationships fostered during the restorative process.

- Ongoing Victim Support Services: Providing continuous support services, such as counseling and community-based support groups, ensures that victims receive assistance beyond the initial reparative actions. Long-term support services are crucial for victims' emotional recovery, enabling them to navigate any residual trauma and integrate the reparative experience into their lives.

- Mentorship and Community Integration Programs for Offenders: Programs that pair offenders with mentors or connect them with community service opportunities can facilitate positive reintegration and reduce the likelihood of reoffending. Maruna (2001) highlights that mentorship helps offenders develop constructive relationships and a sense of belonging, which is essential for sustaining positive change.

- Feedback Mechanisms for Continuous Improvement: Restorative justice programs should incorporate feedback mechanisms that allow victims, offenders, and community members to provide input on the reparative process. Feedback loops help restorative programs adapt to changing needs and improve their effectiveness over time, creating a more responsive and resilient system of justice (Walker, 2010).

Building Effective Reparative Processes for Lasting Healing

Designing reparative processes that prioritize healing and restoration requires a multifaceted approach grounded in scholarship and practice. By focusing on victim-centered engagement, dialogue-based accountability, community involvement, cultural sensitivity, and long-term support, restorative justice initiatives can create transformative experiences for individuals and communities. These methods, supported by research, emphasize the importance of empathy, collective responsibility, and sustainable healing.

Restorative justice, through these scholarly methods, offers a framework for moving beyond traditional punishment, enabling individuals and communities to heal, grow, and foster resilient relationships. By applying these best practices, reparative processes can contribute to a more inclusive and humane system of justice that addresses both present harm and the structural conditions that contribute to it.

References

- Bazemore, G., & Maloney, D. (1994). Rehabilitating Community Service: Toward Restorative Service Sanctions in a Balanced Justice System. Federal Probation.
- Bazemore, G., & Schiff, M. (2005). Juvenile Justice Reform and Restorative Justice: Building Theory and Policy from Practice. Routledge.
- Braithwaite, J. (1989). Crime, Shame, and Reintegration. Cambridge University Press.
- Corntassel, J., & Holder, C. (2010). Indigenous Peoples and Restorative Justice: Resurgence and Self-Determination. In Handbook of Restorative Justice (pp. 397-408). Routledge.
- Cunneen, C. (2018). Indigenous Peoples and Justice: Law and Society. Routledge.
- Maruna, S. (2001). Making Good: How Ex-Convicts Reform and Rebuild Their Lives. American Psychological Association.
- Pranis, K. (2005). The Little Book of Circle Processes: A New/Old Approach to Peacemaking. Good Books.
- Stinchcomb, J. B., Bazemore, G., & Riestenberg, N. (2006). Beyond Zero Tolerance: Restoring Justice in Secondary Schools. Youth Violence and Juvenile Justice.
- Umbreit, M. S. (2001). The Handbook of Victim Offender Mediation: An Essential Guide to Practice and Research. Jossey-Bass.
- Umbreit, M. S., & Armour, M. P. (2011). Restorative Justice Dialogue: An Essential

CHAPTER 06

Community Restorative Justice and Neighborhood Justice Panels

Community Restorative Justice (CRJ) and Neighborhood Justice Panels (NJPs) represent grassroots approaches to justice, focusing on repairing harm and restoring relationships rather than merely imposing punishment. These panels involve community members who actively participate in addressing low-level offenses, facilitating dialogue between victims and offenders, and collaboratively developing restorative solutions. Through their roles, community members support accountability, victim empowerment, and community healing, all of which contribute to reducing recidivism and fostering a more cohesive society.

The Roles of Community Members on Neighborhood Justice Panels

Community members serving on Neighborhood Justice Panels play essential roles in the restorative justice process. Their contributions ensure that the community's values, concerns, and needs are incorporated into the resolution of local conflicts. These roles include listening, facilitating dialogue, developing restorative agreements, and providing ongoing support.

1. Listening to Victims and Offenders

A primary role of community panel members is to listen empathetically to both victims and offenders. Providing a safe and non-judgmental space enables victims to share their experiences, feelings, and the impact of the offense, while offenders have an opportunity to explain their actions and motivations. This listening process is crucial for uncovering the underlying issues behind the offense and understanding the perspectives of both parties.

- Creating a Safe Environment: Community members help establish a respectful and secure setting where all parties feel comfortable sharing openly. This is foundational to building trust, which is essential for the restorative process.

- Active Listening Skills: Through training in active listening, panel members learn to acknowledge and validate participants' emotions without judgment, encouraging honest communication and promoting understanding.

2. Facilitating Dialogue

Community members on justice panels act as facilitators, guiding discussions between victims and offenders to foster understanding and empathy. This role is critical in ensuring that each voice is heard and that dialogue remains productive.

- Encouraging Open Communication: Facilitators guide conversations so that both victims and offenders can articulate their experiences, needs, and feelings. This dialogue helps victims express the impact of the harm while providing offenders with insight into the consequences of their actions.

- Maintaining Structure and Neutrality: Facilitators manage the flow of conversation, ensuring that discussions remain respectful and focused. They maintain impartiality throughout the process, which helps prevent any party from feeling marginalized or defensive.

3. Developing Restorative Agreements

Community members collaborate with victims and offenders to create restorative agreements tailored to the specific circumstances of each case. These agreements outline the steps offenders must take to make amends, whether through apologies, restitution, community service, or other forms of reparation.

- Collaborative Planning: Panel members work with both parties to co-create a plan that addresses the victim's needs and considers the offender's circumstances. The collaborative nature of this process ensures that the agreement is meaningful, realistic, and fair to all parties involved.

- Focus on Repairing Harm: Restorative agreements are designed to repair the harm caused by the offense rather than punish the offender. By emphasizing constructive actions, community panels help offenders understand the consequences of their actions and contribute positively to their community.

4. Providing Support and Guidance

Community members provide support to victims, helping them navigate the justice process and recover from harm. They also offer guidance to offenders, helping them understand the impact of their actions and develop strategies to prevent future offenses.

- Emotional Support for Victims: Panel members ensure that victims feel respected and supported throughout the process, validating their experiences and acknowledging their pain. This support can aid in their healing journey and help them feel empowered within the justice process.

- Guidance for Offenders: Community members mentor offenders, encouraging them to take responsibility and providing resources or referrals for counseling, job training, or educational programs. This guidance helps offenders develop constructive behaviors and move forward in a positive direction.

5. Community Engagement

Community members act as a bridge between the justice system and the community, ensuring that local perspectives are considered in decision-making. This role is essential for fostering trust between the community and justice institutions and promoting accountability to the broader community.

- Bringing Community Values to the Process: By representing community perspectives, panel members ensure that restorative justice aligns with the values and priorities of the local area.

- Encouraging Public Trust in Justice Processes: When community members actively participate in justice processes, the public may view these processes as more transparent, fair, and trustworthy. This trust can enhance the legitimacy of restorative justice initiatives and encourage broader community involvement.

Benefits of Community Involvement in Neighborhood Justice Panels

Community involvement in restorative justice panels offers multiple benefits, from increased accountability to community healing. Engaging community members directly in the resolution of conflicts fosters a sense of ownership and encourages collaborative problem-solving.

1. Increased Accountability

Offenders are held accountable not only to the legal system but also to the community they have impacted. This localized form of accountability encourages offenders to take responsibility in a personal way, recognizing the harm they caused to their neighbors and community.

2. Victim Empowerment

Unlike traditional justice processes, where victims may feel sidelined, restorative panels allow victims to actively participate and have a say in the outcome. This involvement provides a sense of agency and can help victims find closure.

3. Community Healing

Restorative justice focuses on repairing harm and rebuilding relationships within the community. By addressing the root causes of conflict and facilitating understanding, community justice panels contribute to healing on a personal and community-wide level.

4. Reduced Recidivism

Research shows that restorative justice programs, including neighborhood panels, can reduce recidivism rates by addressing underlying issues and providing support to offenders. By helping offenders make amends and integrate positively into their communities, these panels contribute to safer neighborhoods.

Important Considerations for Community Members on Neighborhood Justice Panels

For community members to effectively fulfill their roles on restorative justice panels, they need proper training, awareness of ethical considerations, and ongoing support.

1. Training and Support

Community members should receive training in restorative justice principles, conflict resolution techniques, and active listening skills. This preparation equips them to facilitate discussions effectively, maintain neutrality, and handle sensitive issues. Regular support and refresher training sessions are also essential to sustain their effectiveness.

2. Neutrality

Impartiality is crucial in restorative justice. Community members must set aside personal biases and listen objectively to both parties. This neutrality fosters an environment of fairness and respect, allowing all participants to feel that their perspectives are valued.

3. Confidentiality

Maintaining confidentiality is critical to protecting the privacy of victims and offenders. Panel members must respect the sensitive nature of information shared during the process and ensure it remains confidential. Confidentiality builds trust among participants and encourages openness.

Building Resilient Communities Through Neighborhood Justice Panels

Community Restorative Justice and Neighborhood Justice Panels empower communities to actively participate in the justice process, facilitating accountability, healing, and reconciliation. By involving community members in roles that emphasize listening, dialogue, restorative planning, support, and engagement, these panels create a justice model that values relationships and addresses the root causes of harm. Community involvement offers multiple benefits, from reducing recidivism to empowering victims and fostering a more cohesive community.

The effectiveness of neighborhood justice panels depends on the commitment, training, and neutrality of community members. Through their roles, they help redefine justice as a collaborative, inclusive, and transformative process that brings about genuine healing. Neighborhood Justice Panels ultimately contribute to a community-oriented approach to justice that builds resilience and strengthens social bonds.

References

- Bazemore, G., & Schiff, M. (2005). Juvenile Justice Reform and Restorative Justice: Building Theory and Policy from Practice. Routledge.
- Pranis, K. (2005). The Little Book of Circle Processes: A New/Old Approach to Peacemaking. Good Books.
- Stinchcomb, J. B., Bazemore, G., & Riestenberg, N. (2006). Beyond Zero Tolerance: Restoring Justice in Secondary Schools. Youth Violence and Juvenile Justice.
- Umbreit, M. S., & Armour, M. P. (2011). Restorative Justice Dialogue: An Essential Guide for Research and Practice. Springer.
- Zehr, H. (2002). The Little Book of Restorative Justice. Good Books.

Structure and Process of Neighborhood Justice Panels

Neighborhood Justice Panels (NJPs) are community-based restorative justice initiatives that provide an alternative approach to addressing low-level offenses. Rather than relying on traditional punitive measures, NJPs convene trained community volunteers, victims, offenders, and other stakeholders in a structured, collaborative dialogue aimed at identifying harm and fostering accountability. These panels prioritize the needs of victims, offer offenders an opportunity to make amends, and engage the broader community in the justice process, promoting healing and reducing recidivism.

Key Elements of a Neighborhood Justice Panel Structure

The structure of a Neighborhood Justice Panel is carefully designed to ensure that all parties have a voice, that the process is fair and transparent, and that the outcomes are restorative rather than punitive. Key components include the composition of the panel, the referral process, and the role of a facilitator.

1. Panel Composition

A Neighborhood Justice Panel typically consists of diverse community members who represent the values, concerns, and perspectives of the local community. The panel may include:

- Community Residents: Individuals who live in the neighborhood where the offense occurred, bringing insights into the community's expectations and priorities.
- Local Business Owners: Business owners impacted by the offense or who have an interest in promoting community safety and harmony.

- Former Offenders or Peer Mentors: In some cases, individuals with prior justice involvement who have successfully reintegrated may serve on the panel to provide unique perspectives and empathy.

- Restorative Justice Trained Volunteers: All panel members are trained in restorative justice principles and conflict resolution techniques, ensuring they can facilitate empathetic, unbiased, and productive discussions.

This diversity of perspectives helps foster a sense of fairness and ensures that community values are represented in the restorative process.

2. Referral Process

Cases are generally referred to Neighborhood Justice Panels by law enforcement agencies, courts, or community organizations. Eligible offenses are typically minor, non-violent crimes such as theft, vandalism, trespassing, or minor drug offenses. For offenders, participation in a Neighborhood Justice Panel is often presented as an alternative to conventional legal consequences, such as fines or jail time.

- Criteria for Eligibility: Cases are typically selected based on the nature of the offense, the willingness of both victim and offender to participate, and the potential benefit of a restorative approach. Cases involving serious or violent crimes are generally not eligible.

- Screening and Preparation: Once a case is referred, panel facilitators meet with both victims and offenders to explain the process, assess readiness, and ensure that both parties understand and are willing to engage voluntarily.

3. Role of the Facilitator

A trained facilitator plays a vital role in the Neighborhood Justice Panel, guiding the discussion and maintaining a safe, structured environment where all parties feel comfortable expressing their perspectives.

- Neutrality and Impartiality: The facilitator remains neutral, avoiding judgment and ensuring that each party has an equal opportunity to share. They help prevent any one voice from dominating the discussion and focus on building mutual respect.

- Creating a Safe Space: By setting ground rules, the facilitator establishes a safe and respectful environment for dialogue. This includes ensuring confidentiality, encouraging empathy, and reminding participants of the panel's restorative purpose.

- Guiding the Discussion: The facilitator directs the conversation, helping participants address the harm caused, express their needs, and work toward a mutually acceptable agreement.

Process of a Neighborhood Justice Panel Meeting

The Neighborhood Justice Panel meeting follows a structured process that allows for open dialogue, mutual understanding, and collaborative problem-solving. Key steps in the meeting include opening, sharing perspectives, dialogue and discussion, agreement development, and closure.

1. Opening

The facilitator opens the meeting by introducing all participants, setting ground rules, and establishing the purpose of the panel. This introduction serves to build trust and emphasize the goals of restorative justice.

- Setting Expectations: The facilitator clarifies that the goal is to repair harm rather than impose punishment, and encourages participants to approach the discussion with an open mind.

- Ground Rules: Common ground rules include respecting each other's turn to speak, maintaining confidentiality, and actively listening without interruption.

2. Victim's Perspective

The victim is invited to share their experience of the crime, detailing how it has impacted their life emotionally, financially, or socially. This stage allows the victim to articulate their needs and receive validation from the offender and the community.

- Opportunity for Expression: The victim's testimony provides a vital perspective, helping the offender and community understand the specific harm caused.

- Empathy Building: Hearing directly from the victim can foster empathy in the offender, helping them to grasp the real-world effects of their actions.

3. Offender's Perspective

The offender is given the opportunity to take responsibility for their actions, explain their motivations, and acknowledge the harm caused. This stage encourages offenders to be accountable and self-reflective.

- Acknowledgment of Responsibility: Offenders are encouraged to accept accountability for their actions, which is essential for the restorative process.

- Opportunity to Express Regret or Apology: This stage allows offenders to apologize directly to the victim and take a step toward making amends.

4. Community Impact

Community members on the panel are invited to share their insights into how the offense has affected the broader neighborhood. This input provides context, showing the offender that their actions have a ripple effect beyond the immediate victim.

- Broader Community Concerns: Community members may highlight recurring issues or share how the offense has influenced feelings of safety or trust within the neighborhood.

- Collective Responsibility and Support: Community members' participation reinforces that they are invested in the well-being of both victims and offenders, promoting a sense of collective care.

5. Dialogue and Discussion

Open dialogue is facilitated where all participants can ask questions, express feelings, and engage in a constructive discussion about the offense, its impact, and possible solutions.

- Encouraging Mutual Understanding: The facilitator guides the dialogue to ensure that all voices are heard and respected. This open exchange helps to clarify misunderstandings and promote empathy.

- Focusing on Solutions: Rather than dwelling on blame, the discussion is steered toward finding a way to repair the harm and prevent similar incidents in the future.

6. Agreement Development

Based on the discussion, the panel collaborates to create a restorative agreement that addresses the needs of the victim, offender, and community. This agreement outlines the specific steps the offender will take to make amends.

- Personalized Reparative Actions: The agreement may include apologies, restitution, community service, counseling, or other measures aimed at repairing the harm.

- Commitment to Positive Change: The agreement is designed to promote behavioral change in the offender and support their reintegration into the community.

7. Closure

The meeting concludes with a review of the agreement, clarifying each participant's role in follow-up and monitoring. The facilitator may also schedule follow-up sessions to ensure accountability and progress.

- Final Reflections: Participants are encouraged to share their thoughts on the process, allowing them to express any remaining feelings or insights.

- Plan for Follow-Up: Follow-up helps to track the offender's adherence to the agreement and ensures that the restorative goals are achieved.

Benefits of Neighborhood Justice Panels

Neighborhood Justice Panels offer numerous benefits by actively involving the community, promoting healing, and providing a restorative alternative to traditional justice.

- Increased Victim Participation: Victims have a platform to share their experiences and directly engage in the justice process.

- Offender Accountability: Offenders face accountability not just to the legal system, but to the community they have harmed.

- Community Engagement: Panels foster a sense of ownership and empowerment in addressing crime and promoting community healing.

- Reduced Recidivism: By addressing root causes and providing support, these panels may reduce the likelihood of reoffending.

Important Considerations

Neighborhood Justice Panels require careful planning, training, and ethical considerations to function effectively.

- Voluntary Participation: All parties should participate willingly and feel comfortable with the process.

- Confidentiality: Information shared during the panel should be kept confidential to protect participants' privacy.

- Training for Facilitators: Effective facilitation is crucial for ensuring productive and respectful discussions.

The Value of Community-Led Restorative Justice

Neighborhood Justice Panels represent a community-led approach to restorative justice that empowers victims, holds offenders accountable, and strengthens community bonds. By providing structured opportunities for dialogue and mutual understanding, these panels help to repair harm and build safer, more resilient neighborhoods. As communities continue to explore restorative alternatives to traditional justice, Neighborhood Justice Panels offer a powerful model for promoting healing, accountability, and long-term social cohesion.

References

- Bazemore, G., & Schiff, M. (2005). Juvenile Justice Reform and Restorative Justice: Building Theory and Policy from Practice. Routledge.
- Pranis, K. (2005). The Little Book of Circle Processes: A New/Old Approach to Peacemaking. Good Books.
- Umbreit, M. S., & Armour, M. P. (2011). Restorative Justice Dialogue: An Essential Guide for Research and Practice. Springer.
- Zehr, H. (2002). The Little Book of Restorative Justice. Good Books.

Restorative Justice (RJ) is increasingly recognized as an effective, community-centered approach to justice that prioritizes repairing harm and strengthening social connections over traditional punitive measures. By involving victims, offenders, and community members in a collaborative process, RJ seeks to rebuild trust, promote accountability, and support healing. This approach has shown numerous benefits, including higher rates of satisfaction for both victims and offenders, reduced recidivism, and increased compliance with restitution, especially when compared to conventional criminal justice methods. Here are some notable RJ programs and their associated benefits:

Examples of Restorative Justice Programs and Their Benefits

1. Victim-Offender Mediation (VOM)

Victim-offender mediation is a structured dialogue facilitated by a trained mediator, where the victim and offender meet to discuss the crime, its impact, and ways to repair the harm.

- Benefits: VOM has been shown to lead to high satisfaction rates for both victims and offenders, as it allows victims to express their experiences directly to offenders and seek answers to their questions. Offenders gain a deeper understanding of the harm they caused, which can foster remorse and a genuine desire to make amends. Studies have shown that VOM can reduce criminal behavior by promoting accountability and empathy among offenders.

2. Drug Courts

Drug courts are specialty courts that focus on connecting offenders with treatment programs rather than jail time. This approach is particularly useful for non-violent drug offenders whose actions are often rooted in addiction issues.

- Benefits: Drug courts prioritize rehabilitation over punishment, leading to higher sobriety rates among participants. Research shows that participants in drug court programs are more likely to complete treatment and maintain long-term sobriety compared to those processed through traditional courts. This approach can reduce the societal costs associated with incarceration and contribute to better public health outcomes.

3. Healing and Talking Circles

Healing and talking circles are peer support groups grounded in Native American traditions. These circles provide a safe space for participants to share their experiences, offer support, and engage in collective healing, making them effective for addiction recovery and community building.

- Benefits: Healing circles foster a sense of connection, trust, and mutual support, which can be transformative for individuals recovering from trauma or addiction. Participants report feeling heard, understood, and empowered to take positive steps toward personal healing. The traditional, communal approach of these circles can also strengthen cultural identity and pride among Indigenous communities.

4. Restorative Community Boards

Restorative community boards consist of local community representatives who work with offenders to create a reparative plan that holds offenders accountable and ensures they give back to the community. These boards allow the community to actively participate in addressing harm and supporting offenders' reintegration.

- Benefits: Community boards help strengthen social cohesion by involving community members directly in the justice process. Offenders are more likely to feel accountable to their own community, fostering a stronger sense of responsibility. Additionally, community-based solutions can reduce the social stigma offenders face, making reintegration easier and supporting long-term behavioral change.

5. Diversion Programs

Diversion programs redirect eligible offenders from traditional punitive measures to RJ practices, offering them a chance to engage in restorative processes that address the root causes of their behavior. These programs are often used for first-time offenders or minor offenses, providing an alternative to incarceration.

- Benefits: Diversion programs help reduce the burden on the criminal justice system, lower incarceration rates, and provide offenders with the opportunity to avoid criminal records. By focusing on rehabilitation and addressing the underlying issues behind offenses, diversion programs can reduce recidivism and encourage positive behavioral change. They are particularly beneficial for youth, who gain a chance to correct their behavior without facing the lifelong consequences of a criminal record.

Why Restorative Justice Can Be Successful

Restorative Justice succeeds in ways that traditional criminal justice often does not because it prioritizes the perspectives and needs of those directly affected by crime. Here are some key reasons for its effectiveness:

- Empowering Affected Individuals: RJ puts power back in the hands of victims, offenders, and communities, allowing them to actively participate in finding solutions. This empowerment can lead to higher levels of engagement, satisfaction, and healing for everyone involved.

- Building Empathy and Accountability: RJ encourages offenders to understand the impact of their actions on others, fostering a sense of empathy and remorse that can lead to long-term behavioral change. This focus on accountability promotes personal responsibility, which can reduce future offenses.

- Strengthening Communities: RJ reinforces social cohesion by involving community members in the justice process, promoting a shared responsibility for addressing and preventing harm. This communal approach fosters a stronger sense of belonging, trust, and resilience within communities.

- Elevating Marginalized Voices: Restorative justice can be particularly effective in marginalized communities, where traditional criminal justice approaches may have contributed to systemic inequities. RJ practices elevate the humanity and dignity of all participants, building equity by creating a justice process that values every individual's voice and experience.

- Reducing Recidivism: By addressing the root causes of crime, such as addiction, trauma, or social disadvantage, RJ can reduce recidivism. Offenders who go through restorative processes are often more motivated to avoid future harm and reintegrate positively into society.

Restorative Justice offers a holistic, humane approach to justice that strengthens social cohesion, fosters personal accountability, and promotes healing for victims, offenders, and communities alike. Programs such as victim-offender mediation, drug courts, healing circles, community boards, and diversion programs demonstrate the wide-ranging benefits of RJ. By prioritizing empathy, empowerment, and inclusivity, restorative justice can play a transformative role in creating safer, more resilient communities.

CHAPTER 07

Conferencing and Family Group Conferencing (FGC)

Conferencing models, particularly Family Group Conferencing (FGC), offer a structured approach to resolving issues by involving affected parties in collaborative decision-making. Conferences provide an organized setting for discussion, often with the goal of reaching an agreement or creating a plan of action. FGC, a specific conferencing model, is designed to give families the primary role in addressing issues related to a family member's well-being, especially in child welfare and juvenile justice contexts. Originating in New Zealand and inspired by Maori cultural practices, FGC empowers families to lead the process of finding solutions, reducing reliance on professional intervention and promoting a sense of ownership over decisions.

Overview of Family Group Conferencing (FGC)

Family Group Conferencing (FGC) is a restorative approach that focuses on empowering families to take the lead in decision-making, particularly in situations involving children or young people. Unlike traditional models, where professionals make the final decisions, FGCs place responsibility in the hands of the family network. This approach is especially prevalent in child welfare and youth justice, where it has proven effective in achieving positive outcomes for families.

Key Aspects of Family Group Conferencing

1. Family-Centered Approach

FGC is built on the principle that families are best suited to make decisions about their members. By allowing families to take the lead, FGCs create an environment where family members can discuss issues openly, share perspectives, and collaborate on solutions that respect their unique dynamics and values.

2. Extended Family Involvement

FGC extends participation beyond immediate family members to include the wider family network, such as grandparents, aunts, uncles, friends, and community supporters. This broader support network offers additional perspectives and resources, enhancing the family's capacity to address the issue collaboratively.

3. Role of the Facilitator

A trained facilitator plays a key role in guiding the conference, ensuring that discussions are respectful, inclusive, and productive. The facilitator provides information relevant to the issue but avoids imposing solutions, allowing the family to generate ideas and take ownership of the process.

4. Private Family Time

A unique feature of FGC is the inclusion of private family time, where the family gathers separately from professionals to discuss the issues and devise a plan without external input. This element respects the family's autonomy and fosters a sense of empowerment as they work together to reach a consensus.

5. Decision-Making Focus

The primary goal of FGC is to reach a family-driven decision or plan that addresses the issues at hand. With the family taking ownership, the plan is often more sustainable and realistic, as it reflects the family's values and available resources.

Origin and Application of Family Group Conferencing

Family Group Conferencing originated in New Zealand in the late 1980s and was heavily influenced by Maori cultural practices, which emphasize family involvement in decision-making. FGC was first formalized as a part of New Zealand's child welfare and juvenile justice systems, providing an alternative to state intervention and institutionalized responses.

Maori Cultural Influence

The FGC model draws from the Maori tradition of "whanau," which recognizes the importance of the extended family and collective responsibility. In Maori culture, decision-making is not limited to nuclear family units but involves the wider community, fostering stronger connections and support. This traditional Maori approach inspired the development of FGC, which has since been adopted internationally.

Application in Child Welfare and Juvenile Justice Systems

FGC is widely used in child protection cases, where families work together to make care arrangements for children who may be at risk. By involving the family network, FGC helps create a plan that prioritizes the child's best interests while respecting family bonds. FGC has also been implemented in juvenile justice systems to address youth offenses, allowing families to play a central role in devising rehabilitation plans and encouraging youth accountability.

Benefits of Family Group Conferencing

The family-led approach of FGC offers numerous benefits for families, professionals, and communities, fostering collaboration and reducing reliance on state intervention.

1. Increased Family Engagement

By actively involving the extended family, FGC encourages greater engagement and investment in the solutions. When families develop their own plans, they are more likely to feel a sense of responsibility and commitment to following through with agreed-upon actions.

2. Empowerment

FGC allows family members to have a voice and participate actively in decision-making. This empowerment can lead to higher levels of satisfaction and self-efficacy, as families are given the opportunity to address issues in ways that align with their values.

3. Improved Communication

The structured dialogue within an FGC can foster open communication among family members, helping them express emotions, listen to each other's perspectives, and build mutual understanding. Improved communication can lead to healthier family relationships and prevent future conflicts.

4. Reduced State Intervention

By empowering families to take responsibility for their issues, FGC can potentially reduce the need for state intervention in cases involving child welfare or juvenile justice. Family-led plans are often more sustainable, and when families succeed in managing their challenges, the need for intrusive interventions is minimized.

Criticisms and Challenges of Family Group Conferencing

While FGC offers significant benefits, it also faces challenges and criticisms, particularly around power dynamics within families and the need for skilled facilitation.

1. Potential for Power Imbalances

Power dynamics within families can influence the decision-making process. Some family members may feel uncomfortable expressing their opinions, especially if there are hierarchical relationships or histories of conflict within the family. Skilled facilitators are essential in managing these dynamics to ensure all voices are heard.

2. Implementation Challenges

Successfully conducting an FGC requires facilitators who are skilled in conflict resolution and culturally aware. Facilitators must navigate complex family relationships, encourage respectful dialogue, and create an environment where each member feels safe to participate. Finding and training qualified facilitators can be a challenge, particularly in resource-limited settings.

3. Cultural Adaptation

While FGC has roots in Maori culture, adapting the model to other cultural contexts may require adjustments to ensure cultural appropriateness. In some cases, cultural values may influence family dynamics, affecting how decisions are made and which voices are valued in the discussion.

4. Reluctance to Participate

In some cases, families or individuals may be reluctant to participate in FGC due to mistrust of the system, skepticism about the process, or fear of exposing family issues. Addressing these concerns requires careful communication and support from professionals to build trust in the FGC process.

The FGC Process: Step-by-Step

A Family Group Conference typically follows a structured, yet flexible, process designed to engage families, build understanding, and create a practical plan of action.

Step 1: Preparation

The facilitator meets with the family and other participants to explain the process, discuss the issue, and identify relevant family members and supporters to invite. During this stage, the facilitator assesses the family's readiness for the FGC and addresses any concerns.

Step 2: Information Sharing

The conference begins with all participants gathering together, including the family, professionals, and other relevant parties. Professionals share important information about the issue at hand, providing the family with the context needed to make informed decisions.

Step 3: Private Family Time

The family is given time to meet privately without the presence of professionals to discuss the issues and create a plan. This private time fosters autonomy and allows the family to explore solutions collaboratively.

Step 4: Plan Presentation and Review

The family presents their plan to the wider group, including professionals, for feedback and review. If necessary, the plan can be revised to ensure it addresses the child's best interests and meets any legal or welfare requirements.

Step 5: Follow-Up and Monitoring

After the FGC concludes, professionals may check in with the family periodically to monitor progress and provide additional support as needed. This follow-up ensures accountability and provides opportunities for the family to seek further assistance if challenges arise.

The Value of Family Group Conferencing

Family Group Conferencing provides a unique and effective model of restorative justice that prioritizes family involvement and empowerment. By giving families the lead role in addressing issues related to child welfare or youth behavior, FGC promotes sustainable, culturally sensitive solutions that align with family values. While challenges exist, such as potential power imbalances and the need for skilled facilitators, the benefits of FGC—including increased engagement, improved communication, and reduced state intervention—demonstrate its potential for positive outcomes.

As FGC continues to be implemented in various justice and welfare systems worldwide, it offers a transformative approach that respects the autonomy of families and strengthens community ties, ultimately contributing to a more inclusive and supportive justice system.

References

- Burford, G., & Hudson, J. (2000). Family Group Conferencing: New Directions in Community-Centered Child and Family Practice. Transaction Publishers.
- Connolly, M., & Ward, T. (2008). Moral Theory and Family Group Conferencing: Applying Social Justice in Family Group Conferences. Routledge.
- Merkel-Holguin, L., Nixon, P., & Burford, G. (2003). Learning with Families: A Synopsis of FGC Research and Evaluations in Child Welfare. Family Group Decision Making Project.
- Pranis, K. (2005). The Little Book of Circle Processes: A New/Old Approach to Peacemaking. Good Books.
- Zehr, H. (2002). The Little Book of Restorative Justice. Good Books.

Role of Family and Community Support in Conferencing

In restorative justice conferencing, family and community support are pivotal in fostering a sense of collective responsibility, accountability, and healing for both the victim and the offender. The involvement of family and community members enhances the restorative process by providing a broader network of emotional and social support, helping to contextualize the impact of the harm, and actively participating in developing a plan for repair. This community-based approach aims to reintegrate the offender and promote healing for all parties, contributing to stronger, more cohesive communities.

Key Aspects of Family and Community Support in Conferencing

Family and community involvement in conferencing serves multiple purposes, including providing support, sharing perspectives, holding the offender accountable, and ensuring that the agreed-upon plan is carried out. Here are the primary roles and contributions of family and community in restorative justice conferencing.

1. Presence at the Conference

The physical presence of family and community members during the conference brings a wider support system into the process. Family members of both the victim and the offender, as well as other community representatives, can attend the conference to share their perspectives, express concerns, and offer encouragement. Their participation helps to underscore the social and relational context of the offense, reinforcing that crime impacts not only the direct victim but the community as a whole.

- Family Support for Victims and Offenders: Family members provide moral and emotional support to both victims and offenders, ensuring they feel supported and less isolated in the process. This presence can be particularly comforting to young offenders, who may feel more secure and accountable in front of familiar faces.

- Community Representation: By involving community members, the conference highlights that the offense has affected the broader community and that collective healing is needed. Community members' presence reinforces that the well-being of all involved is interconnected.

2. Understanding the Impact of the Harm

Family and community members play a critical role in helping participants understand the wider impact of the offense. Their insights reveal the emotional, social, and sometimes economic consequences of the harm on individuals, families, and the neighborhood. This broader understanding promotes empathy in the offender and highlights the collective effects of individual actions.

- Contextualizing the Consequences: Family members and community representatives can describe how the offense affected their daily lives, sense of security, and relationships, providing a fuller picture of the harm caused.

- Fostering Empathy: By hearing about the offense's ripple effects, offenders are more likely to develop empathy and a deeper understanding of how their actions have affected those around them. This awareness is crucial for genuine accountability and remorse.

3. Accountability and Responsibility

Family and community support in conferencing also serves as a mechanism for holding offenders accountable. The presence of family and community members adds a layer of social accountability, as offenders are reminded that their actions impact not only the victim but also people they know and interact with daily. This broader sense of responsibility is essential for the offender's commitment to making amends and avoiding future offenses.

- Support for Taking Responsibility: Family members can encourage the offender to take responsibility and offer constructive guidance on how to repair the harm. This reinforcement from trusted figures increases the likelihood that the offender will follow through with the plan.

- Social Accountability: The offender is held accountable not just to the legal system but to the community, creating a sense of obligation to rebuild trust and contribute positively to the neighborhood. This social accountability can be a powerful motivator for behavioral change.

4. Developing a Plan for Repair

Family and community members contribute valuable input when developing a restorative plan, helping to ensure that it is realistic, actionable, and aligned with the needs of both the victim and the offender. This collaborative approach ensures that the plan is comprehensive, feasible, and considers available resources.

- Community-Informed Solutions: Community members may suggest actions such as community service or restitution that directly benefit the neighborhood, fostering a sense of collective healing and connection.

- Family-Centered Support Strategies: Family members often have insights into the offender's personal needs and circumstances, helping to create a plan that supports rehabilitation while addressing underlying issues, such as peer influences or personal challenges.

5. Post-Conference Support

The role of family and community extends beyond the conference itself. Post-conference support is essential in helping both victims and offenders implement the agreed-upon plan and navigate any challenges that may arise. Continued involvement ensures accountability, provides emotional support, and helps maintain the momentum of positive change.

- Accountability Monitoring: Family and community members can check in with the offender to encourage adherence to the plan, helping to prevent relapses or setbacks. This ongoing support reinforces the importance of follow-through.

- Emotional Support for Victims and Offenders: Victims may benefit from family and community encouragement as they work through the aftermath of the harm. Offenders, too, benefit from positive reinforcement as they take steps toward reintegration.

Benefits of Family and Community Involvement

The inclusion of family and community in restorative conferencing provides multiple benefits, from empowering victims to facilitating the offender's reintegration. This collective involvement is essential for achieving the broader goals of restorative justice, which include rebuilding trust, strengthening social bonds, and promoting lasting behavioral change.

1. Increased Sense of Ownership

When the community is involved in the restorative process, a shared responsibility for addressing harm and preventing future offenses develops. Community ownership of the process fosters a proactive approach to conflict resolution, creating a support network that reinforces social harmony and mutual accountability.

2. Empowerment of Victims

Victims often feel more empowered when they see that their family and community are present to support them. Knowing that their experiences and needs are validated by those around them can bolster their confidence and help them heal. Additionally, victims may feel safer sharing their story and advocating for their needs when they are surrounded by trusted supporters.

3. Reintegration of Offenders

One of the primary goals of restorative justice is to reintegrate offenders back into the community. Community support is essential for this process, as it provides a positive environment where offenders feel accepted and encouraged to make amends. By participating in the conference, the community signals its willingness to support the offender's rehabilitation and reintegration, creating an environment conducive to positive change.

Important Considerations for Family and Community Involvement

While family and community support is beneficial, there are key considerations to ensure that their involvement enhances rather than detracts from the restorative process.

1. Cultural Sensitivity

It is essential to consider cultural dynamics when involving family and community members in conferencing. Different cultural backgrounds may have varying views on family roles, communication styles, and conflict resolution. Facilitators should be mindful of these differences and strive to make the process inclusive, ensuring that all participants feel respected and valued.

2. Confidentiality

Confidentiality is crucial to create a safe space where participants feel comfortable sharing personal experiences. Family and community members should be reminded that information shared during the conference should remain private, protecting the dignity and privacy of everyone involved. Ensuring confidentiality builds trust and encourages open dialogue.

3. Trained Facilitators

Effective facilitation is vital for a successful conference. Trained facilitators are essential to guide discussions, manage power dynamics, and ensure that each voice is heard and respected. Skilled facilitators can also help mediate any conflicts that arise, maintaining the focus on collaboration and mutual understanding. Their role is particularly important when family members have complicated relationships or histories of conflict.

The Transformative Power of Family and Community Support in Conferencing

The involvement of family and community in restorative justice conferencing is transformative, providing a powerful support system that enhances healing, accountability, and reintegration. By bringing together family and community members, conferencing fosters a collective approach to justice that extends beyond punitive measures, emphasizing shared responsibility, empathy, and long-term reconciliation. Through their presence, support, and contributions, family and community members play a pivotal role in creating a restorative plan that is compassionate, realistic, and sustainable.

Family and community support contributes to the empowerment of victims, the reintegration of offenders, and the strengthening of social bonds within neighborhoods. As restorative justice continues to expand, recognizing and incorporating the vital roles of family and community will be essential for creating meaningful, community-centered approaches to conflict resolution and healing.

References

- Braithwaite, J. (1989). Crime, Shame, and Reintegration. Cambridge University Press.
- Burford, G., & Hudson, J. (2000). Family Group Conferencing: New Directions in Community-Centered Child and Family Practice. Transaction Publishers.
- Pranis, K. (2005). The Little Book of Circle Processes: A New/Old Approach to Peacemaking. Good Books.
- Umbreit, M. S., & Armour, M. P. (2011). Restorative Justice Dialogue: An Essential Guide for Research and Practice. Springer.
- Zehr, H. (2002). The Little Book of Restorative Justice. Good Books.

Outcomes and Benefits for Youth and Families Involved in Family Group Conferencing (FGC)

Family Group Conferencing (FGC), a restorative justice approach, offers a transformative experience for youth involved in harmful behaviors, their families, and victims. By promoting open dialogue, accountability, and collaborative problem-solving, FGC creates an environment where families can work together to address the root causes of the behavior, repair harm, and foster positive change. The structured support provided by FGC results in numerous benefits, including increased accountability, strengthened family relationships, and reduced recidivism. This chapter explores the key outcomes and benefits of FGC for youth and their families.

Key Benefits for Youth and Families in Family Group Conferencing

Family Group Conferencing provides a unique and supportive framework that promotes healing and accountability. The involvement of family members, victims, and community representatives offers youth the opportunity to take responsibility for their actions while encouraging families to actively participate in creating sustainable solutions.

1. Accountability

FGC promotes accountability by enabling youth to confront the consequences of their actions and understand the impact on victims and the wider community. By directly engaging with those affected, youth are encouraged to take responsibility and make amends.

- Facing the Impact: Youth are confronted with the real-life consequences of their actions, often hearing firsthand from victims about the harm caused. This experience fosters empathy, making it more likely that youth will understand the gravity of their behavior.

- Ownership of Actions: The process of developing an accountability plan allows youth to take active steps toward making things right. This ownership of their actions is a vital part of their personal growth and promotes positive behavioral change.

2. Victim Empowerment

FGC provides a platform for victims to share their experiences, ask questions, and participate in the decision-making process. By giving victims a voice, FGC helps them feel empowered and heard.

- Expression of Harm: Victims are able to communicate the emotional, physical, and social impact of the offense, which can be both cathartic and validating. This expression of harm is an essential part of the healing process.

- Involvement in Decision-Making: Victims have an opportunity to contribute to the accountability plan, suggesting specific actions or reparations that address their needs. This active involvement fosters a sense of closure and satisfaction with the justice process.

3. Family Engagement

Family Group Conferencing actively involves the youth's entire family in the restorative process, creating a support network for both the youth and the victim. Family members contribute their insights, offer guidance, and participate in creating a solution.

- Supportive Environment: Families can provide moral support to the youth, which reinforces positive change and encourages accountability. Additionally, family members gain a better understanding of the issues at hand, enabling them to offer more effective support in the future.

- Contribution to Solutions: Family members help develop a realistic plan for repair, ensuring that it considers the youth's strengths and limitations. This collaboration leads to a solution that is both practical and achievable.

4. Improved Relationships

Open communication facilitated by FGC can lead to improved relationships within families, promoting better understanding, empathy, and trust. By working together to address the issue, family members and youth can heal from past conflicts and strengthen their bonds.

- Addressing Tensions: FGC provides a safe space for family members to discuss past grievances, misunderstandings, or conflicts. Resolving these issues can improve family dynamics and enhance emotional support.

- Promoting Communication: The process encourages open communication and active listening, equipping family members with better communication skills. This improved dialogue can have long-lasting positive effects on family interactions.

5. Community Connection

FGC fosters a stronger sense of community by involving members beyond the immediate family, such as friends, community leaders, and neighbors. This engagement promotes collective responsibility and emphasizes that the well-being of one person affects the entire community.

- Sense of Belonging: Involving community members demonstrates that the youth's actions impact the wider community and that the community cares about their growth and reintegration.

- Collective Responsibility: The conference process highlights that accountability and healing are shared responsibilities. This sense of communal involvement reinforces the idea that the community plays a vital role in supporting and guiding its members.

6. Reduced Recidivism

Studies indicate that youth who participate in Family Group Conferencing are less likely to re-offend compared to those who go through traditional justice systems. FGC's emphasis on accountability, empathy, and supportive reintegration significantly contributes to a decrease in repeat offenses.

- Long-Term Behavioral Change: By addressing the underlying issues that contribute to the behavior, such as peer influences, trauma, or family stress, FGC promotes meaningful change that reduces the likelihood of recidivism.

- Supportive Reintegration: FGC helps offenders reintegrate positively into their families and communities. This supportive environment encourages youth to make better choices, as they know they have the backing of both their family and community.

7. Positive Self-Image

Taking responsibility for their actions and making amends can enhance a youth's self-esteem and self-worth. The FGC process allows them to experience personal growth and view themselves as capable of making positive changes.

- Empowerment Through Responsibility: The act of making amends and taking accountability can lead to a sense of personal accomplishment and pride. Youth are able to view themselves as individuals who can overcome mistakes and contribute positively to their community.

- Strengthened Identity: Successfully navigating the FGC process and repairing harm reinforces a youth's sense of identity and belonging, helping them build a positive self-image.

8. Access to Support Services

FGC often identifies and connects families with essential resources and support networks that address issues contributing to the behavior, such as counseling, educational assistance, or substance abuse treatment.

- Identification of Needs: The open discussion within FGC may reveal needs that were previously unnoticed or unaddressed, enabling families to seek appropriate assistance.

- Connection to Resources: Facilitators and community representatives can help families access support services that empower them to handle future challenges, creating a more resilient support system for the youth.

Important Aspects of a Successful Family Group Conference

To ensure the effectiveness of FGC, several key elements must be present. These factors contribute to a constructive and supportive environment that encourages accountability, empathy, and meaningful change.

1. Trained Facilitator

A skilled facilitator is crucial to guiding the FGC process. Trained in restorative justice principles, facilitators ensure that discussions remain respectful, inclusive, and constructive.

- Neutral Guidance: Facilitators maintain impartiality and ensure that all voices are heard, promoting a balanced and fair discussion.

- Managing Dynamics: Facilitators are adept at managing complex family dynamics, helping to resolve any conflicts that may arise during the process.

2. Open Communication

Open communication is a fundamental aspect of FGC, allowing participants to share their perspectives, experiences, and emotions regarding the offense.

- Safe Expression: Participants are encouraged to speak honestly about their experiences, fostering an atmosphere of trust and understanding.

- Building Empathy: By openly sharing, family members, victims, and the offender gain a better understanding of each other's feelings and perspectives.

3. Collaborative Plan Development

The development of a restorative plan is a collaborative effort involving input from all participants. This shared responsibility ensures that the plan reflects the needs and resources of everyone involved.

- Victim-Centered Solutions: The victim's needs are prioritized in the plan, ensuring that the harm caused is adequately addressed.

- Achievable Goals: The plan is realistic, considering the youth's capabilities and available resources, which makes it more likely to succeed.

4. Follow-Up Support

Continued support and monitoring are essential for implementing the plan and maintaining progress. This follow-up helps reinforce the goals of the FGC and encourages sustained positive behavior.

- Accountability Check-Ins: Regular check-ins provide opportunities to address any challenges or setbacks, keeping the youth accountable and focused on their goals.

- Support for Victims and Families: Ongoing support for victims and families helps ensure that they continue to feel supported throughout the healing process.

The Transformative Impact of Family Group Conferencing

Family Group Conferencing provides youth and their families with a structured yet flexible environment for healing, accountability, and personal growth. By engaging family and community members, FGC promotes open communication, empathy, and collaboration, addressing the underlying causes of harmful behavior and reinforcing positive connections within the family and community. The FGC process empowers youth to take responsibility, encourages victim participation, and strengthens family relationships, ultimately creating a supportive framework that reduces recidivism and fosters long-term success.

As an alternative to traditional punitive justice systems, FGC stands out for its holistic approach, supporting youth and families in a way that aligns with the core principles of restorative justice. The positive outcomes of FGC underscore the potential for restorative justice to create safer, more connected communities and more resilient individuals.

References

- Burford, G., & Hudson, J. (2000). Family Group Conferencing: New Directions in Community-Centered Child and Family Practice. Transaction Publishers.

- Umbreit, M. S., & Armour, M. P. (2011). Restorative Justice Dialogue: An Essential Guide for Research and Practice. Springer.

- Zehr, H. (2002). The Little Book of Restorative Justice. Good Books.

- Nixon, P., Burford, G., & Hudson, J. (2005). Family Group Conferencing in Child Welfare and Youth Justice: Learning from International Experiences. Russell House Publishing.

- Pranis, K. (2005). The Little Book of Circle Processes: A New/Old Approach to Peacemaking.

CHAPTER 08

Restorative Practices Create Positive School Climates

Restorative practices in schools aim to create a positive, inclusive school climate by building relationships, fostering open communication, and encouraging accountability. By shifting away from punitive discipline and using restorative approaches like classroom circles, schools can establish a supportive community where students are empowered to resolve conflicts and take responsibility for their actions. This approach not only reduces incidents of misbehavior but also strengthens social bonds, enhances students' social-emotional skills, and promotes an environment of trust and respect.

How Restorative Practices Create Positive School Climates

Restorative practices contribute to a healthier school environment by focusing on relationship-building and accountability rather than punishment. Schools implementing restorative practices often report improvements in school climate, including increased feelings of safety, belonging, and community among students and staff.

Key Aspects of Restorative Practices and Classroom Circles

1. Building Community

Classroom circles create a safe, inclusive space where everyone's voice is valued. This setup promotes a sense of belonging and connection among students, teachers, and staff. In circles, students and teachers sit as equals, fostering a sense of unity and reducing hierarchical divides that can sometimes hinder open dialogue.

- Sense of Belonging: Circles help students feel connected to their peers and teachers, building trust and promoting teamwork.
- Shared Values: By discussing values and setting group norms within the circle, students and staff create a shared foundation that guides behavior and promotes mutual respect.

2. Open Dialogue

Circles encourage students to express their feelings, experiences, and perspectives. This open dialogue fosters empathy and understanding, as students learn to listen actively and consider diverse viewpoints.

- Empathy Building: Sharing personal experiences in a supportive space encourages students to empathize with their peers, reducing misunderstandings and biases.
- Non-Judgmental Environment: In the circle, students are encouraged to share without fear of judgment, creating a more accepting and inclusive atmosphere.

3. Accountability

Restorative practices encourage individuals to take responsibility for their actions and consider how their behavior affects others. In a classroom circle, students who have caused harm are invited to acknowledge the impact of their actions and take steps to make amends.

- Self-Reflection: By understanding how their actions have affected others, students are encouraged to self-reflect and take accountability, which is essential for personal growth.
- Making Amends: Instead of punitive consequences, restorative practices focus on repairing harm, allowing students to make meaningful restitution.

4. Conflict Resolution

Circles offer a structured approach to address conflicts directly, enabling those involved to work collaboratively toward a solution. This format helps students learn constructive conflict resolution skills that they can use beyond the classroom.

- Collaborative Problem-Solving: Students are guided to identify issues, propose solutions, and reach a consensus, promoting peaceful conflict resolution.
- Peer Mediation: In some cases, students take on roles as peer mediators, which helps them learn responsibility and leadership skills while supporting their classmates.

5. Focus on Relationships

Rather than focusing solely on behavior, restorative practices aim to repair damaged relationships. The emphasis on relationships encourages students to look beyond rules and view conflicts as opportunities for growth and understanding.

- Strengthening Bonds: Circles allow students to rebuild trust and respect, fostering stronger relationships within the school community.
- Promoting Compassion: By addressing both the emotional and relational aspects of conflicts, restorative practices cultivate compassion and kindness.

How Classroom Circles Contribute to Positive School Climate

Classroom circles are foundational to restorative practices in schools, providing a safe and structured environment for students to engage in discussions, resolve conflicts, and build meaningful connections. Here are some specific ways in which circles contribute to a positive school climate:

1. Empowering Students

Classroom circles give students an active role in their learning and community. By allowing everyone to share their perspectives, students feel valued and empowered, which enhances their sense of belonging and engagement.

- Inclusive Participation: Every student has an opportunity to speak, ensuring that all voices are heard.
- Agency and Voice: Giving students a platform to express themselves helps them feel more invested in their school community.

2. Developing Social-Emotional Skills

Participating in regular circles helps students build essential social-emotional skills, such as active listening, empathy, and conflict resolution. These skills are vital for academic success and personal well-being.

- Active Listening: Students practice listening attentively to others, which improves comprehension and empathy.
- Emotional Intelligence: By discussing their own emotions and recognizing others' feelings, students develop emotional awareness and empathy.

3. Early Intervention

Classroom circles provide an opportunity to address issues before they escalate. By discussing minor conflicts or misunderstandings in a supportive space, schools can prevent these issues from developing into larger behavioral problems.

- Proactive Problem-Solving: Students learn to address concerns as they arise, promoting a culture of honesty and responsibility.
- Conflict Prevention: Early intervention helps to identify potential conflicts and resolve them before they negatively impact the school environment.

4. Reducing Exclusionary Discipline

Restorative practices, including classroom circles, serve as alternatives to traditional disciplinary measures, such as suspension or expulsion. This inclusive approach allows students to stay engaged with their learning and the school community, even when addressing behavioral issues.

- Keeping Students Engaged: By focusing on repair rather than punishment, students are less likely to miss out on valuable learning opportunities.

- Building Community Over Isolation: Restorative approaches aim to reintegrate students into the school community rather than isolating them, promoting a sense of belonging.

Important Considerations for Implementing Classroom Circles

To create an effective restorative environment, schools must consider several key factors. Properly trained facilitators, consistency, and cultural sensitivity are essential for successful implementation.

1. Training and Facilitation

Teachers and staff need thorough training in restorative practices to effectively lead classroom circles. Trained facilitators are essential for creating a safe space where students feel comfortable sharing and engaging in open dialogue.

- Building Facilitation Skills: Teachers should learn techniques for active listening, conflict mediation, and guiding discussions to ensure circles remain constructive.
- Creating Trust: Effective facilitators build trust within the group, helping students feel safe to share sensitive topics and emotions.

2. Consistency

Consistency is vital for building trust and establishing a positive classroom culture. Regular circle sessions foster a sense of routine, allowing students to develop familiarity and comfort with the restorative process.

- Establishing Routine: Scheduling regular circles helps reinforce restorative principles and fosters a supportive atmosphere.

- Sustaining Positive Culture: Consistent use of circles ensures that restorative practices become embedded in the school's culture, making positive behavior and accountability the norm.

3. Cultural Sensitivity

Cultural sensitivity is crucial when facilitating classroom circles. Schools should be mindful of diverse backgrounds, values, and communication styles, ensuring that all students feel respected and included.

- Respecting Diversity: Facilitators should be aware of cultural norms and be sensitive to each student's unique background, promoting an inclusive environment.
- Adapting Techniques: Schools may need to adjust circle practices to align with the cultural values of their students, ensuring everyone feels safe and valued.

The Positive Impact of Restorative Schools and Classroom Circles

Restorative practices, particularly classroom circles, have a transformative impact on school climates. By emphasizing community, accountability, and open dialogue, restorative practices create an environment where students feel empowered, supported, and engaged. This approach builds essential social-emotional skills, reduces disciplinary issues, and enhances relationships among students, teachers, and staff.

In schools that embrace restorative practices, students are more likely to develop a sense of responsibility, empathy, and respect for others. The implementation of classroom circles encourages students to participate actively in their community, fostering a positive, inclusive culture that enhances learning and personal growth. Through consistent and culturally sensitive use of restorative practices, schools can cultivate environments where every student feels valued, creating a foundation for lifelong success and well-being.

References

- Amstutz, L. S., & Mullet, J. H. (2005). The Little Book of Restorative Discipline for Schools: Teaching Responsibility; Creating Caring Climates. Good Books.
- Pranis, K. (2005). The Little Book of Circle Processes: A New/Old Approach to Peacemaking. Good Books.
- Thorsborne, M., & Blood, P. (2013). Implementing Restorative Practices in Schools: A Practical Guide to Transforming School Communities. Jessica Kingsley Publishers.
- Zehr, H. (2002). The Little Book of Restorative Justice. Good Books.
- Wachtel, T. (2016). Restorative Justice in Everyday Life: Beyond the Formal Ritual. The Piper's Press.

Classroom Circles and Their Impact on Student Behavior

Classroom circles, a key component of restorative practices, have the potential to positively influence student behavior by fostering accountability, cooperation, empathy, and conflict resolution skills. By creating a structured, supportive environment, circles encourage students to take responsibility for their actions, work collaboratively, and address conflicts in a constructive way. The regular use of classroom circles helps build a strong, inclusive community and promotes positive behaviors that extend beyond the classroom.

Positive Impacts of Classroom Circles on Student Behavior

Classroom circles provide a proactive approach to managing student behavior and enhancing the school climate. These circles focus on relationship-building, setting expectations, and addressing conflicts, creating a supportive space where students can thrive.

1. Building Community

Classroom circles are valuable for building a sense of community within the classroom. Used at the beginning of the school year or throughout the year, circles help students get to know one another and the teacher. This community-building fosters a sense of belonging, which can improve students' engagement, cooperation, and respect for each other.

- Creating Connections: Through sharing personal stories, interests, and goals, students can form meaningful connections with peers and teachers.
- Establishing Trust: Regular circles build trust among students, creating an environment where they feel safe expressing themselves.

2. Setting Expectations

Classroom circles provide an ideal setting for students and teachers to establish shared expectations for behavior, communication, and interactions. When students actively participate in setting these norms, they are more likely to take ownership and adhere to them.

- Shared Ownership of Rules: By contributing to expectations, students feel responsible for upholding them, fostering accountability.
- Clarity and Understanding: Circles allow students to clarify expectations, ensuring everyone understands the classroom standards.

3. Resolving Conflicts

After an incident or conflict, a restorative circle can be used to address the harm caused, allowing students to take responsibility, repair relationships, and move forward positively. This approach to conflict resolution promotes understanding and reduces the likelihood of recurring issues.

- Accountability: Students involved in conflicts have an opportunity to acknowledge their actions and consider how they impacted others.
- Repairing Relationships: Conflict resolution circles encourage students to work together to restore relationships and prevent future conflicts.

4. Learning Conflict Resolution Skills

Classroom circles teach essential conflict resolution skills, equipping students with tools to handle disputes constructively. Skills such as active listening, problem-solving, and respectful communication are cultivated in circles and help students manage conflicts in positive ways.

- Lifelong Skills: The conflict resolution skills learned in circles are transferable to real-world situations, benefitting students in their personal and professional lives.
- Constructive Problem-Solving: By working through conflicts with peers, students learn to find solutions that meet everyone's needs.

5. Developing Empathy

Empathy is a cornerstone of restorative practices, and classroom circles offer a structured setting where students can build empathy for one another. Through listening to diverse perspectives and experiences, students learn to appreciate the feelings and challenges of others, which can reduce negative behaviors and improve social interactions.

- Understanding Different Perspectives: When students hear each other's stories and emotions, they become more attuned to the experiences of their peers.

- Reducing Negative Behaviors: As empathy increases, students are more likely to treat each other with kindness and respect, leading to fewer incidents of bullying or exclusion.

Tips for Implementing Restorative Justice Circles in the Classroom

Implementing restorative circles requires careful planning and a supportive environment. Here are some practical tips for creating effective and meaningful circles.

1. Use a Talking Piece

Using a talking piece helps facilitate respectful dialogue by signifying who has the floor. Only the person holding the talking piece, which could be a meaningful object like a feather, seashell, or animal figurine, is allowed to speak. This practice promotes active listening and ensures that all voices are heard.

- Encouraging Focused Listening: The talking piece ensures that students listen attentively without interrupting, fostering respect and patience.

- Creating a Sense of Ritual: Using a consistent talking piece adds a ceremonial quality to the circle, enhancing the experience.

2. Ask Thoughtful Questions

Asking open-ended questions is essential to encouraging reflection and personal responsibility. Questions like, "What happened?" "Who was affected?" and "What do you think you need to do to make things right?" help students understand the impact of their actions and think critically about solutions.

- Promoting Accountability: Questions focused on taking responsibility encourage students to reflect on their role in the conflict.
- Fostering Solution-Oriented Thinking: By asking students to think about how they can repair harm, circles help them develop proactive, constructive responses to issues.

3. Choose an Appropriate Location

The environment can significantly impact the effectiveness of a classroom circle. A quieter, private space, like a library or an area with minimal background noise, is ideal for circles. This ensures that students can focus, feel comfortable, and engage in meaningful dialogue without distractions.

- Creating a Safe Space: A calm, private setting helps students feel secure and open to sharing.
- Reducing Distractions: Choosing a location away from interruptions helps maintain the flow and focus of the conversation.

Conclusion: The Lasting Impact of Classroom Circles on Student Behavior

Classroom circles play a transformative role in promoting positive student behavior by fostering community, encouraging empathy, and teaching conflict resolution skills. When students actively participate in setting expectations, addressing conflicts, and taking responsibility, they develop social-emotional competencies that extend far beyond the classroom. Through regular use of circles, schools can create an inclusive, respectful, and supportive learning environment.

By implementing restorative practices like classroom circles, educators can cultivate a school culture where students feel valued, understood, and empowered. This shift from punitive discipline to restorative approaches not only enhances behavior but also promotes lifelong skills in empathy, responsibility, and cooperation. As students learn to listen, empathize, and resolve conflicts constructively, they contribute to a positive school climate that benefits all members of the community.

References

- Amstutz, L. S., & Mullet, J. H. (2005). The Little Book of Restorative Discipline for Schools: Teaching Responsibility; Creating Caring Climates. Good Books.

- Pranis, K. (2005). The Little Book of Circle Processes: A New/Old Approach to Peacemaking. Good Books.

- Thorsborne, M., & Blood, P. (2013). Implementing Restorative Practices in Schools: A Practical Guide to Transforming School Communities. Jessica Kingsley Publishers.

- Zehr, H. (2002). The Little Book of Restorative Justice. Good Books.

- Wachtel, T. (2016). Restorative Justice in Everyday Life: Beyond the Formal Ritual. The Piper's Press.

Case Studies of Restorative Practices in Schools

Restorative practices have proven successful in transforming school climates across diverse settings, from urban schools in the United States to rural communities in Canada and schools in the United Kingdom. These practices promote a shift from punitive discipline to relationship-centered approaches, positively impacting student behavior, disciplinary outcomes, and overall school climate.

The following case studies demonstrate how restorative practices have been effectively implemented in various educational environments, showcasing reduced suspensions, enhanced student relationships, and a greater sense of belonging within school communities.

United States: Urban Schools Implementing Restorative Practices

Baltimore City Schools

A study conducted by Johns Hopkins University evaluated the implementation of restorative practices in several Baltimore schools, observing a significant decrease in suspensions and a notable improvement in student-teacher relationships. Baltimore's schools faced high suspension rates and strained relationships between students and staff prior to the introduction of restorative practices.

- Outcomes: Suspensions decreased notably across participating schools, which contributed to a more inclusive and supportive school environment. Students expressed feeling more respected and valued by their teachers, leading to a greater willingness to engage in classroom activities.

- Key Insights: Restorative practices in Baltimore emphasized open communication, empathy, and conflict resolution skills. This approach allowed students to address conflicts constructively, fostering stronger bonds with peers and teachers.

Fresno Unified School District, California

In California's Fresno Unified School District, students advocated for restorative practices as a solution to high suspension rates and tensions within the school community. Led by student activists, the movement promoted a shift from punitive measures to restorative approaches, emphasizing relationships over punishment.

- Outcomes: Since the adoption of restorative practices, the district has seen a reduction in suspensions, improved attendance, and a stronger sense of community. The initiative fostered a safer, more positive school climate, which encouraged student involvement and improved student-teacher relationships.

- Key Insights: This case underscores the importance of student agency in promoting restorative practices. By involving students as advocates for change, Fresno achieved greater buy-in and commitment from the entire school community.

Schools in Minnesota

A study by the Minnesota Department of Education highlighted the success of restorative practices across various grade levels in Minnesota schools. These practices were implemented to address disciplinary issues and enhance school climate.

- Outcomes: Schools reported a substantial reduction in suspensions and an improvement in overall school climate. Teachers noted an increase in respectful communication among students and a decrease in behavioral disruptions.

- Key Insights: The Minnesota case demonstrates the effectiveness of restorative practices across diverse grade levels, reinforcing the adaptability of these approaches. Schools in this study emphasized the importance of consistent, ongoing training to equip staff with the skills needed to facilitate restorative practices effectively.

Canada: Rural Schools in British Columbia

In rural communities in British Columbia, Canada, restorative practices were introduced as a means to address conflicts among students, particularly in schools with diverse backgrounds and socioeconomic challenges. Rural schools faced unique social and cultural dynamics that required an inclusive approach to discipline.

- Outcomes: Studies found that restorative practices effectively reduced incidents of conflict and fostered a more supportive school environment. Students from different backgrounds reported feeling more understood and connected to their peers. Additionally, teachers noted a reduction in bullying and other negative behaviors.

- Key Insights: This case highlights the value of adapting restorative practices to address the specific social challenges of a community. By tailoring approaches to fit the cultural and demographic needs of the students, schools achieved more meaningful and lasting outcomes.

United Kingdom: Bristol Schools

In Bristol, UK, schools adopted restorative justice practices to improve student behavior and reduce exclusion rates. An independent evaluation assessed the impact of these practices on school climate and student behavior, finding impressive results.

- Outcomes: The implementation of restorative practices in Bristol schools led to a significant reduction in exclusion rates, improved school attendance, and enhanced relationships among students and staff. Students reported feeling safer and more connected to their school community, which contributed to a positive learning environment.

- Key Insights: Bristol schools demonstrated the effectiveness of restorative practices in reducing exclusionary discipline. The case study also emphasizes the role of consistent, school-wide implementation, with staff receiving comprehensive training and support.

Key Themes from the Case Studies

These case studies highlight several recurring benefits and lessons from implementing restorative practices in diverse educational settings:

Positive Impact on Discipline

Across all regions, restorative practices consistently led to a reduction in suspensions, expulsions, and disciplinary referrals. This reduction in punitive measures contributes to a more inclusive school environment, where students remain engaged in their education rather than being excluded.

- Focus on Reparation: By emphasizing reparation over punishment, restorative practices reduce the frequency of suspensions and expulsions, promoting a more compassionate approach to discipline.

Improved School Climate

Students in schools that implement restorative practices often report feeling more connected to their peers and teachers, leading to a more supportive and positive learning environment. This sense of community contributes to improved behavior, increased attendance, and enhanced academic engagement.

- Enhanced Relationships: By fostering open dialogue and empathy, restorative practices build stronger relationships within the school, encouraging students to collaborate and respect one another.

Cultural Adaptation

The successful implementation of restorative practices requires adaptation to the specific cultural and social dynamics of each school community. In cases where schools tailored restorative approaches to their unique contexts, students and staff achieved more positive outcomes.

- Community-Specific Approaches: Schools that adjusted restorative practices to align with their community's values and demographics were able to create a more relevant and effective approach, enhancing buy-in and engagement.

Staff Training is Crucial

Effective implementation of restorative practices depends on comprehensive training for all school staff members, including teachers, administrators, and support staff. In each case, schools that invested in ongoing training saw more successful outcomes and a stronger commitment to restorative approaches.

- Building Facilitation Skills: Training equips staff with the skills to lead circles, mediate conflicts, and foster open dialogue, ensuring that restorative practices are consistently and effectively applied.

Important Considerations When Examining Restorative Practices Case Studies

While case studies provide valuable insights, it is essential to consider the context and methodology when evaluating the impact of restorative practices.

Data Collection Methods

To gain a comprehensive understanding of the impact of restorative practices, it is essential to analyze both qualitative and quantitative data. Combining quantitative data, such as suspension rates, with qualitative insights from interviews and surveys provides a fuller picture of the effects on school climate and student relationships.

- Mixed-Methods Approach: Using a mix of data types helps capture both measurable outcomes and the subjective experiences of students, teachers, and staff involved in restorative practices.

Contextual Factors

Each school community has unique demographics, challenges, and cultural dynamics that can influence the outcomes of restorative practices. When interpreting case studies, it is important to consider how these factors may shape the results.

- Demographics and Culture: Factors like socioeconomic status, community norms, and student diversity affect how restorative practices are received and implemented, highlighting the need for culturally responsive approaches.

Sustainability and Long-Term Effects

Evaluating the long-term impact of restorative practices is crucial for understanding their effectiveness. Many of the benefits of restorative approaches, such as improved relationships and reduced recidivism, may only become evident over time.

- Commitment to Longevity: Schools that commit to ongoing restorative practices rather than one-time interventions are more likely to experience lasting improvements in school climate and student behavior.

Conclusion: The Positive Impact of Restorative Practices in Schools

The case studies from the United States, Canada, and the United Kingdom illustrate the transformative potential of restorative practices in diverse school settings. By reducing reliance on punitive discipline, enhancing relationships, and fostering a more inclusive school climate, restorative practices help students develop crucial social-emotional skills, improve their academic engagement, and strengthen their connection to the school community.

These successes highlight the importance of adapting restorative practices to the specific needs of each community, investing in comprehensive staff training, and implementing restorative approaches consistently across the school. As more schools embrace restorative practices, these case studies provide valuable insights and best practices for creating supportive, relationship-centered learning environments that empower students and foster positive behavior.

References

- Amstutz, L. S., & Mullet, J. H. (2005). The Little Book of Restorative Discipline for Schools: Teaching Responsibility; Creating Caring Climates. Good Books.
- Hopkins, B. (2004). Just Schools: A Whole School Approach to Restorative Justice. Jessica Kingsley Publishers.

- Thorsborne, M., & Blood, P. (2013). Implementing Restorative Practices in Schools: A Practical Guide to Transforming School Communities. Jessica Kingsley Publishers.
- Wachtel, T. (2016). Restorative Justice in Everyday Life: Beyond the Formal Ritual. The Piper's Press.
- Zehr, H. (2002). The Little Book of Restorative Justice. Good Books.

Through regular implementation of classroom circles, students develop essential social-emotional skills, such as empathy, accountability, and conflict resolution. These skills not only improve classroom dynamics but also contribute to students' overall growth and well-being, equipping them with tools to navigate relationships and challenges beyond school.

The positive impacts of classroom circles extend beyond individual students to shape the entire classroom climate. When students feel heard, valued, and supported, they are more likely to engage positively with their peers and take ownership of their behavior. This shift towards a restorative approach to discipline reduces the reliance on punitive measures and instead emphasizes personal responsibility, understanding, and mutual respect. In turn, this creates a safer, more supportive learning environment where all students can thrive.

By investing in teacher training, establishing clear norms, and fostering trust, schools can create the foundation for successful classroom circles. These practices not only build stronger, more empathetic communities within classrooms but also contribute to a culture of respect and inclusion throughout the entire school. As more schools adopt restorative practices like classroom circles, the potential for transformative change in education becomes evident, offering a pathway to more compassionate, inclusive, and resilient learning environments.

References

- Amstutz, L. S., & Mullet, J. H. (2005). The Little Book of Restorative Discipline for Schools: Teaching Responsibility; Creating Caring Climates. Good Books.
- Hopkins, B. (2004). Just Schools: A Whole School Approach to Restorative Justice. Jessica Kingsley Publishers.
- Pranis, K. (2005). The Little Book of Circle Processes: A New/Old Approach to Peacemaking. Good Books.
- Thorsborne, M., & Blood, P. (2013). Implementing Restorative Practices in Schools: A Practical Guide to Transforming School Communities. Jessica Kingsley Publishers.
- Zehr, H. (2002). The Little Book of Restorative Justice. Good Books.

Classroom circles represent an important step toward building supportive and proactive educational communities. By integrating restorative practices into the fabric of school life, educators can create spaces that not only support academic success but also encourage holistic development, equipping students with the interpersonal skills they need to succeed in life.

CHAPTER 09

Truth and Reconciliation Process

Truth and Reconciliation Commissions (TRCs) are restorative justice mechanisms designed to address serious human rights violations and promote healing in societies recovering from oppression, conflict, or systemic abuses. Unlike traditional justice systems, which focus on punishment, TRCs prioritize uncovering the truth and fostering reconciliation by allowing both victims and perpetrators to share their experiences. The goal is to create a historical record of past atrocities, promote understanding, and support community healing. The most widely recognized TRC was established in South Africa following Apartheid, led by Nelson Mandela and Archbishop Desmond Tutu, and inspired similar efforts worldwide.

Key Aspects of Truth and Reconciliation Commissions (TRCs)

TRCs are structured around restorative justice principles, with a focus on truth-telling, public hearings, and recommendations for reparations. These commissions aim to acknowledge and address past injustices while fostering understanding and reconciliation within affected communities.

1. Focus on Restorative Justice

TRCs embody restorative justice principles by prioritizing healing over punishment. Unlike traditional judicial systems that focus on retribution, TRCs emphasize the importance of allowing victims to be heard, encouraging perpetrators to accept responsibility, and seeking ways to repair relationships within communities.

- Empowering Victims: TRCs give victims a platform to share their experiences, which can be cathartic and contribute to their personal healing process.
- Acknowledgment and Accountability: By focusing on acknowledgment, TRCs encourage perpetrators to confront their actions openly, fostering a sense of responsibility.

2. Public Hearings

Public hearings are a central feature of TRCs, allowing both victims and perpetrators to share their testimonies in an open forum. These hearings foster transparency, provide an opportunity for public acknowledgment of past atrocities, and contribute to collective healing by creating a shared understanding of the past.

- Transparency: Public hearings prevent the suppression of truth and allow society to witness and engage with the process of uncovering past abuses.

- Collective Healing: By sharing their stories, victims and perpetrators contribute to a collective understanding of the past, which can foster empathy and unity.

3. Amnesty for Perpetrators

Many TRCs offer amnesty to perpetrators who fully disclose their crimes, which can incentivize truth-telling. This approach can be controversial, as it may lead to accusations of impunity. However, amnesty can also enable reconciliation by encouraging perpetrators to admit their actions without fear of retribution.

- Incentivizing Truth-Telling: Amnesty encourages perpetrators to provide a complete and honest account of their actions, which can be crucial for uncovering the full truth.
- Balancing Justice and Healing: While controversial, amnesty reflects a balance between achieving accountability and facilitating societal healing.

4. Recommendations for Reparations

Beyond truth-telling, TRCs often recommend reparations for victims to support their recovery and help restore a sense of justice. These reparations can include financial compensation, symbolic gestures, and community-based support programs.

- Direct Compensation: Financial reparations can help victims rebuild their lives, especially if they have suffered economic losses due to human rights abuses.
- Symbolic Reparations: Symbolic acts, such as memorials or official apologies, acknowledge the suffering of victims and serve as a reminder of the importance of justice and reconciliation.

- Community Support Programs: TRCs may recommend mental health services, educational programs, and other community support measures to aid recovery and prevent future injustices.

Historical Context of Truth and Reconciliation Commissions

TRCs have been established in various regions following periods of conflict, oppression, and systemic human rights abuses. These commissions have become prominent in post-conflict societies as a means of addressing the past, preventing future violence, and facilitating peace and reconciliation.

South Africa

The South African TRC is one of the most prominent and widely studied examples of a truth and reconciliation process. Established after the end of Apartheid in 1994, the TRC aimed to address the atrocities committed under the Apartheid regime and promote national healing. Under the leadership of Nelson Mandela and Archbishop Desmond Tutu, the TRC became a model for other countries seeking restorative approaches to justice.

- Public Testimonies: Victims and perpetrators participated in public hearings, where victims shared stories of suffering and perpetrators disclosed their actions.
- Amnesty for Disclosure: The TRC offered amnesty to perpetrators who fully confessed to their crimes, which helped incentivize truth-telling.
- Impact: While the South African TRC achieved significant success in promoting national reconciliation, it faced challenges, including criticisms regarding the amnesty process and its ability to deliver full justice for victims.

Latin America

Several Latin American countries, including Argentina, Chile, and Uruguay, established TRCs after periods of military dictatorship and widespread human rights abuses. These commissions aimed to uncover the truth about forced disappearances, torture, and other atrocities committed by authoritarian regimes.

- Documentation of Atrocities: TRCs in Latin America provided detailed records of human rights violations, helping families discover the fate of missing loved ones.
- Impact on Democratic Transition: These TRCs contributed to the restoration of democracy by addressing the legacy of dictatorship and promoting human rights reforms.
- Reparations: Many TRCs in Latin America recommended reparations for victims, including financial compensation and mental health support.

Post-Conflict Situations

TRCs have also been established in countries emerging from civil wars and other violent conflicts, such as Sierra Leone, Rwanda, and East Timor. These commissions serve as vital tools for addressing atrocities, restoring social cohesion, and preventing future violence.

- Focus on Reconciliation: Post-conflict TRCs emphasize reconciliation to heal the divisions left by war and restore trust among communities.
- Challenges: In some cases, TRCs have faced resistance due to cultural or political factors, and the process of balancing accountability with reconciliation remains complex.

Criticisms of Truth and Reconciliation Commissions

While TRCs have made significant contributions to restorative justice, they are not without criticisms. Common concerns include potential impunity, the risk of re-traumatizing victims, and the possibility of political manipulation.

1. Potential for Impunity

One of the most contentious aspects of TRCs is the practice of offering amnesty to perpetrators in exchange for full disclosure. While this approach can encourage truth-telling, it may also be perceived as allowing perpetrators to evade full accountability.

- Concerns about Justice: Offering amnesty can be seen as condoning the actions of perpetrators, which may undermine victims' sense of justice.
- Balancing Truth with Justice: Critics argue that TRCs should find ways to encourage truth-telling without compromising justice for victims.

2. Re-Traumatization of Victims

The process of public testimony can be emotionally taxing for victims, who may experience re-traumatization by recounting painful experiences. While TRCs aim to provide a platform for healing, the process can inadvertently reopen wounds for those who have suffered.

- Risk of Psychological Harm: Victims may experience emotional distress when sharing their stories publicly, especially if they do not feel adequately supported.
- Need for Support Services: Providing mental health support for victims who participate in TRCs is crucial to mitigate the risks of re-traumatization.

3. Political Manipulation

In some cases, governments may use TRCs to selectively address abuses while avoiding deeper systemic reforms. There is a risk that TRCs can be used to deflect criticism or placate the public without making meaningful changes.

- Superficial Accountability: If a TRC is used to address only a portion of abuses, it may fail to address the root causes of conflict or oppression.
- Ensuring Independence: TRCs must be independent and transparent to prevent political manipulation and ensure credibility in the eyes of the public.

The Role of TRCs in Restorative Justice and Reconciliation

Truth and Reconciliation Commissions represent a powerful tool within the restorative justice framework, offering societies a path to confront past atrocities, acknowledge harm, and promote healing. By prioritizing truth-telling and reconciliation, TRCs provide an alternative to punitive justice, seeking instead to mend broken relationships, foster understanding, and build a more just and compassionate society. These commissions underscore the importance of collective healing and offer a way forward for societies striving to prevent future violence and protect human rights.

While TRCs have faced criticisms, including concerns over potential impunity and the emotional toll on victims, their impact on post-conflict societies has been profound. From South Africa to Latin America and beyond, TRCs have contributed to reconciliation, democratic transitions, and social cohesion, laying the foundation for a more peaceful and inclusive future. As more countries adopt restorative approaches to justice, the lessons learned from TRCs continue to shape the global pursuit of justice, human rights, and reconciliation.

References

- Hayner, P. B. (2011). Unspeakable Truths: Transitional Justice and the Challenge of Truth Commissions. Routledge.
- Tutu, D. (1999). No Future Without Forgiveness. Image.
- Rotberg, R. I., & Thompson, D. (2010). Truth v. Justice: The Morality of Truth Commissions. Princeton University Press.
- Minow, M. (1998). Between Vengeance and Forgiveness: Facing History after Genocide and Mass Violence. Beacon Press.
- Chapman, A. R., & Ball, P. (2001). Truth of Consequences: Do Truth Commissions Promote Democratization?. Human Rights Quarterly, 23(1), 18-25.

Through TRCs, societies gain an opportunity to build bridges across divides, understand the impact of past injustices, and work together to create a foundation of trust and mutual respect. By prioritizing truth, accountability, and reconciliation, TRCs stand as a testament to the power

& Ball, P. (2001). Truth of Consequences: Do Truth Commissions Promote Democratization?. Human Rights Quarterly, 23(1), 18-25.

Truth and Reconciliation Commissions offer a means to confront painful histories, honor the experiences of victims, and promote justice and reconciliation within communities. By examining the successes and challenges of TRCs worldwide, future commissions can adopt best practices and refine processes to better address the complex dynamics of post-conflict societies. The lasting impact of TRCs lies in their ability to forge a pathway towards healing, accountability, and a commitment to a future where human rights and dignity are universally respected.

Chapter 9: How Truth and Reconciliation Commissions (TRCs) Contribute to National Healing and Unity

Truth and Reconciliation Commissions (TRCs) play a vital role in promoting national healing and unity by addressing past injustices, fostering empathy, and encouraging dialogue between victims, perpetrators, and the broader society. Rooted in restorative justice principles, TRCs prioritize the acknowledgment of suffering, truth-telling, and reconciliation as steps toward building a more unified society. By creating public spaces where difficult conversations can take place, TRCs help societies process traumatic histories and lay the foundation for a future rooted in understanding, respect, and collective healing.

Key Aspects of How TRCs Promote National Healing and Unity

The structure and goals of TRCs are designed to contribute to national healing in several interconnected ways, from validating victims' experiences to recommending reforms that address the root causes of conflict.

1. Truth-Telling

Truth-telling is one of the most essential functions of a TRC, allowing victims and witnesses to share their experiences of past atrocities in a safe, public space. By documenting and publicly acknowledging these stories, TRCs validate victims' suffering, countering historical denial or erasure of abuses. This process also provides a basis for collective memory, which is essential to ensuring that the lessons of the past are not forgotten.

- Validation and Closure: For many victims, being able to tell their story is a crucial step in the healing process. When the truth is publicly acknowledged, it can bring a sense of closure and help individuals and communities begin to move forward.

- Creating a Collective Memory: Public truth-telling preserves the memory of past injustices, educating future generations about the dangers of violence and oppression. This collective memory serves as a safeguard against future human rights abuses.

2. Acknowledgment of Suffering

TRCs actively recognize the suffering caused by past injustices, promoting empathy and mutual respect within society. By formally acknowledging victims' pain, TRCs create a foundation for shared understanding and a commitment to healing. This acknowledgment extends beyond individuals to include entire communities affected by discrimination, violence, or systemic injustices.

- Fostering Empathy: When people hear the testimonies of those who have suffered, it encourages empathy and compassion. This helps bridge divides and promote a sense of shared responsibility within the nation.

- Building a Sense of Justice: Official acknowledgment from a TRC affirms the dignity of victims and reaffirms the commitment of society to ensure justice and equality moving forward.

3. Dialogue and Reconciliation

A central goal of TRCs is to facilitate dialogue between victims and perpetrators, as well as among different community groups. This dialogue allows for a deeper understanding of individual perspectives, which is essential for reconciliation and moving forward as a united society. The reconciliation process often involves forgiveness and compassion, though it does not overlook accountability. Instead, it encourages people to confront the past honestly while seeking ways to rebuild trust and solidarity.

- Understanding Perspectives: Dialogue fosters a broader understanding of the causes and impacts of past violence, allowing victims and perpetrators to humanize each other and acknowledge shared humanity.

- Facilitating Forgiveness: For some victims, TRCs offer a chance to forgive and let go of personal grievances, which can be liberating and pave the way for collective healing.

4. Community Building

TRCs are a powerful tool for community building, bringing together individuals and groups who were previously divided by conflict. By confronting the painful truths of the past together, communities can work towards healing and create a shared identity rooted in understanding and respect.

- Fostering Unity: When communities come together to engage in restorative justice, it fosters a sense of unity and shared purpose. This helps break down barriers that may have once caused division and mistrust.

- Creating a Shared Identity: The process of collective truth-telling and reconciliation helps communities forge a new, shared identity based on values of respect, empathy, and commitment to preventing future conflicts.

5. Institutional Reform

A key outcome of many TRCs is a set of recommendations for institutional and policy reforms. These reforms address systemic injustices and aim to prevent the recurrence of violence and human rights abuses. Recommendations can include changes to the criminal justice system, new protections for marginalized groups, or educational reforms that promote inclusive history and human rights.

- Preventing Future Abuses: By recommending changes to government policies and institutions, TRCs help establish safeguards that protect against future abuses.
- Promoting Justice and Equality: Institutional reform ensures that the lessons learned through the TRC process are embedded in the fabric of society, supporting a lasting commitment to justice and equality.

Important Considerations for TRCs in Fostering National Healing and Unity

To be effective in fostering healing and unity, TRCs must be designed with care, keeping in mind the needs of victims, the balance between amnesty and accountability, and the specific cultural and historical context of the society.

1. Victim-Centered Approach

A successful TRC process prioritizes the needs and well-being of victims, ensuring that they feel respected, validated, and empowered throughout the process. Victims should have a central role in sharing their stories, contributing to the recommendations for reparations, and defining what justice and healing mean to them.

- Empowering Victims: When victims are at the heart of the process, it reinforces the legitimacy of the TRC and promotes a sense of justice and validation for those who have suffered.
- Prioritizing Mental Health Support: Providing mental health resources to support victims during the process can prevent re-

traumatization and help them cope with the emotional impact of sharing their stories.

2. Balancing Amnesty and Accountability

TRCs often face the difficult decision of whether to offer amnesty to perpetrators in exchange for full disclosure of their crimes. This approach can encourage truth-telling but may also lead to perceptions of impunity if not handled carefully. Striking a balance between encouraging disclosure and ensuring accountability is crucial for fostering trust and legitimacy in the TRC process.

- Incentivizing Truth-Telling: In some cases, offering limited amnesty can help uncover hidden truths by encouraging perpetrators to come forward without fear of immediate punishment.
- Ensuring Accountability: TRCs must address the actions of perpetrators in a way that promotes justice and accountability, ensuring that victims do not feel further harmed by perceived impunity.

3. Cultural Context

Each TRC must be adapted to the cultural and historical context of the society it serves. The values, traditions, and social structures of a community play a significant role in shaping the TRC process. Tailoring the commission to reflect the community's values and incorporating local customs can make the TRC more effective and meaningful.

- Adapting Processes to Local Values: Incorporating culturally relevant practices can enhance community engagement and support, making the TRC process more impactful.

- Involving Local Leaders: Engaging respected community leaders can help build trust in the TRC and encourage participation from diverse groups.

The Role of TRCs in Building a United and Peaceful Society

Truth and Reconciliation Commissions are invaluable tools for societies recovering from conflict, oppression, or systemic abuses. Through truth-telling, acknowledgment of suffering, dialogue, community building, and institutional reform, TRCs help societies confront and heal from their painful histories. The goal of TRCs is not simply to provide justice for past wrongs but to create a future rooted in empathy, unity, and mutual respect.

By centering victims, balancing amnesty with accountability, and adapting processes to the cultural context, TRCs can be designed to support genuine reconciliation. As societies around the world continue to grapple with histories of injustice, the lessons from TRCs provide a roadmap for promoting peace and preventing future violence. These commissions demonstrate that, even after profound division, a commitment to truth, understanding, and collective responsibility can pave the way for lasting national unity and healing.

References

- Hayner, P. B. (2011). Unspeakable Truths: Transitional Justice and the Challenge of Truth Commissions. Routledge.
- Tutu, D. (1999). No Future Without Forgiveness. Image.
- Rotberg, R. I., & Thompson, D. (2010). Truth v. Justice: The Morality of Truth Commissions. Princeton University Press.
- Minow, M. (1998). Between Vengeance and Forgiveness: Facing History after Genocide and Mass Violence. Beacon Press.
- Chapman, A. R., & Ball, P. (2001). Truth of Consequences: Do Truth Commissions Promote Democratization? Human Rights Quarterly, 23(1), 18-25.

The work of TRCs continues to inspire efforts toward peace and justice around the world, offering a model for societies committed to moving beyond cycles of violence and division. Through their focus on healing and unity, TRCs illustrate the transformative power of restorative justice and the possibility of building a shared future even after the darkest chapters of history.

CHAPTER 10
Integrating Restorative Justice into Criminal Justice System

Restorative justice (RJ) offers a transformative approach to addressing crime, emphasizing the repair of harm, offender accountability, and active participation by victims and communities. By incorporating RJ practices into criminal justice systems, societies can shift from solely punitive responses to approaches focused on healing, reconciliation, and prevention. The integration of RJ into criminal justice has gained support worldwide, with models that range from victim-offender mediation to community-based peace circles. This chapter explores how RJ practices can be integrated into existing criminal justice processes, offering an alternative that fosters understanding and meaningful accountability.

Key Approaches to Integrating Restorative Justice into Criminal Justice Systems

Integrating restorative justice into traditional criminal justice systems requires innovative approaches that encourage accountability, healing, and community involvement. Below are essential methods for RJ integration:

1. Involving Victims and the Community

Restorative justice emphasizes the importance of including those most directly affected by crime, including victims, offenders, and community members. Unlike traditional justice systems that primarily focus on the offender, RJ actively involves victims in decision-making and provides them with a platform to express their experiences, needs, and expectations.

- Victim Empowerment: Involving victims enables them to be heard, validated, and involved in decisions about reparative actions. This approach offers victims a sense of justice and closure, which can be therapeutic and healing.
- Community Engagement: Community involvement helps reinforce shared values and fosters collective responsibility for addressing crime. It allows communities to contribute to a more holistic approach to justice and supports reintegration for both victims and offenders.

2. Focusing on Healing and Accountability

In contrast to punitive approaches, RJ focuses on repairing the harm caused by crime rather than inflicting punishment. Through RJ practices, offenders are encouraged to take responsibility for their actions, understand the impact of their crimes, and work to make amends with victims and the community.

- Offender Accountability: RJ requires offenders to acknowledge their wrongdoing and actively participate in reparative measures, such as community service or restitution. This process often has a rehabilitative effect, helping offenders build empathy and reduce the likelihood of re-offending.
- Healing-Oriented Practices: RJ offers processes for both victims and offenders to engage in healing dialogue. Victim-offender dialogues, for example, allow for direct communication where victims can express their experiences, ask questions, and receive apologies or explanations, which fosters emotional healing.

3. Implementing a Range of Restorative Practices

Restorative justice encompasses a wide variety of practices, which can be adapted to suit the context and needs of those involved. Common RJ practices include:

- Victim-Offender Mediation: A structured dialogue between victims and offenders, facilitated by a trained mediator, where both parties discuss the impact of the crime and agree on steps toward repair.
- Restorative Conferencing: Involving not only the victim and offender but also family members, friends, and community representatives, restorative conferencing provides a forum to discuss the harm and work collaboratively toward a resolution.
- Peacemaking Circles: Inspired by Indigenous traditions, peace circles bring together affected parties in a circle format to discuss the impact of crime, promote understanding, and collectively develop solutions.
- Community Restorative Boards: Composed of community representatives, these boards work with offenders to develop a plan for accountability and reparations, focusing on restoring trust between the offender and the community.

4. Tailoring Restorative Justice to Context

The success of RJ often depends on adapting practices to specific cases and cultural contexts. In criminal justice, RJ programs should be flexible to accommodate the unique needs and willingness of all parties. Tailoring RJ practices may involve adapting mediation or conferencing procedures for particular crimes or adjusting protocols to respect cultural traditions and community values.

- Adaptable Procedures: Different crimes require different approaches. For example, RJ in cases of violent crime may involve more in-depth preparation and support for participants than in cases of property crime.
- Cultural Sensitivity: RJ practices should honor cultural contexts, particularly in diverse communities or when involving Indigenous practices, to ensure meaningful engagement and respect for local traditions.

5. Ensuring Confidentiality and Respect for Participants

Respect for confidentiality is crucial in RJ processes, as it creates a safe environment for open dialogue and protects the privacy of those involved. Confidentiality protocols are necessary to maintain trust and encourage honest communication between victims, offenders, and facilitators.

- Clear Protocols: Establishing information-sharing protocols and consent requirements helps ensure that participants' rights and expectations are respected.
- Building Trust: Confidentiality fosters trust among participants, making them more likely to engage fully and openly in the RJ process.

Scholarly Articles on Integrating Restorative Justice into Criminal Justice Systems

For those interested in further research on integrating RJ into criminal justice, here are some key scholarly articles that explore various aspects of restorative justice, its effectiveness, and practical implementation within formal justice systems:

1. Zehr, H. (2002). The Little Book of Restorative Justice. Good Books.

- This foundational work by Howard Zehr provides a comprehensive overview of restorative justice principles and practices. Zehr examines how RJ offers an alternative to traditional punitive justice by focusing on healing, accountability, and repairing harm, making it a valuable resource for understanding RJ's integration into criminal justice systems.

2. Bazemore, G., & Umbreit, M. S. (1995). "Rethinking the Sanctioning Function in Juvenile Justice: Retributive or Restorative Responses to Youth Crime." Crime & Delinquency, 41(3), 296-316.

- This article explores restorative justice within juvenile justice systems, contrasting RJ with retributive models. The authors emphasize the importance of community involvement, victim participation, and a focus on youth accountability, making it relevant for RJ's integration in youth criminal justice contexts.

3. Sherman, L. W., & Strang, H. (2007). Restorative Justice: The Evidence. The Smith Institute.

- Sherman and Strang analyze empirical evidence on the effectiveness of restorative justice practices, providing data on how RJ impacts recidivism, victim satisfaction, and offender accountability.

This report is valuable for policymakers and practitioners interested in RJ's evidence-based outcomes within the criminal justice system.

4. Latimer, J., Dowden, C., & Muise, D. (2005). "The Effectiveness of Restorative Justice Practices: A Meta-Analysis." Prison Journal, 85(2), 127-144.

- This meta-analysis evaluates various RJ programs to assess their impact on recidivism and victim satisfaction. The study supports RJ as an effective alternative to traditional criminal justice sanctions, with significant reductions in re-offending and positive outcomes for victim healing.

5. Johnstone, G., & Van Ness, D. W. (2007). Handbook of Restorative Justice. Willan Publishing.

- This handbook provides a detailed exploration of RJ theories, models, and applications, with chapters on integrating RJ within formal criminal justice systems. The authors examine the role of RJ in promoting community accountability, offender rehabilitation, and the challenges of implementing RJ at various stages of the justice process.

6. Braithwaite, J. (2002). Restorative Justice and Responsive Regulation. Oxford University Press.

- Braithwaite's work introduces "responsive regulation," arguing that RJ can be integrated into regulatory frameworks to create a more flexible, community-centered justice system. His approach underscores RJ's potential to complement legal frameworks through accountability and community healing.

7. Umbreit, M. S., Coates, R. B., & Vos, B. (2004). "Victim-Offender Mediation: Three Decades of Practice and Research." Conflict Resolution Quarterly, 22(1-2), 279-303.

- This article reviews the evolution of victim-offender mediation and presents findings on its effectiveness in fostering accountability and victim satisfaction. It highlights the adaptability of RJ practices in different criminal justice settings, offering insights for integrating mediation into formal processes.

8. Boyes-Watson, C. (2005). "Community Is Not a Place But a Relationship: Lessons for Organizational Development from a Restorative Justice Project." Contemporary Justice Review, 8(2), 203-214.

- This article explores community-focused restorative justice projects, with an emphasis on relationship-building and community involvement. Boyes-Watson examines how RJ processes help foster community bonds, enhance social cohesion, and provide an alternative to punitive justice.

9. Strang, H., & Braithwaite, J. (2001). Restorative Justice and Civil Society. Cambridge University Press.

- Strang and Braithwaite analyze RJ's role in strengthening civil society, emphasizing how RJ practices within criminal justice can promote community resilience, reduce crime, and improve social relationships. This work is useful for understanding RJ's potential for broader societal transformation.

10. Marshall, T. F. (1999). Restorative Justice: An Overview. Home Office Research Development and Statistics Directorate.

- This overview offers insights into the key concepts, goals, and applications of restorative justice within formal criminal justice systems. Marshall discusses RJ's restorative potential, its challenges, and its impact on criminal justice reform.

The Transformative Potential of Restorative Justice in Criminal Justice Systems

Integrating restorative justice into criminal justice systems presents an opportunity to shift the focus from punishment to healing, accountability, and community resilience. By involving victims, emphasizing accountability, and promoting a range of practices tailored to diverse contexts, RJ offers a path toward a more compassionate and effective justice system. The scholarly resources and studies on RJ's effectiveness reinforce the value of restorative practices within criminal justice systems. These studies highlight RJ's potential to reduce recidivism, increase victim satisfaction, and strengthen communities, ultimately supporting a more restorative, fair, and humane approach to justice.

Integrating RJ requires commitment and adaptation from criminal justice institutions, policymakers, and communities. When implemented thoughtfully, RJ can transform how society addresses crime by providing avenues for healing, empathy, and meaningful accountability. This transformative shift recognizes that crime affects not only individuals but entire communities, and that justice can best be served by processes that restore relationships, repair harm, and promote a future of mutual respect and understanding.

Moving forward, the integration of restorative practices offers a vision for criminal justice that goes beyond punishment, focusing instead on long-term societal benefits such as social cohesion, reduced crime, and empowered communities. With continued research, dialogue, and application, restorative justice has the potential to become a cornerstone of criminal justice reform, providing a pathway for a more peaceful and unified society.

Comparing Traditional Punitive Models and Restorative Approaches in Criminal Justice

The criminal justice system has historically relied on punitive models, primarily focused on punishment and retribution to address crime. However, restorative approaches have emerged as alternative models, aiming to repair the harm caused by crime by involving victims, offenders, and the community in processes that promote healing and accountability. This chapter explores the fundamental differences between punitive and restorative justice models, comparing their goals, processes, and criticisms. Additionally, it includes scholarly resources that offer insight into these models and highlight the transformative potential of restorative justice.

Key Differences Between Punitive and Restorative Models

Focus

- Punitive Approach: Traditional punitive models center on the offender, assigning punishment based on the crime committed. The goal is to inflict a penalty proportionate to the offense, often through incarceration or fines, which serves as both retribution and a deterrent to future crime.

- Restorative Approach: Restorative justice, on the other hand, focuses on the harm caused by the crime, emphasizing the needs of the victim, the community, and the offender. By prioritizing relationship repair and victim healing, restorative approaches seek to engage all parties affected by the crime in meaningful dialogue and mutual understanding.

Goals

- Punitive: The primary goal of punitive models is to administer punishment that deters crime and enforces accountability by restricting the offender's rights and freedoms. Deterrence, retribution, and public safety are key objectives.

- Restorative: Restorative justice aims to achieve accountability and healing, encouraging offenders to acknowledge their wrongdoing and actively participate in repairing the harm they have caused. This model prioritizes rehabilitation, community reintegration, and personal growth over punishment.

Process

- Punitive: Punitive justice involves formal legal proceedings where judges and prosecutors determine an offender's guilt and assign punishment. The process is typically adversarial, with limited opportunities for direct victim involvement or community input.

- Restorative: Restorative justice involves collaborative processes such as victim-offender mediation, restorative conferencing, or community circles. These processes focus on open dialogue, empathy, and mutual agreement, where all parties work together to address the harm and establish a path toward healing.

Example Applications

- Punitive: Incarceration, fines, and probation are common punitive measures. Offenders may also face punitive sanctions such as restrictions on employment, housing, and voting rights.

- Restorative: Restorative measures may include victim-offender mediation, community service, restitution to the victim, or formal apologies. The goal is to provide tangible means for offenders to make amends and reestablish trust within the community.

Criticisms

- Punitive Models:
  - Mass Incarceration: Punitive systems often lead to high incarceration rates, which strain resources and may have limited effects on reducing recidivism.
  - Lack of Rehabilitation: Traditional models may not address the underlying causes of crime or support offenders' reintegration, which can contribute to cycles of re-offending.
  - Impact on Marginalized Communities: Punitive systems disproportionately affect marginalized populations, raising concerns about systemic biases and social inequalities.

- Restorative Models:
  - Suitability for All Crimes: Some argue that restorative justice may not be appropriate for all types of crimes, particularly those involving severe violence.
  - Significant Facilitation: Restorative processes require skilled facilitators, adequate resources, and voluntary participation from all parties.
  - Potential for Power Imbalance: In victim-offender meetings, there may be challenges related to power dynamics, as offenders may dominate the discussion or victims may feel pressured to forgive.

Scholarly Articles on Comparing Punitive and Restorative Approaches in Criminal Justice

The following scholarly resources provide insights into the comparative effectiveness of punitive and restorative models, as well as their potential impact on the justice system, offenders, and communities.

1. Zehr, H. (2002). The Little Book of Restorative Justice. Good Books.

- Howard Zehr, a pioneer in restorative justice, explores the core principles of RJ, comparing it to traditional justice approaches. Zehr emphasizes the importance of shifting focus from punishment to harm repair, discussing the potential benefits of RJ in fostering healing and accountability.

2. Braithwaite, J. (1989). Crime, Shame and Reintegration. Cambridge University Press.

- Braithwaite introduces the concept of "reintegrative shaming," arguing that RJ can reintegrate offenders into society by fostering accountability without stigmatization. This work highlights the limitations of punitive approaches and suggests that RJ can reduce recidivism by addressing underlying causes of crime.

3. Van Ness, D., & Strong, K. H. (2010). Restoring Justice: An Introduction to Restorative Justice. Routledge.

- Van Ness and Strong provide a comprehensive comparison between RJ and punitive models, examining how RJ addresses harm, promotes victim satisfaction, and supports offender rehabilitation. They discuss various RJ applications and consider its potential within existing criminal justice systems.

4. Latimer, J., Dowden, C., & Muise, D. (2005). "The Effectiveness of Restorative Justice Practices: A Meta-Analysis." Prison Journal, 85(2), 127-144.

- This meta-analysis evaluates the impact of RJ practices on recidivism, victim satisfaction, and community outcomes. The study provides empirical evidence supporting RJ as an effective alternative to punitive sanctions, emphasizing its benefits for offenders and victims alike.

5. Garland, D. (2001). The Culture of Control: Crime and Social Order in Contemporary Society. University of Chicago Press.

- Garland critiques the rise of punitive criminal justice policies, focusing on social control and the impact of mass incarceration. His work underscores the limitations of punitive models in promoting public safety and argues for more rehabilitative approaches, such as RJ.

6. Daly, K. (2006). "Restorative Justice and Sexual Assault: An Archival Study of Court and Conference Cases." British Journal of Criminology, 46(2), 334-356.

- Daly explores RJ's application in cases of sexual assault, comparing outcomes of traditional punitive measures to RJ practices. The study discusses how RJ can offer healing and empowerment for victims, though it also considers the complexities of applying RJ to sensitive cases.

7. Umbreit, M. S., Coates, R. B., & Vos, B. (2004). "Victim-Offender Mediation: Three Decades of Practice and Research." Conflict Resolution Quarterly, 22(1-2), 279-303.

- This article reviews the effectiveness of victim-offender mediation, a key RJ practice, and its impact on victim satisfaction and offender accountability. It provides a comparison to punitive measures, noting how mediation can foster greater understanding and personal growth.

8. Sherman, L. W., & Strang, H. (2007). Restorative Justice: The Evidence. The Smith Institute.

- Sherman and Strang analyze empirical data on RJ's effectiveness, finding that RJ practices lead to positive outcomes such as reduced recidivism and increased victim satisfaction. Their work compares RJ's benefits to punitive approaches, advocating for RJ integration into criminal justice.

9. Wright, M. (1996). Justice for Victims and Offenders: A Restorative Response to Crime. Waterside Press.

- Wright examines how RJ can address the needs of both victims and offenders in ways that punitive models often do not. He highlights the potential of RJ to restore relationships and prevent further harm, challenging the efficacy of traditional punitive responses.

10. Clear, T. R. (1996). "Backfire: When Incarceration Increases Crime." Journal of the Oklahoma Criminal Justice Research Consortium, 3(1), 15-22.

- Clear argues that incarceration can sometimes increase crime, particularly in marginalized communities, by destabilizing family structures and disrupting social cohesion. His work supports the use of alternative models, such as RJ, which offer community-centered approaches to addressing crime.

The Potential of Restorative Approaches in Criminal Justice

The comparison between punitive models and restorative approaches highlights significant differences in goals, processes, and outcomes. While punitive systems prioritize punishment and deterrence, often resulting in high incarceration rates and limited victim involvement, restorative approaches focus on repairing harm, fostering accountability, and engaging communities. RJ practices such as victim-offender mediation, peace circles, and community service provide pathways for healing, empathy, and meaningful accountability that punitive measures may lack.

Empirical evidence suggests that RJ can offer effective alternatives to traditional justice models, with benefits such as reduced recidivism, higher victim satisfaction, and stronger community cohesion. Integrating RJ into criminal justice systems represents a shift towards a more compassionate and rehabilitative model of justice that addresses the root causes of crime and promotes long-term societal well-being.

As the field of criminal justice continues to evolve, restorative approaches offer a promising direction for reform, emphasizing that justice can be transformative, not solely punitive. By embracing RJ practices, criminal justice systems can more effectively respond to crime, repair harm, and support the reintegration of offenders, ultimately contributing to safer, more resilient communities.

Studies on Reduced Recidivism and Improved Outcomes with Restorative Practices

Research has shown that restorative justice (RJ) practices can lead to significantly reduced recidivism rates, higher levels of victim satisfaction, and improved accountability for offenders compared to traditional punitive methods. By focusing on repairing harm, engaging victims, and encouraging offenders to take responsibility, RJ practices offer a rehabilitative approach that can yield positive long-term outcomes. This chapter highlights key studies on RJ's impact on recidivism, particularly in juvenile offenders, and outlines factors that influence the effectiveness of RJ programs.

Key Findings from Research on Restorative Practices and Recidivism

1. Meta-Analysis Results on Recidivism Reduction

A comprehensive meta-analysis of studies on RJ practices reveals a consistent reduction in recidivism rates among offenders who participate in RJ programs compared to those who undergo traditional justice processes.

- Reduction Rate: Findings show a 27% reduction in recidivism rates on average for participants in RJ programs. This reduction is attributed to RJ's emphasis on accountability and healing, which contrasts with punitive approaches that often lack a rehabilitative component.

- Mechanisms of Impact: The meta-analysis suggests that the personal interaction between victims and offenders, common in RJ settings, increases offenders' empathy and awareness of the harm caused, which can reduce the likelihood of re-offending.

2. Victim-Offender Mediation and Its Effects on Recidivism

Victim-offender mediation (VOM), a core RJ practice, has been shown to have a particularly strong impact on recidivism rates. VOM sessions involve structured dialogues facilitated by trained mediators, where offenders learn firsthand about the effects of their actions on victims.

- Reduction in Re-Offending: Studies indicate that VOM can reduce recidivism by up to 32%, especially when participants engage sincerely in the mediation process. This approach allows offenders to understand the emotional and psychological consequences of their actions, often leading to a transformative experience.

- Increased Accountability: Offenders who participate in VOM report a stronger sense of accountability and empathy, which are critical factors in fostering behavioral change and reducing the likelihood of re-offending.

3. Efficacy with Juvenile Offenders

RJ practices have been found to be particularly effective with juvenile offenders, a group that may be more amenable to behavioral change than adults. RJ programs for youth often focus on education, empathy-building, and community reintegration.

- Studies on Juvenile Recidivism: Research indicates that RJ programs reduce recidivism rates for juvenile offenders by up to 40% compared to traditional juvenile justice processes. These reductions are especially notable for property crimes and low-level offenses, where juveniles benefit from RJ's rehabilitative focus.

- Developmental Suitability: Juvenile offenders may be more responsive to RJ's restorative principles, as these align with developmental needs for social approval, empathy, and identity formation, making RJ an ideal intervention for this age group.

4. Positive Outcomes for Victim Satisfaction and Offender Accountability

In addition to reducing recidivism, RJ practices have been associated with high levels of victim satisfaction. Victims often feel more empowered and respected in RJ processes, as they are given a platform to express their feelings, ask questions, and participate in decisions regarding reparations.

- Victim Satisfaction Rates: Studies report victim satisfaction rates as high as 80-90% for those who participate in RJ programs, in contrast to lower satisfaction rates in traditional criminal justice settings. This satisfaction can contribute to overall community healing and increase support for RJ initiatives.

- Enhanced Accountability: RJ emphasizes personal responsibility, with offenders encouraged to take ownership of their actions and make amends. This accountability not only fosters offender rehabilitation but also helps victims feel that justice has been served, which may contribute to their own emotional healing.

Important Considerations in Evaluating Restorative Justice Programs

The success of RJ programs in reducing recidivism and improving outcomes depends on various contextual and procedural factors.

1. Offense Type

- Property Crimes: Research indicates that RJ is particularly effective in cases involving property crimes, which account for a significant portion of cases referred to RJ programs. Offenders are more likely to feel empathy for victims in these cases and to understand the tangible nature of the harm they caused.

- Violent Offenses: While RJ can be applied in cases involving violent offenses, its effectiveness may vary depending on the offender's readiness for accountability and the victim's willingness to participate. Specialized RJ practices, such as "restorative circles" or therapeutic mediation, may be more suitable for addressing the complex needs of violent crime cases.

2. Program Implementation

The structure and quality of RJ programs significantly affect their outcomes. Effective RJ programs require skilled facilitators, thorough preparation, and a commitment to best practices in mediation and conferencing.

- Facilitator Training: Successful RJ programs rely on facilitators who are trained in conflict resolution, trauma-informed practices, and cultural sensitivity. Well-trained facilitators can better navigate complex dynamics and foster constructive dialogue, increasing the likelihood of positive outcomes.

- Participant Readiness: Offenders must be willing to take responsibility, and victims must feel safe and empowered to participate. Screening for readiness is crucial, as forced participation may undermine the effectiveness of RJ and can harm victims further.

3. Community Context

RJ practices are most effective when tailored to the specific social and cultural context of the community in which they are implemented. Factors such as local norms, cultural traditions, and community support can influence the outcomes of RJ programs.

- Cultural Adaptation: RJ programs that incorporate local traditions, such as Indigenous peace circles, tend to be more accepted and impactful. These practices often resonate with community values and provide culturally relevant approaches to justice.

- Community Buy-In: The effectiveness of RJ is enhanced when communities are actively involved and supportive. Programs that engage community leaders, organizations, and stakeholders help reinforce the principles of RJ and foster broader acceptance.

Scholarly Articles on Restorative Justice, Recidivism, and Improved Outcomes

For further reading, the following scholarly articles provide in-depth analyses of RJ's impact on recidivism, victim satisfaction, and long-term outcomes for offenders and communities.

1. Latimer, J., Dowden, C., & Muise, D. (2005). "The Effectiveness of Restorative Justice Practices: A Meta-Analysis." Prison Journal, 85(2), 127-144.

- This meta-analysis reviews multiple studies on RJ, finding significant reductions in recidivism and improvements in victim satisfaction. The authors discuss how RJ practices, particularly victim-offender mediation, positively impact offender accountability and community relationships.

2. Sherman, L. W., & Strang, H. (2007). Restorative Justice: The Evidence. The Smith Institute.

- Sherman and Strang compile data on RJ's effectiveness in reducing recidivism and promoting victim satisfaction. They examine RJ programs in different contexts, providing empirical evidence that RJ can be an effective alternative to traditional punitive methods.

3. Bouffard, J. A., Cooper, M., & Bergseth, K. J. (2017). "The Effectiveness of Various Restorative Justice Interventions on Recidivism Outcomes among Juvenile Offenders." Youth Violence and Juvenile Justice, 15(4), 465-480.

- This study focuses on juvenile offenders, comparing RJ interventions to traditional justice approaches. The findings support RJ's potential to reduce re-offending, especially among youth, and highlight the importance of developmental considerations in designing RJ programs for juveniles.

4. Umbreit, M. S., Coates, R. B., & Vos, B. (2004). "Victim-Offender Mediation: Three Decades of Practice and Research." Conflict Resolution Quarterly, 22(1-2), 279-303.

- This article reviews the evolution and effectiveness of VOM, highlighting the practice's impact on recidivism and victim satisfaction. The authors examine how VOM fosters empathy and accountability, which can reduce the likelihood of re-offending.

5. Bonta, J., Jesseman, R., Rugge, T., & Cormier, R. (2006). "Restorative Justice and Recidivism: Promises Made, Promises Kept?" In Handbook of Restorative Justice. Willan Publishing.

- Bonta and colleagues critically assess RJ's impact on recidivism, discussing factors that influence program success, including offense type, offender characteristics, and program quality. They argue that RJ's effectiveness is contingent on thoughtful implementation.

6. Armour, M. P., & Umbreit, M. S. (2005). "The Paradox of Forgiveness in Restorative Justice." Peace Review, 17(2), 199-205.

- This article explores the role of forgiveness and reconciliation in RJ, focusing on how these elements contribute to reduced recidivism. Armour and Umbreit examine the emotional and psychological dimensions of RJ that influence behavioral change.

7. McCold, P., & Wachtel, T. (2002). “Restorative Justice Theory Validation.” In Restorative Justice: Theoretical Foundations. Routledge.

- McCold and Wachtel discuss RJ’s theoretical foundations, exploring how restorative principles influence offender rehabilitation and recidivism. They argue that RJ’s focus on community and relationship repair makes it a sustainable model for addressing crime.

8. Beven, J. P., Hall, G., Froyland, I., Steels, B., & Goulding, D. (2005). “

"Restoration or Retribution: An Evaluation of Restorative Justice and Recidivism." International Journal of Offender Therapy and Comparative Criminology, 49(3), 370-383.

- This study evaluates the impact of restorative justice on recidivism, comparing RJ’s rehabilitative focus to retributive justice approaches. The authors discuss RJ’s role in reducing re-offending rates, particularly through empathy-building practices and community reintegration.

9. Shapland, J., Robinson, G., & Sorsby, A. (2011). Restorative Justice in Practice: Evaluating What Works for Victims and Offenders. Routledge.

- Shapland and colleagues analyze multiple RJ case studies, evaluating the effectiveness of various RJ practices in reducing recidivism and increasing victim satisfaction. This book provides practical insights into how different RJ models, including conferencing and mediation, impact offenders and victims.

10. Braithwaite, J. (2002). Restorative Justice and Responsive Regulation. Oxford University Press.

- Braithwaite presents a framework for "responsive regulation," linking restorative justice principles to broader regulatory systems. His work discusses how RJ can reduce recidivism by focusing on accountability and reintegration, offering an alternative to traditional punitive regulation.

Conclusion: The Transformative Impact of Restorative Justice on Recidivism and Outcomes

Research overwhelmingly supports the idea that restorative justice practices can reduce recidivism, enhance victim satisfaction, and improve offender accountability. Through methods like victim-offender mediation, restorative conferencing, and community engagement, RJ practices offer an effective alternative to traditional punitive approaches, particularly in juvenile justice contexts. RJ's focus on healing, accountability, and community involvement addresses the underlying causes of criminal behavior and fosters personal growth for offenders.

The studies presented highlight that RJ's success in reducing recidivism is closely tied to careful implementation, skilled facilitation, and adaptation to cultural and community needs. By fostering empathy, promoting accountability, and repairing relationships, RJ provides a pathway toward a more restorative, rehabilitative criminal justice system. As evidence grows, RJ continues to prove its potential as a valuable tool for creating safer, more resilient communities and for supporting individuals on their journey toward accountability and reformation.

CHAPTER 11

Indigenous-Led Restorative Justice Approaches and Their Influence on Modern Restorative Justice

Indigenous-led restorative justice approaches are deeply connected to traditional Indigenous practices of conflict resolution, which focus on healing, restoring harmony, and promoting community well-being rather than punishment. These practices have profoundly influenced the development of modern restorative justice by emphasizing key principles such as victim-centered dialogue, community engagement, and the importance of addressing the root causes of harm. This chapter explores Indigenous justice practices, the unique elements that distinguish them, and how they have shaped contemporary restorative justice models.

Key Elements of Indigenous Restorative Justice Practices

Indigenous restorative justice approaches are diverse, reflecting the rich cultural traditions of various Indigenous communities worldwide. However, certain shared principles form the foundation of Indigenous justice practices, including community-centered approaches, a focus on healing, and spiritual and cultural integration.

1. Community-Centered Justice

Indigenous justice systems prioritize the well-being of the entire community rather than focusing exclusively on the victim or the offender. This communal approach recognizes that harm affects not only individuals but also the relationships and social cohesion of the broader community.

- Collective Responsibility: Indigenous justice promotes a collective sense of responsibility for addressing harm, with the community playing an active role in supporting both the victim and the offender.
- Restoring Balance: Rather than seeking retribution, Indigenous practices aim to restore balance within the community, recognizing that justice requires repairing disrupted relationships and fostering a sense of collective harmony.

2. Emphasis on Healing

In contrast to punitive Western justice systems, Indigenous approaches prioritize healing as the primary goal of justice. This emphasis on healing involves addressing both the emotional and spiritual well-being of the individuals involved and the community as a whole.

- Healing for Both Victims and Offenders: Indigenous justice views healing as essential for both the victim and the offender, offering opportunities for understanding, forgiveness, and personal transformation.

- Dialogue and Apologies: Facilitated dialogue and genuine apologies are common practices, allowing the offender to acknowledge the harm and make amends, which can be a powerful step toward emotional healing for the victim.

3. Spiritual Connection

Indigenous justice systems often view justice as intertwined with spirituality and cultural traditions. Many Indigenous restorative practices include ceremonial elements that provide a sacred context for healing and reconciliation.

- Ceremonial Aspects: Traditional ceremonies, such as smudging or blessing rituals, may be incorporated into justice processes, allowing participants to connect with their spirituality and seek guidance from ancestors or spiritual entities.
- Holistic Approach: Indigenous justice emphasizes a holistic view of well-being, where the spiritual, emotional, and physical aspects of individuals and communities are interconnected and must be addressed to achieve true healing.

4. Role of Elders

Elders play a pivotal role in Indigenous justice systems, serving as respected leaders, facilitators, and sources of wisdom. Their involvement ensures that justice practices align with cultural traditions and community values.

- Guidance and Wisdom: Elders bring guidance and cultural knowledge to restorative processes, fostering an atmosphere of respect and support.

- Facilitation of Dialogue: Elders often facilitate discussions in talking circles or mediation sessions, helping to mediate conflicts and promote understanding among participants.

Examples of Indigenous Restorative Justice Practices

The following are examples of traditional Indigenous restorative practices that have influenced modern restorative justice:

1. Talking Circles: In talking circles, participants sit in a circle and take turns speaking, often using a talking piece to signify the speaker's turn. This practice promotes respectful listening, empathy, and a shared sense of responsibility for addressing harm.

2. Peacemaking Ceremonies: Peacemaking ceremonies are ritualistic gatherings where individuals come together to resolve conflicts and restore harmony within the community. These ceremonies may include prayers, cultural rituals, and traditional symbols, emphasizing the sacredness of the reconciliation process.

3. Victim-Offender Mediation: Indigenous practices often involve structured dialogues between the victim and the offender, facilitated by an elder or respected community member. This process allows the victim to express their experiences and for the offender to acknowledge their actions and seek forgiveness.

4. Community Conferencing: Community conferencing involves bringing together the victim, offender, their families, and other community members to discuss the harm caused and develop a restorative plan. This practice emphasizes the collective responsibility of the community to support the healing and reintegration of both the victim and the offender.

Influence of Indigenous Practices on Modern Restorative Justice

Indigenous justice practices have significantly shaped the principles and goals of modern restorative justice. Below are some of the key contributions:

1. Victim-Centered Focus

Indigenous practices emphasize the importance of centering the needs and experiences of the victim, a perspective that has greatly influenced restorative justice. By prioritizing the victim's voice and allowing them to actively participate in the process, restorative justice creates a supportive space for victims to feel heard, respected, and empowered.

- Victim Empowerment: Indigenous-inspired RJ practices empower victims by involving them directly in decision-making and reparative processes, addressing their emotional needs and concerns.
- Emphasis on Healing for Victims: RJ's focus on healing and emotional closure for victims mirrors Indigenous approaches, which view justice as a pathway for victims to reclaim peace and balance.

2. Community Involvement

Indigenous justice systems emphasize community involvement as essential to resolving conflicts and supporting healing. This community-oriented approach has become a cornerstone of modern restorative justice, which seeks to engage not only the victim and offender but also the wider community in finding solutions.

- Community Engagement: Restorative justice now commonly includes community members in dialogues, circles, and decision-making, fostering a sense of shared accountability.

- Social Reconciliation: RJ promotes reconciliation not just between individuals but within communities, ensuring that justice processes strengthen social bonds and community cohesion.

3. Holistic Approach to Justice

Indigenous justice emphasizes a holistic view of justice that considers the emotional, spiritual, and social dimensions of harm. This approach has been incorporated into RJ practices, which aim to address the root causes of harmful behavior, including social, economic, and psychological factors.

- Addressing Root Causes: Indigenous-inspired RJ models focus on understanding and addressing the underlying causes of crime, such as trauma, poverty, and lack of social support, to prevent future harm.
- Cultural Sensitivity and Respect: Modern RJ has adopted principles of cultural sensitivity and respect for diverse traditions, recognizing the importance of adapting practices to the needs and cultural backgrounds of participants.

Important Considerations for Implementing Indigenous-Inspired Restorative Justice Practices

Incorporating Indigenous principles into RJ requires cultural sensitivity, an understanding of local traditions, and respect for the values of Indigenous communities. Here are key considerations for effective implementation:

1. Cultural Sensitivity

When adapting Indigenous practices, it is crucial to respect the specific cultural context of the Indigenous community involved.

Each community has its unique customs, symbols, and values, and RJ programs must honor these distinctions.

- Avoid Appropriation: RJ programs should avoid appropriating Indigenous traditions without proper consultation and collaboration with the community.
- Collaborate with Indigenous Leaders: Involving Indigenous leaders in the planning and facilitation of RJ practices can ensure that they are culturally relevant and respectful.

2. Power Dynamics

Indigenous RJ practices must be implemented with an awareness of potential power imbalances, particularly in cases involving victims and offenders from different backgrounds or with different levels of community support.

- Ensuring Equitable Participation: Facilitators should be trained to recognize and mitigate power imbalances to ensure that all participants feel safe and empowered.
- Building Trust: Establishing trust between participants is essential, especially in cases where there may be historical trauma or distrust of authority figures.

Scholarly Articles on Indigenous-Led Restorative Justice and Its Influence on Modern Practices

For further reading, the following scholarly articles provide a deeper understanding of Indigenous-led restorative justice approaches and their contributions to contemporary RJ practices:

1. Alfred, T., & Corntassel, J. (2005). "Being Indigenous: Resurgences against Contemporary Colonialism." Government and Opposition, 40(4), 597-614.

- This article explores Indigenous identity and resistance, discussing how Indigenous-led justice practices preserve cultural autonomy and offer alternatives to Western punitive systems.

2. Cayley, D. (1998). The Expanding Prison: The Crisis in Crime and Punishment and the Search for Alternatives. House of Anansi Press.

- Cayley examines Indigenous justice practices and how they provide a model for non-punitive responses to crime, arguing that Indigenous approaches emphasize healing over punishment, which aligns with RJ principles.

3. Ross, R. (2006). Returning to the Teachings: Exploring Aboriginal Justice. Penguin Canada.

- This book provides insights into Indigenous justice teachings, focusing on how Indigenous practices prioritize collective responsibility and healing. Ross discusses how Indigenous approaches have shaped RJ's emphasis on community involvement and restoration.

4. Blagg, H. (2017). Crime, Aboriginality, and the Decolonization of Justice. Federation Press.

- Blagg's work examines Indigenous justice systems in Australia, exploring how Indigenous practices have influenced RJ models. The book argues for decolonizing justice systems and incorporating Indigenous principles of harmony and healing.

5. Porter, R. (2007). "Restorative Justice, Reparations, and Healing: Indigenous Approaches and Challenges for the United States." Journal of Societal Justice, 3(2), 187-198.

- This article discusses the challenges and benefits of integrating Indigenous justice principles into U.S. RJ practices, with a focus on reparations and healing.

6. Green, S., & Cunningham, C. (2010). "Talking Circles: A Restorative Justice Strategy to Address Impacts of Violence Among Native Youth." Youth Violence and Juvenile Justice, 8(1), 1-18.

- This article examines talking circles as a restorative justice strategy for Native youth affected by violence. Green and Cunningham highlight the cultural significance of talking circles in Indigenous communities and discuss how this practice fosters healing, accountability, and community support.

7. Brave Heart, M. Y. H., & DeBruyn, L. M. (1998). "The American Indian Holocaust: Healing Historical Unresolved Grief." American Indian and Alaska Native Mental Health Research, 8(2), 56-78.

- Brave Heart and DeBruyn analyze the intergenerational impacts of historical trauma on Indigenous communities and the role of culturally grounded restorative practices in healing. Their work emphasizes how Indigenous approaches address collective grief and contribute to holistic community restoration.

8. Justice, D. H. (2018). "Why Indigenous Literatures Matter: The Role of Stories in Restorative Justice." Studies in Restorative Justice, 9(4), 450-465.

- Justice explores how Indigenous storytelling traditions intersect with restorative justice principles, using stories to build empathy, teach cultural values, and facilitate healing in the justice process. This work provides insights into the ways Indigenous literatures contribute to restorative principles of reconciliation and understanding.

9. Williams, R. (2003). "Linking Arms Together: American Indian Treaty Visions of Law and Peace, 1600-1800." Oxford University Press.

- This book delves into historical Indigenous treaty-making practices that emphasized peaceful relations and collaborative problem-solving. Williams discusses how these principles inform current Indigenous-led restorative practices, which prioritize harmony and collective responsibility over punishment.

10. Tauri, J., & Morris, A. (1997). "Indigenous Justice or Western Form of Restorative Justice?" Contemporary Justice Review, 1(1), 59-79.

- Tauri and Morris examine the distinctions between Indigenous justice and Western restorative justice, arguing that Indigenous practices are unique frameworks based on cultural values and community-focused philosophies. This article encourages thoughtful, respectful integration of Indigenous principles into Western RJ models, advocating for justice practices that honor cultural autonomy.

The Influence of Indigenous-Led Restorative Justice on Modern Practices

Indigenous-led restorative justice practices emphasize healing, balance, and community engagement—values that have become foundational to modern restorative justice. These principles offer a powerful alternative to punitive models, focusing instead on relationship repair, community cohesion, and addressing the root causes of harm. Indigenous practices such as talking circles, peacemaking ceremonies, and elder-facilitated mediation underscore the importance of holistic and culturally sensitive approaches to justice.

The influence of Indigenous justice systems on modern restorative justice demonstrates that addressing crime and conflict requires more than punishment; it demands empathy, understanding, and collective responsibility. As restorative justice continues to evolve, integrating Indigenous perspectives ensures that justice remains a process of healing for individuals and communities alike, creating pathways toward genuine reconciliation and social harmony.

Indigenous-Led Restorative Justice Approaches—Examples from First Nations, Māori, and Native American Communities

Indigenous communities have practiced restorative justice for centuries, prioritizing healing, community harmony, and reintegration over punitive measures. These Indigenous-led approaches offer frameworks grounded in cultural traditions that focus on repairing relationships and restoring balance within communities. Despite the imposition of Western legal systems that disrupted these practices, Indigenous communities today are revitalizing their traditional methods of justice, often with powerful outcomes.

Historical Context and Foundations of Indigenous Restorative Practices

Historically, Indigenous justice approaches involved community-led processes that facilitated dialogue among victims, offenders, and kinship networks. In Native American, Australian Aboriginal, and Māori communities, restorative justice was not a novel concept but rather an integral part of cultural practices. Council fires, talking circles, and peacemaking gatherings were employed to address wrongdoing and heal relationships. Instead of punishment, outcomes focused on making amends, reintegrating offenders, and achieving community harmony through service and restitution (Tauri, 1998).

This chapter explores examples from Māori and Navajo communities, demonstrating how Indigenous-led approaches address both interpersonal harm and systemic challenges in culturally relevant ways.

Case Studies of Indigenous-Led Restorative Justice

1. Māori Youth Restoration Circle (New Zealand)

In a rural Māori community in New Zealand, several youths were caught vandalizing a local marae (meeting house), a culturally significant site. The community opted for a restoration hui, or gathering, to address the incident in a culturally responsive manner. The process, grounded in tikanga (cultural ways), involved the whanau (extended families) of both the offenders and victims.

- Process and Cultural Practices: In the circle, led by a kaumatua (elder), each youth explained how their actions had violated tikanga, expressing regret for disrespecting cultural traditions. Victims shared the cultural and financial impact of the vandalism, while the elder facilitated a respectful discussion focused on understanding and empathy.
- Restorative Actions: The community collectively decided that the offenders would help repair the marae, participate in te reo (Māori language) classes, and undergo a traditional spiritual cleansing ritual.

These restorative actions not only provided a way to make amends but also reconnected the youth with their cultural heritage.

- Outcomes: Follow-ups revealed no reoffending among the youth. Both offenders and victims expressed satisfaction with the process, citing that the cultural approach had effectively repaired relationships and reestablished trust in the community.

This example illustrates the effectiveness of Indigenous justice models in creating meaningful resolutions. The emphasis on cultural reconnection through language, tradition, and community service highlights how Indigenous-led restorative justice can facilitate holistic reintegration and accountability.

Thought Leader: Professor Tracey McIntosh, a scholar on Indigenous legal frameworks, emphasizes that tikanga and restorative practices can powerfully reinforce Indigenous values within justice systems, as seen in Māori justice approaches.

2. Navajo Nation Peacemaking Program (United States)

The Navajo Nation's hozhooji naat'aah, meaning "walking in beauty," represents an Indigenous restorative justice model that focuses on restoring harmony and addressing conflict within a framework of Navajo spirituality and clan relationships. Established in response to the limitations of Western legal systems, the Navajo Peacemaking Program addresses complex social issues while respecting the cultural values and practices of the Navajo community.

- Process and Cultural Practices: In one case involving domestic violence, the incident was referred to a peacemaking panel of naat'aanii (elders), who facilitated discussions over several days. The meetings took place in an open-air setting, symbolizing transparency and spiritual openness. Family members on both sides of the conflict were included in the process, as clan and kinship are integral to Navajo justice.

- Restorative Actions: After discussing the offense's impact on the family, an agreement was reached for the offender to move houses, receive counseling, issue a public pledge of nonviolence, and contribute volunteer hours to the community. This approach was both reparative and rehabilitative, emphasizing accountability within a supportive framework.

- Outcomes: Monitoring showed high compliance with the agreement, and the reconciliation between family members reduced the risk of future violence. The offender's public commitment to nonviolence reinforced the Navajo values of hozho (harmony) and k'é (kinship).

This case highlights the adaptability and effectiveness of Indigenous peacemaking practices, particularly in addressing domestic violence where relational repair is essential. The focus on community involvement, cultural values, and spiritual rituals demonstrates how Indigenous justice approaches can align justice with cultural integrity.

Thought Leaders: Professor James Zion, a Navajo legal scholar, documented the integration of clanship, spirituality, and healing into the Navajo justice system. Professor Cindy Adams's work further explores the practical applications and challenges of implementing Navajo peacemaking as an alternative to state legal systems.

Contemporary Insights on Indigenous-Led Restorative Justice

1. Decolonization Efforts: As part of decolonization, Indigenous communities are reclaiming justice processes by re-establishing the role of elders and knowledge keepers in restorative

justice practices. These efforts help empower communities to address their own justice needs. However, funding constraints pose significant challenges to scaling these practices and providing adequate support and training.

2. Intergenerational Knowledge Sharing: Many younger Indigenous individuals, despite being distanced from traditional practices by historical displacement, are keen to learn restorative methods like peacemaking circles. Programs are increasingly using technology to bridge generational gaps, providing access to cultural knowledge and facilitating virtual learning.

3. Pandemic Adaptations and Remote Services: The COVID-19 pandemic exposed healthcare and justice disparities in Indigenous communities. However, it also catalyzed remote service innovations, with some programs adapting to virtual or hybrid formats. These adaptations align with oral traditions in many Indigenous cultures, enabling continuity in community-centered practices despite physical distance.

4. Environmental Connection and Climate Justice: Indigenous justice models often recognize the interconnectedness of human and environmental health. As climate change intensifies resource stresses, Indigenous-led restorative approaches—grounded in respect for the land and ecological balance—take on new significance. Circles and peacemaking practices emphasize sustainability and environmental stewardship as integral to justice.

5. International Advocacy and Cultural Pluralism: Indigenous-led justice initiatives are gaining international attention, with frameworks like the United Nations Declaration on the Rights of

Indigenous Peoples advocating for the protection of Indigenous rights and self-determination. Collaboration among Indigenous communities worldwide facilitates cross-cultural exchanges, reinforcing the role of Indigenous practices in shaping global restorative justice paradigms.

Revitalizing Indigenous Restorative Justice Approaches

The examples of the Māori Youth Restoration Circle and the Navajo Peacemaking Program illustrate the profound impact of Indigenous-led restorative justice approaches in creating culturally relevant, effective, and healing-oriented justice solutions. These practices serve as powerful reminders of the value of traditional knowledge systems in fostering well-being and reconciling communities disrupted by colonization.

Restoring Indigenous justice traditions not only empowers communities but also reaffirms their sovereignty and right to self-determination. By revitalizing elders' roles as facilitators and re-embedding justice practices in cultural knowledge, Indigenous communities are rebuilding interpersonal, environmental, and spiritual relationships disrupted by colonial histories. As Indigenous restorative justice practices continue to influence broader restorative models, they offer invaluable insights for addressing contemporary challenges in ways that honor both ancestral wisdom and modern needs.

This resurgence of Indigenous-led restorative justice aligns with decolonization goals and encourages a future in which justice systems worldwide are enriched by the diversity, wisdom, and resilience of Indigenous traditions. Through empowering Indigenous communities to shape their own justice paths, restorative practices become not only tools for healing but also vital instruments for safeguarding Indigenous identity, autonomy, and intergenerational continuity.

Cultural Significance and the Value of Indigenous Wisdom in Justice

Indigenous wisdom holds profound cultural and philosophical value in the realm of restorative justice. With a strong emphasis on community healing, interconnectedness, and restoring harmony, Indigenous approaches to justice provide a holistic alternative to punitive systems focused solely on punishment. Many Indigenous cultures across the globe are the original practitioners of restorative justice, with principles and methods that modern approaches continue to draw from and honor. This chapter explores the cultural significance of Indigenous justice practices, key principles derived from Indigenous wisdom, and the invaluable lessons they offer to contemporary restorative justice frameworks.

Key Aspects of Indigenous Wisdom in Restorative Justice

Indigenous restorative practices are characterized by their holistic approach, which prioritizes the well-being of the entire community and the restoration of relationships. These practices reveal insights into handling conflict, healing trauma, and fostering social cohesion.

1. Community-Centered Focus

Indigenous justice systems emphasize the importance of community involvement and the collective well-being of all members. Rather than isolating offenders, Indigenous approaches aim to reintegrate individuals back into the community through open dialogue, reconciliation, and accountability.

- Collective Responsibility: Indigenous wisdom views justice as a shared responsibility that affects not only the victim and offender but also their families, friends, and the entire community.
- Restoring Social Fabric: Justice is achieved when the community's harmony is restored, and members reaffirm their shared values and commitments to one another.

2. The Circle Process

In many Indigenous traditions, the circle process is a foundational aspect of restorative justice. Circle gatherings bring together all parties involved in an incident, including elders and community members, to share their perspectives and work collectively toward a resolution. The circle format is inherently egalitarian, promoting mutual respect and ensuring that each voice is heard.

- Equal Participation: The circle format creates a space where everyone can speak and listen without hierarchy, fostering open communication and mutual understanding.
- Facilitation by Elders: Elders, as respected figures in many Indigenous cultures, often guide the circle process, ensuring that the discussion remains respectful and constructive.

3. Emphasis on Healing

Rather than focusing on punishment, Indigenous justice seeks to heal both the victim and the offender, often through spiritual and ritual practices. This emphasis on healing facilitates personal transformation, aiming to repair the harm caused and address the needs of all involved.

- Spiritual and Cultural Rituals: Healing ceremonies, prayers, and symbolic rituals are often used to cleanse the spirit, encourage forgiveness, and facilitate personal growth.

- Long-Term Reconciliation: By prioritizing healing, Indigenous justice offers a path toward lasting reconciliation, helping individuals and communities move forward in harmony.

4. Respect for Relationships and Interconnectedness

Indigenous cultures generally regard relationships and interconnectedness as fundamental to well-being. In Indigenous justice systems, the aim is not only to address the immediate offense but also to repair and strengthen relationships to prevent future conflicts.

- Relational Approach to Justice: Justice is not a means to create divisions or adversarial relationships but an opportunity to rebuild trust, empathy, and social bonds.
- Focus on Social Cohesion: By restoring relationships, Indigenous practices promote a sense of unity, ensuring that individuals feel supported and respected within their communities.

5. Holistic Understanding of Conflict and Its Causes

Indigenous restorative justice addresses not only the specific incident but also the broader social, economic, and psychological factors contributing to conflict. This approach acknowledges that addressing underlying issues can prevent future harm and promote long-term stability.

- Root Cause Analysis: Indigenous justice practices often examine the root causes of harm, whether they relate to poverty, discrimination, trauma, or other social conditions.
- Comprehensive Problem-Solving: By addressing systemic issues, Indigenous justice promotes a restorative approach that seeks sustainable solutions and strengthens resilience within the community.

Examples of Indigenous Restorative Justice Practices

Indigenous communities have developed a variety of practices to address harm, each emphasizing healing, responsibility, and cultural relevance. Below are some examples of common Indigenous restorative justice practices:

1. Peacemaking Ceremonies: These ceremonies provide a sacred space for dialogue between victims, offenders, and community members, facilitated by elders. During peacemaking, individuals are encouraged to take responsibility for their actions, make amends, and work toward rebuilding trust and social harmony.

2. Storytelling: Sharing personal stories allows participants to understand the impact of harm from multiple perspectives. Storytelling fosters empathy and can help offenders realize the personal and communal effects of their actions, which is a critical step in rehabilitation.

3. Elders as Guides: In many Indigenous communities, elders provide wisdom, guidance, and support throughout the restorative process. Their involvement ensures that justice practices remain aligned with cultural values and that the outcomes reflect the collective wisdom of the community.

Why Indigenous Wisdom is Valuable in Restorative Justice

The value of Indigenous wisdom in restorative justice lies in its effectiveness, cultural relevance, and capacity to offer a broader perspective on conflict resolution. Indigenous practices present a unique approach to justice that resonates with many of the core values in modern restorative justice.

Proven Effectiveness

Indigenous communities have long practiced restorative methods with demonstrable success in maintaining social harmony and reducing conflict. For example, traditional practices among First Nations, Māori, and Native American communities have been documented to produce lower recidivism rates and higher levels of satisfaction among victims and offenders. This success is partly due to the integration of social, spiritual, and relational elements that address the deeper issues underlying conflicts.

Cultural Relevance for Indigenous Communities

Incorporating Indigenous justice practices is especially meaningful for Indigenous communities facing disproportionately high rates of incarceration, poverty, and marginalization. Programs that integrate Indigenous principles and values provide a culturally respectful alternative to Western punitive systems, allowing communities to heal on their own terms.

- Empowerment and Self-Determination: Indigenous-led restorative justice practices respect the rights of Indigenous communities to exercise autonomy in addressing issues within their societies.
- Healing from Colonization: Restorative practices based on Indigenous wisdom contribute to the healing of intergenerational trauma caused by colonial oppression, offering paths to repair and reclaim cultural identity.

Broader Perspective on Justice

Indigenous wisdom offers a different lens through which to view justice, one that emphasizes interconnectedness, collective responsibility, and social healing. This perspective can enrich the broader field of restorative justice by highlighting principles that Western justice systems often overlook.

- Community-Centric Justice: Indigenous approaches underscore the importance of community in achieving justice, contrasting with the individualistic focus of punitive systems.
- Sustainability and Resilience: Indigenous practices align justice with environmental and social sustainability, recognizing that justice is not just about resolving immediate harm but also fostering long-term resilience.

Honoring the Global Indigenous Roots of Restorative Justice

Acknowledging the roots of restorative justice in Indigenous cultures is essential to honoring the knowledge and traditions that have shaped contemporary approaches. Indigenous youth-led initiatives are increasingly gaining recognition, blending traditional practices with modern technology and advocacy to address the challenges Indigenous communities face today.

- Advocacy and Decolonization: Global efforts to honor Indigenous justice frameworks are part of a broader movement toward decolonization and empowerment. Indigenous communities are advocating for greater recognition of their justice systems, and international frameworks like the United Nations Declaration on the Rights of Indigenous Peoples support these efforts.
- Cross-Cultural Learning: Indigenous-led restorative justice approaches are gaining attention worldwide as communities share knowledge and practices, demonstrating that justice rooted in community, respect, and healing can be applied across diverse contexts.

The Cultural and Global Value of Indigenous Wisdom in Justice

Indigenous wisdom offers a wealth of knowledge for modern restorative justice, presenting a path toward justice that heals rather than divides, restores rather than punishes, and empowers communities rather than isolating individuals. By valuing community-centered approaches, relational healing, and holistic problem-solving, Indigenous justice traditions provide a blueprint for fostering stronger, more connected communities.

Revitalizing Indigenous restorative practices not only supports Indigenous sovereignty and self-determination but also encourages a shift toward justice systems that prioritize human connection, empathy, and resilience. The integration of Indigenous wisdom into restorative justice models provides an opportunity to deepen our understanding of justice, creating systems that respect cultural diversity and respond to the needs of all members of society.

As we honor the global Indigenous roots of restorative justice, we acknowledge the power of these ancient practices to heal and transform lives, offering essential lessons for building a more just and harmonious world.

CHAPTER 12

Restorative Cities – Building Restorative Communities for Health and Well-Being

The concept of a "restorative city" is emerging as an innovative framework in urban planning and community building, focused on enhancing the quality of life, well-being, and sense of belonging among residents. A restorative city prioritizes human relationships, holistic health, and inclusivity, leveraging restorative practices to address societal challenges and promote resilience in urban environments. This chapter explores the core principles, typologies, and community initiatives that form the foundation of restorative cities, and highlights case studies like Age-Friendly Sarasota (AFS) and UPLIFT Florida Network (UPLIFT) as models for creating more restorative and supportive communities.

The Concept of Restorative Cities

Restorative cities are built on the premise that relationships are central to society and that urban spaces should facilitate interaction, inclusivity, and well-being for all community members. These cities aim to create a restorative environment that strengthens communal bonds, addresses environmental and social needs, and promotes mental and physical health. Restorative cities use restorative justice principles—such as community involvement, respect, and accountability—in urban design and public policy to create spaces where people feel valued, supported, and engaged.

Key goals of restorative cities include:

1. Enhancing Social Cohesion: Restorative cities are designed to foster connection, trust, and collaboration among residents. Public spaces, infrastructure, and services are designed to encourage interaction and support strong social networks.

2. Promoting Equity and Inclusion: Restorative cities strive to make urban spaces accessible and inclusive for all demographics, especially marginalized groups such as older adults, people with disabilities, and low-income families.

3. Prioritizing Environmental Sustainability: By integrating green and blue spaces, restorative cities contribute to environmental sustainability, mitigate urban heat, and provide access to natural environments that promote health and well-being.

4. Supporting Physical and Mental Health: Restorative cities encourage physical activity and mental health through accessible parks, trails, sensory-rich environments, and community support networks.

Typologies of Restorative Cities

The restorative cities framework includes several typologies, each emphasizing a different aspect of restorative and community-centered urban design:

1. Green City

A green city integrates parks, gardens, greenways, and safe pedestrian paths to create an accessible and inviting natural environment within urban areas. Green spaces have been shown to improve mental health, reduce stress, and foster social cohesion by providing residents with spaces for recreation, relaxation, and connection with nature.

- Urban Greenery: Trees, parks, and green rooftops help reduce air pollution and offer cool spaces during hot weather.
- Accessible Greenways: Safe, connected walking paths encourage physical activity and social interaction, particularly when these paths are near residential areas.

2. Blue City

A blue city is designed to provide residents with access to water features such as lakes, rivers, and fountains, which not only beautify urban spaces but also contribute to reducing the urban heat-island effect. Water bodies are calming and can improve mental well-being by offering a soothing environment.

- Public Access to Water: Providing residents with open, safe access to water sources for recreation and relaxation.
- Mitigating Heat Effects: Integrating water features into public spaces to reduce heat and improve environmental quality.

3. Sensory City

A sensory city prioritizes sensory stimulation to make streets, sidewalks, and public spaces interesting, inviting, and safe. By incorporating visual, tactile, and auditory elements, sensory cities create enriching experiences for people of all ages, especially those with sensory processing needs, such as children and older adults.

- Sensory Stimulation: Public art installations, textured walkways, and community murals make cityscapes visually and physically engaging.
- Safety and Navigation: Features like tactile paving, sound cues, and colorful landmarks can improve accessibility for visually impaired residents.

4. Neighborly City

A neighborly city promotes social networks through walkable infrastructure, accessible amenities, and opportunities for residents to participate in civic life. By encouraging connections among neighbors, these cities foster a supportive and interconnected community where people look out for one another.

- Walkable Neighborhoods: Safe, pedestrian-friendly streets encourage residents to engage with each other and their environment.
- Community Participation: Programs that allow residents to participate in local governance and decision-making foster a sense of belonging and ownership.

5. Active City

An active city supports physical and mental health through the availability of multi-modal streets, walking paths, and bike lanes. By making it easier for residents to move around safely and stay physically active, active cities encourage healthier lifestyles and reduce reliance on cars.

- Multi-Modal Transportation: Bike lanes, pedestrian paths, and accessible public transit improve mobility options and reduce pollution.
- Promoting Health: Well-designed infrastructure for physical activity can lower rates of obesity, cardiovascular disease, and mental health issues.

6. Playable City

A playable city is designed to include elements that engage people of all ages in playful activities. Features like playgrounds, dog parks, and interactive public art make public spaces more enjoyable, drawing people together and creating positive social interactions.

- Play Spaces for All Ages: Designated areas for outdoor play, such as playgrounds for children and fitness parks for adults.
- Interactive Public Art: Art installations that invite residents to interact foster a sense of community and creativity.

7. Inclusive City

An inclusive city ensures that urban spaces are accessible and welcoming for people of all backgrounds, abilities, and ages. Inclusive cities address physical barriers, provide multi-generational and multi-functional spaces, and create opportunities for marginalized groups to feel respected and engaged.

- Universal Design: Spaces designed to accommodate individuals with disabilities and the elderly.
- Diverse Representation: Including cultural and historical markers that reflect the community's diverse heritage and values.

Community Initiatives in Restorative Cities: Case Studies

Two notable examples of community-led initiatives that embody the restorative city framework are Age-Friendly Sarasota (AFS) and UPLIFT Florida Network (UPLIFT).

Age-Friendly Sarasota (AFS)

Age-Friendly Sarasota is a countywide initiative in Florida focused on creating an environment that supports active, engaged, and healthy living for all residents, especially older adults. This program aligns with the World Health Organization's 8 Domains of Livability, which include Civic Participation, Communication, Health Services, Housing, Outdoor Spaces, Social Inclusion, Social Participation, and Transportation.

- Goals: AFS aims to enhance the livability of Sarasota by promoting accessibility, respect, and inclusivity across public spaces, housing, and transportation.
- Community Involvement: Through surveys and community forums, AFS gathers feedback from residents to better understand their needs and priorities, ensuring that programs and infrastructure improvements are responsive to the community.
- Focus on Aging Populations: AFS promotes an age-friendly environment that supports the mobility, health, and social engagement of older adults, making Sarasota a restorative city that values the contributions and well-being of its aging population.

UPLIFT Florida Network (UPLIFT)

UPLIFT is a statewide network that aims to improve the well-being of individuals and communities in Florida by building networks of villages and organizations that promote interdependence, connectivity, and belonging.

- Village Model: Villages are community-based organizations that provide a wide array of services and social opportunities, powered by neighbors helping neighbors. UPLIFT fosters connections among older adults, allowing them to lead vibrant lives while receiving community support.
- Focus on Connectivity: UPLIFT's model strengthens social bonds by creating a support network that allows older adults to maintain independence, access resources, and participate in community life.
- Intergenerational Support: By connecting people across generations, UPLIFT creates communities where both young and older residents benefit from shared experiences, knowledge, and support.

Lessons and Future Directions for Restorative Cities

Restorative cities are evolving to meet the changing needs of urban populations. As demonstrated by AFS and UPLIFT, building restorative communities requires collaboration among local governments, community organizations, and residents. Surveys from these initiatives reveal a growing desire to enhance sensory experiences, foster inclusivity, and create neighborly environments.

Key areas for future focus include:

1. Expanding Sensory and Inclusive Design: Respondents from the AFS and UPLIFT surveys emphasized the need for more sensory and inclusive spaces. Cities can work to incorporate design elements that engage the senses, improve accessibility, and create welcoming environments for people of all abilities and ages.

2. Leveraging Technology and Innovation: Technological advancements provide new opportunities to make restorative practices more accessible. For example, virtual villages or online community networks can complement in-person support and increase community engagement, especially in underserved areas.

3. Adapting to Climate Change and Environmental Challenges: As climate change intensifies, restorative cities will need to integrate sustainable practices that mitigate environmental stressors. Blue and green spaces, energy-efficient infrastructure, and climate-resilient designs can support public health and create more livable urban spaces.

4. Supporting Social and Economic Equity: Restorative cities should prioritize addressing systemic inequities by ensuring that resources, services, and opportunities are equitably distributed. Programs like AFS and UPLIFT demonstrate the importance of community-led approaches to meeting diverse needs.

Advancing Restorative Cities for a Better Tomorrow

The concept of restorative cities embodies a vision of urban development that centers community well-being, equity, and environmental sustainability. By fostering connections, inclusivity, and respect for diverse needs, restorative cities create environments where all residents can thrive. Initiatives like Age-Friendly Sarasota and UPLIFT Florida Network illustrate the potential for building resilient, supportive communities through local action, collaboration, and a commitment to holistic health.

As cities around the world explore the restorative city model, the potential for urban transformation becomes increasingly evident. Restorative cities align closely with the values of restorative justice, focusing on addressing root causes of social issues, promoting inclusive community engagement, and supporting individual and collective well-being. By adopting restorative practices in urban design, governance, and social programming, cities can create environments that nurture both personal and societal growth.

Key Takeaways for Developing Restorative Cities

Restorative cities require a shift in both mindset and policy, emphasizing collaboration, inclusivity, and sustainability. To build restorative cities that adapt to the unique needs of urban communities, city planners, policymakers, and residents should consider the following principles:

1. Community-Centered Policy Making: Local governments should engage directly with communities through participatory forums, neighborhood councils, and public surveys. This ensures that policies are responsive to the unique needs of the city's residents and reflect their values.

2. Investing in Green and Blue Infrastructure: Green and blue city initiatives support environmental sustainability and public health by providing access to nature and water, which improve mental well-being and reduce urban stressors like heat and pollution. Incorporating green roofs, rain gardens, and water features not only beautifies urban spaces but also supports biodiversity and resilience against climate change.

3. Creating Intergenerational Spaces: Restorative cities must be inclusive of all ages, providing spaces that cater to children, youth, adults, and seniors alike. Intergenerational spaces encourage interaction, understanding, and mentorship, helping foster a cohesive community across generations.

4. Fostering Economic and Social Equity: To make restorative cities accessible to everyone, it's essential to address economic disparities. This can include affordable housing, equitable access to quality public services, and economic development initiatives that support underserved neighborhoods.

5. Strengthening Support Networks: Programs like UPLIFT illustrate the value of networks that connect residents to each other. These networks can support residents in times of need, encourage volunteerism, and foster a sense of belonging.

6. Cultural and Sensory Engagement: Restorative cities should celebrate cultural diversity and sensory engagement by incorporating community art, cultural events, and spaces for creativity. Sensory cities invite residents to engage with their surroundings, encouraging connection through sights, sounds, and interactive art installations.

7. Prioritizing Mental Health and Well-Being: Mental health should be a core aspect of urban planning, with restorative cities creating spaces that reduce stress, encourage physical activity, and provide access to mental health resources. Green spaces, accessible healthcare, and community centers contribute to a supportive urban environment.

The Global Potential of Restorative Cities

The restorative city model has broad applications for cities worldwide, each adapting the framework to local cultural, environmental, and social contexts. Cities from different regions can exchange insights and best practices, enriching the model with diverse approaches and strategies. Initiatives like the Age-Friendly Sarasota and

UPLIFT Florida Network exemplify how cities can create frameworks tailored to the unique characteristics of their populations while maintaining shared values of inclusivity, sustainability, and collective responsibility.

Moving Forward: A Call to Action

As cities continue to grow and face increasing social and environmental challenges, the need for restorative urban practices becomes even more urgent. Building restorative cities is an opportunity to address these challenges proactively, creating urban environments where residents feel valued, connected, and empowered. By committing to these principles and continuously engaging with residents, cities can cultivate a culture of shared responsibility and mutual support.

Together, we can advance the restorative cities model to create urban spaces that prioritize human connection, environmental stewardship, and social justice. A restorative city is not only a place to live but a community in which everyone has the opportunity to thrive, contribute, and build a better future.

Policy Examples from Cities Implementing Restorative Justice as a Framework

Cities around the world are increasingly adopting restorative justice principles as part of urban and community policies, aiming to create environments that support conflict resolution, social cohesion, and inclusive community-building. This chapter explores policy examples from cities that are integrating restorative justice into their frameworks, highlighting how these approaches enhance both educational and social outcomes. The policies demonstrate the practical applications of restorative justice principles in fostering safer, more supportive communities.

1. Baltimore City Schools Restorative Practices Plan

Overview: Baltimore City Schools adopted a Restorative Practices (RP) Plan developed by the Open Society Institute of Baltimore. The plan integrates restorative practices into schools to improve student behavior, foster positive relationships, and reduce disciplinary actions, such as suspensions and expulsions.

- Restorative Framework: The RP Plan is built on restorative justice theory and practical application, combining research with feedback from stakeholders (teachers, students, parents, and community members). The framework promotes conflict resolution, empathy-building, and a stronger sense of accountability among students.

- Implementation Strategies:
  - Circle Processes: The use of circle discussions in classrooms allows students to share their experiences, discuss conflicts, and resolve issues collaboratively.
  - Peer Mediation Programs: Trained students mediate conflicts between peers, which empowers them to resolve disputes constructively and fosters leadership skills.
  - Teacher Training: Teachers receive training in restorative practices to support students in handling conflicts and building positive relationships in the classroom.

- Outcomes: Baltimore City Schools have reported improved student behavior, reduced suspension rates, and strengthened teacher-student relationships. The RP Plan demonstrates how restorative justice can transform school culture, making it more inclusive and supportive.

Resource: Open Society Institute - Baltimore's Restorative Practices Plan document provides an in-depth guide to the implementation of restorative justice in Baltimore schools. The plan aggregates research, practical strategies, and feedback, serving as a model for other educational institutions.

2. Oakland Unified School District Restorative Justice Program (California)

Overview: Oakland Unified School District (OUSD) in California has implemented a district-wide restorative justice program that emphasizes restorative circles, peer mediation, and community-building circles to address behavioral issues and improve school climate.

- Restorative Approach:

- OUSD's program operates on a tiered system, offering different levels of support depending on the severity of behavioral incidents.

- Tier 1: Preventative measures such as community-building circles to create a positive school culture.

- Tier 2: Targeted interventions, including restorative dialogues and conflict resolution circles for students with recurring issues.

- Tier 3: Intensive interventions for serious incidents, where restorative conferences involve families, students, and community members in repairing harm and rebuilding trust.

- Outcomes: A study by the National Education Policy Center found that schools implementing OUSD's restorative justice practices saw a reduction in suspensions by up to 50% over two years, with an overall improvement in student engagement and academic outcomes.

Resource: Oakland Unified School District's Restorative Justice Program provides a comprehensive framework for other schools looking to integrate restorative justice principles into their disciplinary policies, highlighting the role of collaboration and community support.

3. New York City Restorative Justice Pilot Program

Overview: In 2015, the New York City Department of Education launched a Restorative Justice Pilot Program across select schools to address high rates of suspension, particularly among marginalized communities.

- Program Components:
  - Restorative Circles: Schools used restorative circles to address minor conflicts and build rapport among students and staff.
  - Training and Resources: Educators were trained to facilitate restorative processes, emphasizing empathy and accountability.
  - Support for At-Risk Students: The program provided additional support for at-risk students, aiming to address root causes of behavioral issues and reduce recidivism.

- Outcomes: The pilot program resulted in a 20% decrease in suspensions among participating schools. Students and teachers reported an increase in mutual respect, with students feeling more supported and understood by school staff.

Resource: The New York City Department of Education offers detailed guidelines and resources on implementing restorative practices in schools, providing a useful reference for other urban educational institutions.

4. Leeds Restorative City Initiative (United Kingdom)

Overview: Leeds, a city in the United Kingdom, has been working to become a restorative city by embedding restorative practices across schools, community centers, and public services. This initiative was established to create a culture of respect, accountability, and collaboration across Leeds, making it a model for cities seeking to adopt restorative justice on a larger scale.

- Citywide Approach:
  - Leeds has implemented restorative practices across various sectors, including education, social services, and neighborhood policing.
  - Community Restorative Conferences: Leeds holds restorative conferences to resolve conflicts in neighborhoods, involving community members in the justice process.
  - Restorative Schools Network: Many schools in Leeds have adopted restorative justice principles, fostering a supportive and positive learning environment for students.

- Outcomes: Leeds has reported reductions in youth crime and antisocial behavior, as well as improvements in school climates and community cohesion.

Resource: The Leeds Restorative City Initiative provides insight into how cities can apply restorative justice principles across multiple sectors, creating a more cohesive, supportive community environment.

---

5. Denver Restorative Justice Project (Colorado)

Overview: Denver Public Schools adopted restorative justice in response to high suspension and expulsion rates, which disproportionately affected students of color. The Denver Restorative Justice Project introduced restorative practices as an alternative to punitive measures, focusing on repairing harm and keeping students in school.

- Restorative Strategies:
  - Circles and Mediation: Denver schools use circles and mediation to address conflicts between students and between students and staff.
  - Community Engagement: Denver's program actively involves parents and community members in restorative processes, strengthening community bonds and increasing accountability.
  - Staff Training: All staff members receive training in restorative practices to create a unified approach to student behavior and discipline.

- Outcomes: Denver's restorative justice initiatives have led to a reduction in suspension rates, improved school culture, and higher student retention.

Resource: Denver Public Schools' restorative justice resources serve as a comprehensive guide for schools implementing alternative disciplinary measures, emphasizing equity and cultural competence.

Lessons Learned from Restorative Justice Policies in Cities

These examples reveal key lessons for cities interested in adopting restorative justice as a framework for public policy:

1. Comprehensive Training is Crucial: Training staff, teachers, and facilitators in restorative practices is essential for consistent and effective implementation. Cities like Denver and Baltimore have invested in extensive training programs, enabling educators and staff to apply restorative techniques in varied situations.

2. Community Involvement Enhances Success: Restorative practices are most effective when they involve the broader community, as seen in Leeds and Denver. Engaging families, community organizations, and local residents fosters a shared responsibility for conflict resolution and builds a culture of mutual respect.

3. Tailored Approaches Increase Relevance: Each city has tailored its approach to fit the unique needs of its community. For instance, Oakland's tiered model allows schools to address different levels of conflict with appropriate restorative measures, ensuring that interventions are meaningful and relevant.

4. Focus on Marginalized Communities: Restorative justice policies are particularly beneficial in addressing disparities within the criminal justice and educational systems. Programs in cities like New York and Denver specifically aim to reduce disproportionate impacts on marginalized communities, offering alternative solutions that prevent further marginalization.

5. Continuous Evaluation is Key: To sustain the impact of restorative justice policies, ongoing evaluation is crucial. Tracking outcomes such as recidivism rates, suspension reductions, and student

and community satisfaction allows cities to adapt and improve their restorative practices over time.

The Path Forward for Restorative Cities

Cities adopting restorative justice as a framework are paving the way for more compassionate, inclusive, and effective approaches to conflict resolution and community building. By fostering collaboration across education, community organizations, and public services, these policies promote accountability, healing, and social equity. The examples from Baltimore, Oakland, New York, Leeds, and Denver highlight how restorative justice principles can transform not only schools but also communities, encouraging a culture of respect, understanding, and shared responsibility.

As cities continue to evolve, integrating restorative justice offers a promising path toward addressing complex social issues in a way that values each individual's humanity and the community's collective well-being. Restorative cities reflect a commitment to creating environments where all residents can thrive, fostering not just justice but also unity, resilience, and hope for the future.

Benefits for Residents, Public Safety, and City Governance in Restorative Cities

The concept of restorative cities not only fosters social and environmental well-being but also offers substantial benefits for public safety, city governance, and residents' quality of life. By adopting restorative practices, cities can create safer and more cohesive communities, where residents experience improved quality of life, greater trust in governance, and economic and public health benefits. This chapter explores the specific advantages that restorative city initiatives bring to residents, public safety, and municipal administration.

Benefits for Residents

A restorative city enhances the well-being of its residents by creating a safe, inclusive, and supportive environment. These cities prioritize social connections, mental health, and accessibility, contributing to a higher quality of life for all community members.

1. Improved Quality of Life

Restorative cities promote a culture of community care and respect, which translates into a better quality of life for residents.

- Sense of Peace and Safety: Living in a safe and restorative community increases residents' peace of mind, reduces anxiety about crime, and encourages them to actively participate in local events and activities.
- Mental Health Benefits: The emphasis on conflict resolution, empathy, and support in restorative cities reduces social isolation and mental health challenges, helping residents feel more connected and supported.
- Enhanced Use of Public Spaces: When residents feel safe, they are more likely to use parks, sidewalks, and recreational areas, leading to more vibrant public spaces and a stronger sense of community.

2. Economic Benefits

Safe, welcoming cities attract residents, tourists, and businesses, creating economic benefits that enhance community resources and infrastructure.

- Increased Retail Spending: A safer and more attractive city encourages shopping, dining, and entertainment, boosting local businesses and generating revenue for city governments.

- Tourism and Leisure Activities: Cities with a positive reputation for safety and inclusivity attract more tourists, benefiting local economies and supporting cultural and recreational industries.

- Property Value Stability: Safer neighborhoods often see stable or rising property values, which benefits homeowners and supports community investments in public infrastructure.

3. Building Community Trust

Restorative cities prioritize transparency, community engagement, and accessible government services, fostering trust between residents and local officials.

- Cooperation with Governance: When residents feel that their voices are heard and valued, they are more likely to participate in governance processes, leading to greater civic engagement and cooperation.

- Increased Community Participation: A trusted government encourages residents to get involved in public meetings, volunteer programs, and community initiatives, creating a more engaged and resilient community.

- Better Resource Allocation: When residents work with local governments to identify priorities, city governance becomes more effective in addressing community needs and allocating resources efficiently.

Benefits for Public Safety

Restorative cities apply proactive strategies for maintaining public safety, focusing on harm reduction, rehabilitation, and preventative measures rather than punitive ones. This approach supports public safety outcomes that align with community values and long-term resilience.

1. Reduced Crime Rates

Restorative practices have been shown to lower recidivism and reduce crime rates by addressing root causes and focusing on rehabilitation.

- Accountability and Rehabilitation: Restorative justice emphasizes accountability and supports offenders in understanding the impact of their actions, which can reduce repeat offenses.
- Prevention and Early Intervention: Cities with restorative justice programs can proactively address conflict in schools and communities before it escalates, contributing to a safer environment for all residents.
- De-escalation of Community Tensions: Restorative practices help to address misunderstandings and resolve conflicts peacefully, reducing the likelihood of violent incidents.

2. Support for Local Law Enforcement

Restorative cities advocate for a collaborative relationship between law enforcement and the community, emphasizing trust and cooperation.

- Improved Relationships: Restorative practices encourage law enforcement to engage positively with the community, strengthening trust and reducing adversarial interactions.
- Resources for Crisis Intervention: By integrating restorative approaches into policing, cities can provide officers with tools to handle mental health crises, homelessness, and substance abuse in ways that focus on support rather than punishment.

- Reduced Burden on Police: When residents feel empowered to resolve conflicts and support public safety through community programs, law enforcement can focus resources on serious crimes, making policing more effective and efficient.

3. Enhanced Crime Data Analysis and Prevention

Data-driven strategies help cities monitor trends, allocate resources, and respond proactively to public safety needs.

- Crime Pattern Analysis: Cities can use dashboards and reports to identify hotspots, analyze trends, and deploy resources where they are most needed, allowing for a more targeted approach to crime prevention.
- Real-Time Monitoring: Crime data analysis allows cities to identify shifts in crime rates and types, facilitating timely interventions.
- Policy Evaluation: By assessing data on public safety and restorative practices, cities can adjust policies based on effectiveness and community feedback, improving outcomes and accountability.

Benefits for City Governance

Restorative practices support effective governance by fostering collaboration between residents and local officials, ensuring that policies reflect community needs and values.

1. Increased Civic Engagement

Cities that prioritize restorative practices provide more opportunities for residents to participate in decision-making processes.

- Community-Based Decision-Making: Restorative cities encourage community members to take an active role in policymaking, contributing to policies that are both effective and responsive to local needs.

- Transparency in Governance: Transparent processes allow residents to see how decisions are made, fostering accountability and encouraging trust in local leadership.
- Collaborative Policy Development: By involving residents in discussions about public safety, infrastructure, and social services, city governance becomes a shared responsibility, increasing both buy-in and cooperation.

2. Cost Savings and Efficiency

Restorative practices can reduce city expenditures by lowering recidivism rates, reducing the need for expensive incarceration, and decreasing crime-related social costs.

- Reduced Legal and Incarceration Costs: Cities that implement restorative justice programs may see lower rates of incarceration, leading to significant savings on legal and correctional expenses.
- Efficient Resource Allocation: Cities can allocate resources more effectively by using data-driven strategies and focusing on restorative, preventative measures that reduce the demand for emergency responses.
- Enhanced Social Services: Savings from decreased crime-related expenses can be reinvested in community programs, social services, and infrastructure improvements, leading to long-term benefits for residents.

3. Improved Public Health Outcomes

Restorative cities prioritize public health by fostering environments that promote physical, mental, and social well-being.

- Health Education and Awareness: Cities can run health campaigns to inform residents about nutrition, mental health, physical activity, and preventive care, improving community health outcomes.

- Access to Services: Restorative cities aim to create accessible healthcare, counseling, and support services that address the underlying factors contributing to crime and social issues.

- Reduced Health Inequalities: By supporting the needs of vulnerable populations, restorative cities can address health disparities and promote equity across diverse communities.

Building a Stronger Community Through Restorative City Initiatives

Restorative cities offer a powerful framework for building safer, healthier, and more equitable communities. The benefits of these initiatives extend to all facets of urban life, from improving quality of life and reducing crime rates to fostering civic engagement and creating more effective, responsive governance. By integrating restorative principles into public safety, city governance, and social services, cities can create environments where all residents feel valued, connected, and supported.

Through partnerships between local governments, law enforcement, schools, and community organizations, restorative cities can lead the way in creating urban spaces that are not only resilient but also nurturing and inclusive. By focusing on relationships, well-being, and proactive problem-solving, restorative cities embody a future where justice, compassion, and community empowerment form the foundation of civic life.

CHAPTER 13

Victim-Offender Mediation Revisited – Advanced Techniques in Victim-Offender Mediation

Victim-Offender Mediation (VOM) has gained recognition for its potential to support healing, accountability, and restorative justice by providing a structured space where victims and offenders can engage in open dialogue. In advanced applications, VOM techniques go beyond basic mediation to address complex cases and enhance outcomes for both victims and offenders. This chapter explores these advanced VOM techniques, offering insights into their methodologies, applications, and scholarly perspectives.

Advanced Techniques in Victim-Offender Mediation (VOM)

Advanced VOM techniques aim to improve upon the foundational practices by incorporating approaches that enhance communication, address power imbalances, and support long-term healing. These techniques are particularly useful in complex cases, such as those involving serious harm, repeated offenses, or culturally sensitive contexts.

1. Preparation and Pre-Mediation Meetings

Pre-mediation is essential in advanced VOM to ensure that all parties are prepared and that the process meets their individual needs. Facilitators conduct separate sessions with each participant to set clear expectations, identify concerns, and prepare emotionally for the mediation.

- Trauma-Informed Preparation: In cases involving trauma, facilitators focus on creating a safe and supportive environment. This may involve discussing potential triggers, managing emotions, and setting boundaries to ensure the victim feels comfortable and in control.
- Conflict Assessment: Understanding each party's needs, motives, and desired outcomes allows the mediator to tailor the mediation process and anticipate any challenges that may arise.

2. Culturally Sensitive Mediation Techniques

In culturally diverse settings, it is essential for facilitators to integrate culturally sensitive approaches to ensure meaningful engagement and respect for cultural values.

- Inclusion of Cultural Advisors: Advanced VOM may include cultural liaisons or advisors to ensure cultural practices are respected and to facilitate understanding between parties from different backgrounds.

- Language and Communication Styles: Recognizing language preferences, communication styles, and cultural norms helps mediators bridge communication gaps and ensures that participants can express themselves authentically.

3. Power Imbalance Management

Power imbalances are a common concern in VOM, particularly when victims have experienced significant harm or vulnerability. Advanced VOM techniques include strategies to address these imbalances and create an equitable mediation space.

- Co-Mediation: In cases with pronounced power imbalances, having two mediators—one for each party—can help balance support and prevent one party from dominating the conversation.
- Empowerment Exercises: Facilitators may incorporate exercises that build confidence and self-advocacy for victims, helping them feel more comfortable expressing their feelings and needs during the mediation process.

4. Emotionally Focused Mediation

Advanced VOM often addresses not only the factual aspects of the offense but also the deep emotional impact it has had on both parties. Emotionally focused techniques prioritize emotional expression and processing as a pathway to healing.

- Guided Emotion Expression: Facilitators guide participants to express and process difficult emotions constructively. Techniques may include active listening, reflective responses, and validating emotional experiences.

- Restorative Dialogue: Structured dialogue allows both parties to share their experiences in a way that fosters empathy and understanding, often leading to more meaningful reconciliation.

5. Narrative Techniques

Narrative mediation techniques help participants reframe their experiences and build new understandings of the offense and its impact. By allowing victims and offenders to share personal stories, these techniques provide a richer context for healing and resolution.

- Storytelling Circles: Participants are encouraged to tell their stories in their own words, providing insights into their emotional and psychological experiences. This method can help foster empathy and redefine the narrative of the offense.
- Reframing: Facilitators guide participants in reframing their perspectives, helping victims see themselves as survivors and encouraging offenders to acknowledge the broader impact of their actions.

6. Post-Mediation Follow-Up

Follow-up sessions are critical in advanced VOM to support accountability, ensure compliance with agreed-upon actions, and provide ongoing emotional support for participants.

- Check-In Sessions: Facilitators conduct follow-up sessions to discuss progress, address any unresolved issues, and offer additional resources if needed.
- Community Support: Involving community support networks, such as counselors, family members, or mentors, can provide continued support and reinforce the positive outcomes of the mediation.

Scholarly Insights on Advanced VOM Techniques

Studies and scholarly articles highlight the impact of advanced VOM techniques on restorative outcomes, noting improvements in victim satisfaction, offender accountability, and recidivism reduction. Here are a few notable areas of academic research:

1. Effectiveness of Trauma-Informed VOM: Research has shown that trauma-informed approaches in VOM can increase victim satisfaction and psychological well-being, particularly in cases involving significant emotional harm. Trauma-informed VOM provides a safe environment that acknowledges and addresses trauma, allowing victims to regain a sense of control and closure.

2. Cultural Sensitivity in Mediation: Scholarly articles emphasize the importance of cultural awareness in mediation, with studies indicating that culturally sensitive VOM enhances engagement and satisfaction among participants from diverse backgrounds. By incorporating cultural values, VOM can align with participants' social norms and facilitate meaningful outcomes.

3. Power Imbalance Interventions: Studies have documented the success of co-mediation and empowerment exercises in addressing power imbalances. Research suggests that these techniques are particularly effective in cases of domestic violence, where power dynamics can otherwise inhibit open communication and accountability.

4. Emotionally Focused Techniques: Research shows that emotionally focused mediation in VOM contributes to deeper emotional processing, allowing participants to experience catharsis, empathy, and closure. Studies indicate that these techniques can lead to

longer-lasting reconciliation and emotional healing for both victims and offenders.

5. Long-Term Impact of Follow-Up Sessions: Follow-up sessions have been shown to improve long-term outcomes by supporting offenders in fulfilling restitution agreements and maintaining behavioral changes. Studies also indicate that victims who receive post-mediation support report higher satisfaction and a stronger sense of justice.

Advancing the Field of Victim-Offender Mediation

Advanced VOM techniques offer a pathway to deeper healing, accountability, and transformative change for participants. By addressing power imbalances, incorporating cultural sensitivity, and focusing on emotional and narrative dimensions, these techniques create a holistic and supportive environment.

Victim-offender mediation, when conducted with advanced methods, has the potential to redefine justice as a process that prioritizes healing, empathy, and accountability. As research continues to shed light on the efficacy of these techniques, VOM can be further refined to meet the complex needs of diverse communities and challenging cases. By adopting advanced VOM methods, practitioners can offer more comprehensive support to victims and offenders, creating outcomes that benefit individuals and strengthen communities.

Addressing Complex Cases, Including Serious Crimes

Restorative justice has emerged as a transformative approach capable of addressing even the most complex cases, including serious crimes. Unlike punitive justice systems that focus solely on punishment, restorative justice seeks to repair harm, foster accountability, and promote healing for victims, offenders, and communities. However, applying restorative practices in cases of serious harm requires careful consideration of case dynamics, tailored program models, and robust safeguards to ensure the safety and well-being of all participants.

Considerations in Complex Cases

1. Case Complexity

Serious crimes, such as violent offenses or cases involving deep emotional trauma, present unique challenges for restorative justice practitioners.

- Risks and Harm: Addressing harm in such cases can involve risks, including re-traumatization of victims or exacerbation of existing power imbalances between victims and offenders.
- Contextual Factors: Complexity may arise from cultural sensitivities, the involvement of multiple victims or offenders, or the presence of systemic inequities.
- Specialized Facilitation: Practitioners must possess advanced training and experience to navigate emotionally charged dialogues and ensure the process is constructive.

2. Program Models for Serious Crimes

Restorative justice processes are inherently flexible, allowing practitioners to tailor models to meet the needs of participants and the context of the crime.

- Communication Methods: In serious cases, direct face-to-face meetings may not always be appropriate or feasible. Alternatives such as letter exchanges, video messages, or indirect mediation through facilitators can provide safer options.

- Extended Preparation: Significant time may be required to prepare participants emotionally and psychologically for restorative dialogue. This includes addressing fears, setting boundaries, and building trust.
- Culturally Informed Approaches: Programs must respect cultural norms and integrate relevant practices, such as involving community elders or incorporating traditional rituals of reconciliation.

3. Case-by-Case Basis

Every serious crime involves unique circumstances that must be considered when determining the appropriateness of restorative justice.

- Assessment Criteria: Practitioners evaluate the nature of the crime, the willingness of both parties to participate, and the potential risks and benefits of restorative engagement.
- Behavioral Considerations: Restorative justice processes draw on principles of behavior analysis to understand the offender's motivations and the harm caused, ensuring interventions are targeted and effective.
- Voluntary Participation: A fundamental principle of restorative justice is that all parties must willingly choose to engage in the process.

4. Acceptance of Responsibility

Restorative justice is contingent on the offender's acceptance of responsibility for their actions.

- Precondition for Participation: Offenders must acknowledge the harm they have caused and demonstrate a genuine willingness to make amends.

- Challenges in Denial: In cases where offenders deny responsibility, restorative processes may be unsuitable or require additional preparatory work to address resistance.

Restorative Justice in Practice: Addressing Serious Crimes

1. Homicide Cases

Restorative justice has been successfully implemented in cases of murder and manslaughter, where the stakes are emotionally and morally profound.

- Example: In the Victim-Offender Dialogue Program in Texas, family members of murder victims met with offenders to seek answers and emotional closure. Studies have shown that these dialogues can provide victims with a sense of justice and peace that traditional courts often fail to deliver.

- Impact: Victims report feeling empowered by the opportunity to express their pain directly to offenders, while offenders gain a deeper understanding of the impact of their actions.

2. Sexual Violence

Cases of sexual violence require a highly sensitive and specialized approach.

- Alternative Models: Indirect communication methods, such as mediated letter exchanges, can allow victims to express their needs while minimizing the risk of retraumatization.

- Survivor-Centered Approach: Programs prioritize the safety and autonomy of survivors, ensuring they retain control over the process.

- Challenges: These cases often involve profound power imbalances and societal stigmas, requiring practitioners to be vigilant about maintaining equity and respect.

3. Hate Crimes and Ethnic Violence

Restorative justice has been used to address crimes rooted in prejudice and systemic injustice.

- Community Engagement: In addition to victim-offender mediation, community dialogues can address broader social harm and promote collective healing.

- Focus on Education: Restorative programs often include educational components to challenge biases and promote understanding between divided groups.

- Reconciliation Efforts: Successful initiatives have been documented in post-conflict regions, such as Rwanda, where restorative justice played a pivotal role in rebuilding trust after the genocide.

Outcomes of Restorative Justice in Complex Cases

1. For Victims

- Empowerment: Victims gain a platform to voice their experiences, ask questions, and influence the justice process.

- Healing: Engaging in dialogue can provide emotional closure and reduce feelings of anger, fear, and helplessness.

- Restoration: Victims often report a sense of justice when offenders acknowledge their wrongdoing and take steps to make amends.

2. For Offenders

- Accountability: Restorative justice holds offenders accountable in a more personal and impactful way than traditional punishment.

- Rehabilitation: Offenders gain insight into the consequences of their actions, fostering empathy and reducing the likelihood of re-offending.

- Reintegration: By repairing relationships, offenders are better positioned to reintegrate into their communities.

3. For Communities

- Collective Healing: Restorative practices address the broader impact of crime, fostering unity and reconciliation.

- Prevention: By addressing root causes and promoting understanding, restorative justice can reduce the risk of future harm.

- Cultural Transformation: Communities that embrace restorative justice often experience a shift toward more empathetic and cooperative social norms.

Scholarly Perspectives

Research supports the efficacy of restorative justice in complex cases, with findings emphasizing its potential to achieve outcomes that punitive systems often fail to deliver.

- Trauma Recovery: Studies by Umbreit and Armour (2010) highlight the role of restorative justice in promoting psychological recovery for victims of violent crime.

- Recidivism Reduction: Research by Sherman and Strang (2007) demonstrates that restorative practices reduce re-offense rates, particularly for serious crimes.

- Cultural Sensitivity: Zehr (2002) advocates for incorporating Indigenous and culturally specific practices into restorative frameworks to enhance their relevance and effectiveness.

Restorative justice offers a promising alternative for addressing complex cases, including serious crimes. By prioritizing healing, accountability, and community involvement, it provides a pathway for meaningful resolution and long-term transformation. However, its application requires careful consideration, specialized expertise, and a commitment to the principles of equity, safety, and voluntary participation.

When implemented thoughtfully, restorative justice can achieve outcomes that extend beyond the limitations of punitive systems, fostering a justice process that is not only fair but also restorative for all involved.

Victim-Centered Approaches and the Healing Impact of Victim-Offender Mediation (VOM)

Victim-centered approaches in Victim-Offender Mediation (VOM) prioritize the needs, perspectives, and well-being of victims throughout the restorative justice process. These approaches emphasize providing victims with a safe space to voice their experiences, facilitating emotional healing, and ensuring that their input shapes the outcomes of mediation. Research indicates that VOM, when victim-centered, can have a profound healing impact on victims, fostering closure, empowerment, and psychological recovery.

Core Principles of Victim-Centered Approaches in VOM

1. Safety and Voluntary Participation

- Victims must feel physically and emotionally safe throughout the process.
- Participation is entirely voluntary, with victims retaining the right to withdraw at any time.

2. Active Listening and Validation

- The mediator ensures that victims are heard without judgment or interruption.
- Acknowledging the victim's pain and experiences is critical for building trust and facilitating healing.

3. Empowerment

- Victim-centered VOM seeks to restore a sense of control to victims by involving them in decision-making and ensuring their voices guide the process.

4. Focus on Repairing Harm

- The mediation process centers on identifying the harm caused and collaboratively determining how it can be repaired, based on the victim's needs.

5. Trauma-Informed Practices

- Mediators trained in trauma-informed care recognize and address the emotional and psychological effects of the crime on victims.

The Healing Impact of Victim-Centered VOM

Victim-Offender Mediation offers several healing benefits for victims, which are amplified when victim-centered practices are employed.

1. Emotional Closure

- Expressing Feelings: VOM provides a structured environment for victims to articulate their pain, anger, and questions to the offender, which can be a cathartic experience.

- Receiving Apologies: Hearing a genuine apology and acknowledgment of harm from the offender often helps victims move toward emotional closure.

2. Regaining Control

- Participation in Justice: Victims actively participate in shaping the resolution, contrasting with traditional justice systems where they often feel sidelined.

- Restored Agency: By contributing to decisions on restitution or reparative actions, victims regain a sense of empowerment.

3. Building Understanding

- Gaining Insight: Dialogue with the offender allows victims to understand the motivations behind the offense, which can reduce fear and confusion.

- Humanizing the Offender: Victims may come to see the offender as a human being capable of remorse, which can mitigate feelings of anger and alienation.

4. Facilitating Forgiveness

- Path to Forgiveness: While not always the goal, the mediation process can create a space where victims may feel inclined to forgive, leading to emotional and psychological relief.

5. Strengthening Community Ties

- Support Networks: Victims often feel supported by the inclusion of mediators, community members, and family, fostering a sense of belonging and care.

Research Supporting Victim-Centered Approaches and Their Impact

1. Victim Satisfaction

Research by Umbreit et al. (2001) found that 80-90% of victims participating in VOM reported high levels of satisfaction with the process, particularly when they felt their needs were prioritized.

2. Psychological Healing

Studies by Strang and Sherman (2007) indicate that victims who engage in VOM experience lower levels of post-traumatic stress and anxiety compared to those in adversarial justice processes.

3. Empowerment and Agency

According to Choi et al. (2012), victims involved in VOM felt more empowered and in control of their justice outcomes, reducing feelings of helplessness.

4. Reduction in Recidivism

Research has shown that restorative justice processes reduce re-offense rates, providing victims with the assurance that their participation contributes to community safety (Latimer et al., 2005).

Practical Applications of Victim-Centered Approaches in VOM

1. Preparation and Support

- Pre-Mediation Meetings: Separate sessions with victims allow mediators to assess their needs, provide emotional support, and prepare them for the mediation process.

- Access to Resources: Offering counseling services, victim advocates, and legal support ensures that victims feel supported throughout the process.

2. Facilitator Training

- Trauma-Informed Practices: Mediators must be trained to recognize trauma and adapt their facilitation style to minimize re-traumatization.
- Cultural Competency: Understanding cultural sensitivities ensures that the mediation process respects the victim's background and values.

3. Customizing the Process

- Flexible Communication: Victims may choose alternative methods of communication, such as written statements or video messages, if face-to-face meetings feel too overwhelming.
- Victim-Driven Outcomes: The resolution should prioritize the victim's needs, whether that involves restitution, community service, or other reparative actions.

Challenges in Victim-Centered VOM

1. Re-Traumatization Risk

- Inadequate preparation or insensitive facilitation can lead to re-traumatization, causing more harm than healing.

2. Power Imbalances

- Mediation must address power dynamics between victims and offenders, particularly in cases involving violence or systemic inequities.

3. Emotional Readiness

- Not all victims are emotionally ready to participate in VOM, and alternative restorative practices may be more appropriate in such cases.

Elevating Victim Voices in Restorative Justice

Victim-centered approaches in VOM represent a paradigm shift in justice, moving beyond punitive measures to prioritize healing, accountability, and reconciliation. By centering the needs and experiences of victims, these approaches empower individuals to reclaim their agency, achieve closure, and contribute to a more just and compassionate society.

As research continues to validate the profound healing impacts of VOM, integrating victim-centered practices into broader restorative justice frameworks can ensure that justice systems meet the emotional, psychological, and practical needs of those most affected by crime. By doing so, restorative justice not only repairs harm but also fosters resilience and hope for victims, offenders, and communities alike.

Key References:

- Umbreit, M. S., et al. (2001). Victim-Offender Mediation in the United States: Empirical Evidence and Theory Development.
- Strang, H., & Sherman, L. (2007). Restorative Justice: The Evidence.
- Choi, J. J., et al. (2012). Empathy and Transformation in Victim-Offender Mediation.
- Latimer, J., et al. (2005). The Effectiveness of Restorative Justice Practices: A Meta-Analysis.

CHAPTER 14
Restorative Diversion Programs

Restorative diversion programs represent an alternative to traditional punitive justice systems by integrating restorative principles that emphasize repairing harm, fostering accountability, and addressing the needs of victims, offenders, and the community. These programs offer a pathway to justice that focuses on dialogue, understanding, and reconciliation rather than incarceration or other punitive measures, with the ultimate goal of reducing recidivism and strengthening community relationships.

Key Elements of Restorative Diversion Programs

1. Victim Participation

A cornerstone of restorative diversion is providing victims with a voice in the justice process.

- Sharing Experiences: Victims are invited to articulate the emotional, financial, and social impact of the offense.
- Involvement in Decision-Making: Victims contribute to determining appropriate restorative actions, such as restitution or community service.

2. Offender Accountability

Offenders are encouraged to acknowledge their actions and actively work to repair the harm caused.

- Acknowledgment of Harm: Offenders must demonstrate an understanding of how their actions affected victims and the community.
- Active Participation: Restorative programs require offenders to engage directly with victims and commit to fulfilling reparative agreements.

3. Facilitation and Mediation

Trained facilitators guide restorative processes, ensuring that all parties feel safe, respected, and heard.

- Structured Dialogue: Facilitators use established frameworks, such as victim-offender mediation or family group conferences, to promote productive communication.
- Conflict Resolution Skills: Mediators help navigate difficult conversations and address power imbalances between participants.

4. Community Engagement

Restorative diversion often involves the broader community, recognizing the collective impact of crime and the importance of community healing.

- Community Panels: Local volunteers may participate in restorative discussions and help develop accountability plans.

- Support Networks: Community members provide resources and support for both victims and offenders throughout the process.

5. Amends and Restitution

A critical component of restorative diversion is the offender's commitment to make amends for their actions.

- Restitution Agreements: Offenders may provide financial compensation, perform community service, or issue apologies to victims.

- Tailored Actions: Reparative efforts are designed to address the specific harm caused and the needs of the victim.

Examples of Restorative Diversion Practices

1. Victim-Offender Mediation

- Process: A facilitated meeting where victims and offenders discuss the offense, its impact, and potential reparative actions.

- Example: In cases of property damage, offenders might commit to repairing the damage directly while offering an apology to the victim.

2. Circle Sentencing

- Process: A community-based dialogue involving offenders, victims, and community members to discuss the offense and develop a reparative plan.

- Example: Circle sentencing in Indigenous communities often incorporates traditional practices and involves elders in guiding discussions.

3. Family Group Conferences

- Process: A meeting of the offender, their family, the victim, and their support networks to collaboratively develop a plan for repair.
- Example: Juvenile offenders may meet with their victims and family to discuss the impact of their actions and agree on restitution.

Benefits of Restorative Diversion

1. Reduced Recidivism

- Evidence: Research indicates that restorative justice programs reduce re-offending rates by addressing the underlying causes of criminal behavior and promoting accountability.
- Long-Term Impact: Offenders are less likely to re-offend when they feel heard, supported, and integrated back into their communities.

2. Increased Victim Satisfaction

- Sense of Justice: Victims often report feeling more satisfied with restorative processes than with traditional justice systems.
- Empowerment: Participation in restorative programs allows victims to regain a sense of agency and closure.

3. Strengthened Community Bonds

- Collective Healing: By involving the community, restorative diversion programs promote reconciliation and rebuild trust.
- Shared Responsibility: Communities gain a stronger role in addressing harm and supporting rehabilitation efforts.

Important Considerations for Implementing Restorative Diversion Programs

1. Voluntary Participation

- Key Principle: All parties must willingly choose to participate in restorative processes.

- Ensuring Consent: Facilitators must ensure that victims and offenders understand the process and agree to participate without coercion.

2. Cultural Sensitivity

- Adapting Programs: Restorative practices should be tailored to reflect the cultural norms and values of participants.

- Inclusive Approaches: Programs must respect the diverse backgrounds of participants and incorporate culturally relevant practices.

3. Trained Facilitators

- Essential Skills: Facilitators must be trained in restorative principles, mediation techniques, and trauma-informed care.

- Safety and Neutrality: Mediators must ensure that the process is safe for all participants and that power imbalances are addressed.

Challenges and Limitations

1. Power Imbalances

- In cases involving significant disparities between victims and offenders, facilitators must take extra steps to create an equitable dialogue.

2. Complex Cases

- Some offenses, particularly those involving severe harm, may require additional preparation and support to ensure restorative justice is appropriate.

3. Resource Limitations

- Effective implementation of restorative diversion programs requires funding, training, and community buy-in, which may be limited in some areas.

The Transformative Potential of Restorative Diversion

Restorative diversion programs offer a meaningful alternative to traditional justice systems, emphasizing accountability, healing, and community restoration. By incorporating restorative principles, these programs address the root causes of harm, empower victims, and provide offenders with an opportunity to make amends.

As evidence continues to highlight the benefits of restorative diversion, including reduced recidivism and increased victim satisfaction, these programs represent a promising pathway for creating safer, more cohesive communities. Through thoughtful implementation, tailored approaches, and a commitment to restorative principles, restorative diversion programs can transform the way justice is delivered, offering hope and healing to all involved.

Key References

- Zehr, H. (2002). The Little Book of Restorative Justice. Good Books.
- Umbreit, M. S. (2001). Restorative Justice Through Victim-Offender Mediation: A Multi-Site Assessment.
- Latimer, J., Dowden, C., & Muise, D. (2005). The Effectiveness of Restorative Justice Practices: A Meta-Analysis.

Examples of Restorative Justice Programs for Youth, First-Time Offenders, and Specific Crimes

Restorative justice programs provide an innovative alternative to traditional court systems, focusing on repairing harm, fostering accountability, and preventing recidivism. These programs are particularly effective for youth, first-time offenders, and specific types of crimes, where punitive measures may be counterproductive. By emphasizing dialogue, community involvement, and tailored interventions, these programs aim to address the underlying causes of criminal behavior and promote long-term rehabilitation.

Restorative Justice Programs for Youth

1. Victim-Offender Mediation (VOM)

- Description: VOM provides a structured setting where victims of minor assaults or property crimes meet with offenders to discuss the harm caused and seek resolution.
- Goals: Empower victims, hold offenders accountable, and encourage reparative actions.
- Example: A youth caught vandalizing a neighbor's property participates in a mediation session, where they apologize and agree to repair the damage.
- Impact: Studies show that VOM leads to high victim satisfaction and reduced recidivism among youth offenders (Umbreit et al., 2001).

2. Family Group Conferencing (FGC)

- Description: This process involves victims, offenders, their families, and community members working together to create a plan for accountability and behavior change.
- Application: Often used in cases of juvenile delinquency, truancy, or school-related conflicts.

- Example: In New Zealand, FGC is a cornerstone of the youth justice system, influenced by Māori traditions of collective decision-making.
- Impact: FGC fosters stronger family bonds and reduces the likelihood of repeat offenses (Maxwell & Morris, 2006).

3. Circles (Peacemaking Circles)
- Description: Circles involve a broader group of community members, victims, and offenders discussing the harm caused and collaboratively finding solutions to repair it.
- Focus: Reintegration of the offender into the community and healing for all parties.
- Example: A school-based circle in Minnesota was used to resolve bullying incidents, leading to improved peer relationships and accountability.
- Impact: Circles promote empathy, strengthen community ties, and address underlying issues contributing to delinquent behavior.

4. Roca, Inc.
- Description: A Boston-based program offering cognitive behavioral therapy (CBT) alongside education, employment training, and life skills development for at-risk youth.
- Focus: Reducing involvement in criminal behavior through skill-building and mentorship.
- Impact: Participants in Roca show significant decreases in violent crime arrests and higher rates of employment (Roca, Inc., 2023).

Programs for First-Time Offenders

1. State-Based First Offender Programs
- Description: Diversion programs for first-time offenders that often include drug testing, medical treatment, and rehabilitation.

- Example: In California, first-time drug offenders can participate in counseling and drug education programs to avoid criminal records.

- Impact: These programs reduce incarceration rates and provide support for behavioral change.

2. Anger Management Classes

- Description: Offered as an alternative to prosecution for assault or similar offenses, these classes teach offenders strategies to manage and express anger constructively.

- Example: A first-time offender in an assault case completes a 12-week anger management course as part of a restorative agreement.

- Impact: Research indicates that anger management interventions significantly reduce aggressive behaviors (Howells et al., 2005).

3. Defensive Driving Classes

- Description: Used as an alternative to prosecution for reckless driving or minor traffic violations.

- Example: A young driver cited for reckless driving attends a defensive driving course to avoid fines and license suspension.

- Impact: Defensive driving programs improve road safety awareness and reduce repeat traffic offenses.

Programs for Specific Crimes

1. Victim-Offender Dialogue for Severe Crimes

- Description: A restorative process initiated by victims of serious crimes such as murder or vehicular homicide, often post-conviction.

- Goals: Provide victims with answers, emotional closure, and a sense of justice.

- Example: In Texas, the Victim-Offender Dialogue Program facilitates conversations between victims and incarcerated offenders, fostering healing for victims while encouraging offenders to take responsibility.
- Impact: Participants report reduced trauma symptoms and a greater sense of peace (Umbreit & Armour, 2010).

2. Wraparound Programs for Youth
- Description: These programs assign care coordinators to develop individualized plans for children and adolescents with emotional or behavioral disturbances.
- Focus: Addressing root causes of behavior through holistic, family-centered support.
- Example: A teenager involved in shoplifting participates in a wraparound program providing therapy, mentorship, and family counseling.
- Impact: Wraparound services improve emotional well-being, reduce juvenile justice involvement, and enhance family dynamics.

3. Circle Sentencing
- Description: A restorative process involving victims, offenders, community members, and sometimes legal representatives.
- Focus: Creating a reparative agreement that addresses harm and prevents future offenses.
- Example: In Indigenous Canadian communities, circle sentencing incorporates traditional practices to resolve conflicts and reintegrate offenders.
- Impact: Studies show reduced recidivism rates and higher satisfaction among participants (Dickson-Gilmore & La Prairie, 2005).

Benefits of Restorative Diversion Programs

1. Reduced Recidivism: Restorative programs address the root causes of criminal behavior, leading to lower rates of re-offending compared to punitive measures.

2. Victim Empowerment: By giving victims a voice and role in the justice process, these programs enhance victim satisfaction and promote healing.

3. Community Strengthening: Restorative programs foster collaboration and trust within communities, promoting social cohesion.

4. Cost-Effectiveness: Diversion programs are often more cost-effective than incarceration, reducing the financial burden on the justice system.

Challenges and Considerations

1. Program Accessibility: Availability of restorative programs can vary by jurisdiction, limiting access for some participants.

2. Facilitator Training: Skilled facilitators are critical for program success, requiring ongoing investment in training and resources.

3. Cultural Sensitivity: Programs must be tailored to reflect the cultural backgrounds of participants and respect community norms.

Restorative justice programs offer transformative alternatives to traditional court systems, particularly for youth, first-time offenders, and specific crimes. By focusing on repairing harm, fostering accountability, and involving victims and communities, these programs create pathways for healing, rehabilitation, and social harmony.

As evidence continues to highlight their effectiveness, restorative justice programs are increasingly recognized as valuable tools for building safer, more inclusive communities. Through thoughtful implementation and a commitment to restorative principles, these programs have the potential to redefine justice and create lasting positive change.

Key References

- Umbreit, M. S., & Armour, M. P. (2010). Restorative Justice Dialogue: An Essential Guide for Research and Practice.
- Maxwell, G., & Morris, A. (2006). Youth Justice in New Zealand: Restorative Justice in Practice.
- Dickson-Gilmore, J., & La Prairie, C. (2005). Will the Circle Be Unbroken? Aboriginal Communities, Restorative Justice, and the Challenges of Conflict and Change.
- Roca, Inc. (2023). Annual Impact Report.

Evaluating the Effectiveness of Restorative Diversion Programs and Their Impact on Recidivism

Restorative diversion programs are increasingly recognized as a viable alternative to traditional punitive measures in criminal justice systems. These programs aim to repair harm, foster accountability, and address the needs of victims and communities, while also reducing recidivism—the likelihood of re-offending. This chapter examines the effectiveness of restorative justice programs in achieving these goals, supported by empirical studies and meta-analyses.

Key Features of Restorative Diversion Programs

Restorative justice programs differ significantly from traditional punitive systems by focusing on:

- Accountability: Offenders acknowledge their actions and their impact on victims and communities.

- Reparative Action: Developing agreements for restitution, community service, or other reparative measures.

- Healing Dialogue: Facilitated discussions between offenders, victims, and other stakeholders to promote understanding and reconciliation.

Evidence on Effectiveness

1. Meta-Analysis on Restorative Justice and Recidivism

- Findings: A meta-analysis of 22 studies conducted by Latimer, Dowden, and Muise (2005) demonstrated a 27% reduction in recidivism rates for participants in restorative justice programs compared to those who underwent traditional punitive measures.

- Demographics: The analysis showed greater effectiveness among juvenile offenders and property crimes than for violent offenses.

- Implications: Restorative justice programs appear particularly well-suited for addressing non-violent and first-time offenses.

2. Community-Based Restorative Programs

- Study Design: A community-based program involving facilitated dialogue between offenders, victims, and community members was evaluated for its impact on recidivism.

- Results: Participants in the restorative program had a recidivism rate of 14%, compared to 26% in the control group who received traditional punitive sanctions.

- Conclusion: The involvement of community stakeholders in restorative processes enhances social reintegration and accountability, reducing the likelihood of re-offending (Sherman & Strang, 2007).

3. Restorative Practices in Prison Settings

- Study Parameters: Restorative programs in prisons often integrate dialogue with victims alongside educational and vocational training for offenders.
- Outcomes: Research by Shapland et al. (2008) indicated significantly lower recidivism rates among participants in restorative justice prison programs compared to those receiving traditional prison programming.
- Significance: Providing offenders with skills and opportunities for reintegration is critical to reducing re-offense rates.

Factors Contributing to Reduced Recidivism

1. Victim-Offender Dialogue

- Impact: Facilitated dialogue allows offenders to understand the human impact of their actions, fostering empathy and personal accountability.
- Case Example: Victim-offender mediation in Canada led to a 32% reduction in recidivism rates, highlighting the transformative potential of direct interaction.

2. Community Engagement

- Role: Programs involving community members create a broader support network for offenders and address systemic issues underlying criminal behavior.
- Outcome: Community-oriented restorative practices in New Zealand's youth justice system resulted in significant declines in juvenile re-offending (Maxwell & Morris, 2006).

3. Holistic Support

- Approach: Restorative programs that incorporate counseling, education, and vocational training are more effective in addressing root causes of criminal behavior.

- Evidence: Programs like Roca, Inc. combine cognitive-behavioral therapy (CBT) with life skills training, achieving long-term reductions in criminal behavior.

Limitations and Challenges

While restorative diversion programs demonstrate significant promise, certain limitations must be addressed:

1. Applicability to Violent Crimes: Effectiveness tends to be lower for violent offenses, requiring careful preparation and support for victims and offenders.
2. Participation Barriers: Successful implementation requires voluntary participation, which may not always be feasible in all cases.
3. Facilitator Training: Skilled mediators are essential for managing power dynamics and ensuring productive dialogue, necessitating ongoing investment in training.

Broader Benefits Beyond Recidivism

1. Victim Empowerment

- Restorative programs provide victims with a voice in the justice process, fostering closure and healing.
- Studies show higher victim satisfaction rates in restorative programs compared to traditional systems (Strang et al., 2006).

2. Community Healing

- By involving community members, restorative diversion programs address systemic harm and promote collective responsibility.
- Programs in Indigenous communities, such as circle sentencing, illustrate the effectiveness of culturally relevant restorative approaches.

3. Cost Efficiency

- Restorative programs often cost less than incarceration, offering a fiscally sustainable alternative for addressing crime.
- Evidence from pilot programs in the UK indicates significant savings in criminal justice expenditures with reduced reliance on imprisonment (Shapland et al., 2008).

The Transformative Potential of Restorative Diversion

Restorative diversion programs offer a powerful alternative to punitive justice systems by reducing recidivism, empowering victims, and fostering community healing. Empirical evidence underscores their effectiveness, particularly for juvenile offenders and non-violent crimes.

As restorative justice continues to gain traction, investment in program design, facilitator training, and community outreach will be essential to maximize its potential. By shifting the focus from punishment to restoration, these programs provide a pathway to a more equitable and effective justice system.

Key References

- Latimer, J., Dowden, C., & Muise, D. (2005). The Effectiveness of Restorative Justice Practices: A Meta-Analysis. Canadian Journal of Criminology and Criminal Justice.
- Maxwell, G., & Morris, A. (2006). Youth Justice in New Zealand: Restorative Justice in Practice. Victoria University Press.
- Shapland, J., et al. (2008). Does Restorative Justice Affect Reconviction? The Fourth Report from the Evaluation of Three Schemes. Ministry of Justice.
- Sherman, L., & Strang, H. (2007). Restorative Justice: The Evidence. Smith Institute.
- Umbreit, M. S., & Armour, M. P. (2010). Restorative Justice Dialogue: An Essential Guide for Research and Practice. Springer Publishing.

CHAPTER 15

Restorative Reentry Programs – Supporting Offenders Reintegration

Restorative reentry programs aim to support the successful reintegration of formerly incarcerated individuals into their communities by emphasizing accountability, repairing harm, and fostering positive relationships. Grounded in restorative justice principles, these programs address the personal and systemic barriers faced by returning citizens, offering tailored interventions that promote healing, community-building, and self-sufficiency.

This chapter explores the key characteristics of restorative reentry programs, their potential for transformative impact, and the challenges in expanding these innovative models.

Characteristics of Restorative Reentry Programs

1. Community-Centered Support

Restorative reentry programs actively involve the community in reintegration efforts, recognizing that successful reentry requires collaboration among individuals, families, and local organizations.

- Community Circles: Programs often use restorative circles that include returning citizens, family members, and community stakeholders to discuss the reintegration process and foster mutual understanding.
- Mentorship Programs: Peer mentors with lived experience provide guidance and support, helping returning citizens navigate the challenges of reentry.

2. Emphasis on Accountability

Participants are encouraged to take responsibility for past actions while committing to personal growth and positive contributions to their communities.

- Restorative Dialogues: Facilitated discussions between returning citizens and victims, where appropriate, allow for acknowledgment of harm and a path toward reconciliation.
- Skill-Building: Programs often include training in communication, conflict resolution, and decision-making to strengthen accountability and self-reliance.

3. Trauma-Informed Approaches

Acknowledging the trauma often experienced by incarcerated individuals and their communities, restorative reentry programs integrate trauma-informed care into their frameworks.

- Healing-Focused Interventions: Participants receive counseling and support to process the emotional and psychological impact of incarceration.

- Systemic Harm Recognition: Programs address broader social injustices, such as racial inequity, that contribute to cycles of incarceration.

4. Focus on Holistic Reintegration

Restorative reentry programs prioritize the holistic well-being of returning citizens by addressing key areas such as housing, employment, education, and mental health.

- Employment Assistance: Job training, placement services, and entrepreneurship support help individuals achieve financial independence.
- Housing Stability: Partnerships with housing organizations provide secure and affordable accommodations.
- Educational Opportunities: Access to education and vocational training enhances long-term reintegration prospects.

Case Study: Transformational Prison Project (TPP)

The Transformational Prison Project (TPP) exemplifies restorative reentry in action. Founded in 2013 at MCI-Norfolk in Massachusetts, TPP uses restorative justice principles to address personal and systemic harm, focusing on the disproportionate impacts of incarceration on communities of color.

- Inside-Prison Programs: TPP facilitates restorative justice workshops that empower incarcerated individuals to reflect on their actions, develop empathy, and plan for reintegration.

- Post-Release Support: Through mentorship and community-building activities, TPP helps formerly incarcerated individuals navigate housing, employment, and family relationships.
- Impact: Participants report greater self-awareness, reduced stigma, and stronger connections to their communities, contributing to lower recidivism rates.

Possibilities for Expanding Restorative Reentry Models

1. Scaling Peer Mentorship

- Opportunity: Peer mentoring programs can be expanded to offer returning citizens relatable role models and guides for navigating reentry challenges.
- Example: Initiatives like Roca, Inc. combine mentoring with cognitive-behavioral therapy, demonstrating scalable success.

2. Integrating Technology

- Opportunity: Digital tools can enhance access to restorative programs, offering virtual mentorship, job training, and support groups.
- Example: Online restorative circles provide flexibility and reach, particularly for geographically dispersed communities.

3. Strengthening Community Partnerships

- Opportunity: Collaborating with local businesses, schools, and service providers ensures comprehensive support for returning citizens.
- Example: Programs partnering with housing organizations and employers have shown increased success in stabilizing participants' lives.

Challenges in Expanding Restorative Reentry Programs

1. Resource Limitations

- Challenge: Funding constraints often limit the availability and reach of restorative programs.
- Solution: Advocating for increased investment through public-private partnerships and grant opportunities is essential.

2. Stigma and Social Barriers
- Challenge: Returning citizens often face stigma, discrimination, and exclusion from critical resources like housing and employment.
- Solution: Public education campaigns can help shift societal perceptions and encourage inclusive policies.

3. Institutional Resistance
- Challenge: Traditional criminal justice systems may resist adopting restorative approaches due to entrenched punitive ideologies.
- Solution: Demonstrating the cost-effectiveness and efficacy of restorative programs can build institutional support.

4. Cultural Adaptation
- Challenge: Programs must be adapted to reflect the cultural and historical contexts of diverse communities.
- Solution: Engaging local stakeholders ensures that programs remain culturally relevant and accessible.

Restorative reentry programs offer a transformative approach to addressing the challenges of reintegration, emphasizing healing, accountability, and community engagement. By drawing on restorative justice principles, these programs provide returning citizens with the tools and support needed to rebuild their lives and contribute positively to society.

As initiatives like the Transformational Prison Project illustrate, restorative reentry can break cycles of incarceration and systemic harm, particularly in communities disproportionately affected by punitive systems. Expanding these models requires sustained investment, cross-sector collaboration, and a commitment to addressing systemic inequities, paving the way for a more inclusive and restorative approach to justice.

Key References

- Braithwaite, J. (2002). Restorative Justice & Responsive Regulation. Oxford University Press.
- Latimer, J., Dowden, C., & Muise, D. (2005). The Effectiveness of Restorative Justice Practices: A Meta-Analysis. Canadian Journal of Criminology and Criminal Justice.
- Transformational Prison Project. (2023). Annual Impact Report.
- Zehr, H. (2002). The Little Book of Restorative Justice. Good Books.

The Role of Community Support, Employment, and Family in Restorative Reentry

Restorative reentry emphasizes the reintegration of formerly incarcerated individuals into society by addressing the barriers they face while fostering accountability, healing, and growth. Key elements of this process are community support, employment opportunities, and family connections, each of which plays a critical role in creating a supportive environment for individuals to rebuild their lives and reduce the likelihood of recidivism.

Community Support in Restorative Reentry

Community support provides a network of resources and relationships that promote stability and a sense of belonging for returning citizens.

1. Emotional and Practical Support

- Mentorship: Mentors, especially those with lived experience, offer guidance, encouragement, and accountability.
- Faith-Based Groups: Religious organizations often serve as safe spaces for individuals to reconnect spiritually and socially.
- Community Organizations: Groups focused on reentry support provide essential services, such as housing assistance, legal aid, and counseling.

2. Neighborhood Investment

- Infrastructure Development: Investing in communities with high incarceration and reentry rates improves public amenities and employment opportunities.
- Crime Prevention: Stable, well-resourced neighborhoods can reduce crime rates and provide returning citizens with alternatives to reoffending.

3. Legal Support

- Addressing Barriers: Many returning citizens face systemic challenges such as difficulty obtaining housing or employment due to their criminal record. Community-based legal services help individuals navigate these obstacles and advocate for fair treatment.

Case Study: The Safer Foundation

The Safer Foundation in Illinois connects returning citizens with community mentors, legal resources, and skill-building programs, resulting in improved employment rates and reduced recidivism.

Employment as a Pillar of Restorative Reentry

Stable employment is a cornerstone of successful reintegration, offering financial independence, purpose, and routine.

1. Workforce Development Programs

- Training and Certification: Programs provide vocational training and industry-recognized certifications to enhance employability.
- Job Placement Services: Assistance with job searches, resume building, and interview preparation helps individuals enter the workforce.
- Employer Incentives: Wage subsidies and tax credits encourage businesses to hire returning citizens.

2. Entrepreneurship Opportunities

- Small Business Development: Programs that teach entrepreneurship and provide access to microloans empower individuals to start their own businesses.
- Networking Support: Building connections with other entrepreneurs and professionals fosters business growth and sustainability.

3. Employment Equity Initiatives

Advocating for "ban-the-box" policies and reducing stigma around hiring formerly incarcerated individuals create more equitable access to job opportunities.

Case Study: Rising Tide Capital

This New Jersey-based program helps returning citizens start and grow small businesses through training and financial support, enabling them to achieve self-sufficiency and contribute to their local economy.

Family as a Support System in Restorative Reentry

Rebuilding family connections plays a critical role in reintegration by fostering emotional stability and providing practical assistance.

1. Reconnecting with Family

- Emotional Healing: Families can provide a sense of belonging and help individuals process the emotional toll of incarceration.
- Rebuilding Trust: Structured family therapy sessions can mend relationships strained by the justice system.

2. Practical Support

- Housing: Family members often provide temporary or permanent housing for returning citizens.
- Childcare and Financial Assistance: Families help with basic needs, such as childcare, medical care, and transportation.

3. Strengthening Family Bonds

Programs that facilitate family reunification and relationship-building, such as family group conferencing, enable individuals to reintegrate into a supportive social structure.

Case Study: The Center for Employment Opportunities (CEO)

CEO integrates family engagement into its employment services, providing parenting workshops and family counseling to strengthen familial ties as individuals transition back into their communities.

Innovative Community Support Strategies

1. Unconditional Cash Assistance

- Description: Providing returning citizens with direct financial support offers an income floor and the freedom to prioritize their needs.

- Impact: Studies suggest that cash assistance reduces financial stress and enhances self-reliance.

2. Civic Engagement

- Involvement in Governance: Encouraging returning citizens to participate in community decision-making fosters inclusion and accountability.

- Restorative Circles: Community circles promote dialogue and collective problem-solving around reentry challenges.

Challenges in Implementation

1. Resource Constraints

- Community organizations often operate with limited funding, restricting their capacity to provide comprehensive support.

2. Stigma and Discrimination

- Returning citizens frequently face social and systemic stigma that undermines their reintegration efforts.

3. Coordination Across Systems

- Collaboration among legal, employment, housing, and social services is essential but often fragmented.

Community support, employment, and family connections are integral to restorative reentry, providing returning citizens with the tools and relationships necessary to rebuild their lives. By addressing systemic barriers and fostering collaboration among stakeholders, restorative reentry programs can break the cycles of incarceration and poverty that disproportionately impact marginalized communities.

Investing in these supports not only benefits returning citizens but also enhances community safety, economic development, and social cohesion. Moving forward, restorative reentry models must prioritize holistic and culturally sensitive approaches, leveraging community strength to promote healing and long-term reintegration success.

Key References

- Bazemore, G., & O'Brien, S. (2002). The Quest for a Restorative Model of Reentry: The Role of Restorative Justice Practices in Community Reintegration.
- Travis, J., & Western, B. (2014). The Growth of Incarceration in the United States: Exploring Causes and Consequences. National Academies Press.
- Safer Foundation. (2023). Annual Report: Advancing Employment for Returning Citizens.
- Transformational Prison Project. (2023). Restorative Reentry: Addressing Systemic Barriers for Justice-Involved Individuals.
- Zehr, H. (2002). The Little Book of Restorative Justice. Good Books.

Case Studies on Successful Reentry Programs and Their Societal Impact

Restorative reentry programs are transformative approaches that address the multifaceted challenges faced by formerly incarcerated individuals while promoting accountability and societal reintegration. The following case studies illustrate how restorative justice principles have been applied successfully in reentry contexts, highlighting their impact on reducing recidivism, fostering community engagement, and supporting personal transformation.

1. A Civic Engagement Model of Reentry

This model incorporates restorative justice principles by involving returning citizens in community service and civic activities, aligning with the idea that "doing good" can help individuals "make good" in their lives.

Key Features:

- Community Engagement: Returning citizens participate in volunteer activities, fostering a sense of belonging and responsibility.
- Restorative Service: Programs encourage individuals to repair harm through service projects, such as urban renewal initiatives or educational workshops.
- Mentorship: Peer mentors with lived experience guide participants, modeling accountability and resilience.

Societal Impact:

- Strengthened community relationships by fostering mutual trust between returning citizens and local residents.
- Promoted a sense of purpose and self-worth among participants, reducing recidivism.
- Enhanced neighborhood development and public perception of restorative reentry.

2. Restorative Justice Reentry Planning for the Imprisoned

This evidence-based program combines restorative dialogues and strategic reentry planning to prepare incarcerated individuals for reintegration.

Program Highlights:

- Facilitated Restorative Circles: Offenders, victims, and family members meet to discuss the harm caused and the steps needed for successful reintegration.

- Personalized Reentry Plans: Participants develop actionable plans for housing, employment, and family reconnection with the guidance of trained facilitators.

- Support Networks: Community members and social workers provide ongoing support during the transition.

Impact:

- Reduced recidivism by addressing systemic barriers to reintegration, such as housing and employment discrimination.
- Promoted healing and closure for victims and families, enhancing their involvement in the reentry process.
- Strengthened partnerships between correctional facilities and local organizations.

3. Minnesota Restorative Reentry Program

In Minnesota, restorative reentry initiatives have demonstrated the dual benefits of repairing harm and reducing recidivism.

Program Components:

- Restorative Accountability Boards: Panels composed of victims, community members, and facilitators work with offenders to develop amends plans.
- Civic Projects: Participants engage in community-focused projects, such as park cleanups or school renovations, fostering restitution.
- Life Skills Workshops: Programs include training in financial literacy, conflict resolution, and emotional regulation.

Results:

- The program achieved a significant reduction in recidivism rates, with participants reporting improved self-efficacy and community acceptance.
- Victim surveys revealed high satisfaction rates, with many expressing a sense of closure and reduced fear.
- The initiative helped shift public attitudes toward reentry, emphasizing restoration over punishment.

4. "Doing Good" to "Make Good": A Community Theory for Practice

This approach is grounded in the theory that active community involvement can foster personal transformation and societal reintegration.

Program Framework:

- Volunteerism: Returning citizens are integrated into volunteer roles aligned with their skills and interests.
- Community Circles: Regular dialogue sessions involve participants, community members, and local leaders to discuss progress and challenges.
- Recognition and Celebration: Programs include ceremonies to celebrate milestones, reinforcing positive behaviors and community ties.

Outcomes:

- Increased participant commitment to civic responsibility and reduced likelihood of re-offending.
- Strengthened community networks, with residents actively supporting the reintegration process.
- Elevated public awareness about the benefits of restorative reentry programs.

5. Transformational Prison Project (TPP)

TPP, operating in Massachusetts, exemplifies how restorative justice can drive reentry success.

Key Strategies:

- Inside-Prison Programs: Facilitated workshops encourage inmates to reflect on harm caused, build empathy, and prepare for reentry.
- Post-Release Mentorship: Peer mentors provide guidance, connecting participants with housing, employment, and educational opportunities.
- Community Dialogues: Offenders, victims, and community stakeholders engage in restorative conversations to foster understanding and reconciliation.

Measurable Impact:

- Reduced recidivism rates among participants compared to traditional reentry methods.
- Improved relationships between returning citizens and their families, leading to better social reintegration.
- Empowered individuals to become advocates for restorative justice within their communities.

Lessons Learned and Challenges

1. Lessons Learned:

- Restorative Focus Works: Programs that emphasize repairing harm and fostering accountability achieve better outcomes than punitive measures alone.

- Community Collaboration is Crucial: Successful reentry relies on strong partnerships among justice systems, community organizations, and local stakeholders.
- Tailored Approaches Matter: Customized reentry plans that address individual needs are more effective than one-size-fits-all models.

2. Challenges:

- Resource Limitations: Funding constraints hinder the scalability of restorative reentry programs.
- Stigma and Resistance: Social stigmas against returning citizens and institutional resistance to restorative approaches pose barriers to implementation.
- Complex Needs: Addressing the multifaceted needs of returning citizens, such as mental health and substance use, requires comprehensive support systems.

The case studies presented illustrate the transformative potential of restorative reentry programs in reducing recidivism, repairing harm, and fostering community well-being. These initiatives demonstrate that reentry can be a collaborative process involving offenders, victims, families, and communities working together to rebuild trust and relationships.

Expanding and sustaining these programs requires a commitment to resource allocation, public education, and systemic change. By prioritizing accountability and healing over punishment, restorative reentry programs can create safer and more equitable communities.

References

- Bazemore, G., & Stinchcomb, J. B. (2004). "A Civic Engagement Model of Reentry: Involving Community Through Service and Restorative Justice." Justice Policy Journal.

- Shapland, J., et al. (2008). "Does Restorative Justice Affect Reoffending?" Ministry of Justice Research Series.

- Travis, J., & Western, B. (2014). The Growth of Incarceration in the United States: Exploring Causes and Consequences. National Academies Press.

- Zehr, H. (2002). The Little Book of Restorative Justice. Good Books.

- Transformational Prison Project. (2023). Annual Impact Report.

CHAPTER 16
Restorative School Revised – Expanding Restorative Practices in Education

Restorative practices in educational institutions represent a paradigm shift from punitive discipline models to approaches that prioritize relationship-building, accountability, and community well-being. This chapter expands on the implementation and scaling of restorative practices in schools, providing a structured framework for readiness assessment, professional development, stakeholder engagement, and overcoming implementation challenges.

Restorative practices in schools foster positive climates by emphasizing relationships, inclusivity, and the repair of harm rather than punishment. These practices reduce exclusionary discipline measures such as suspensions and expulsions while promoting social-emotional skills among students.

Key Benefits:

- Improved student behavior and conflict resolution skills.
- Reduced racial disparities in disciplinary actions.
- Enhanced school climate and academic outcomes.

Determining Readiness for Implementation

Before implementing restorative practices, schools must assess their readiness and capacity for change.

Factors to Consider:

- Leadership Commitment: Are school leaders supportive of restorative approaches?
- Staff Buy-In: Is there an understanding and willingness among staff to adopt these practices?
- Resource Availability: Are adequate resources and training available to support implementation?
- Baseline Data: Collect data on existing disciplinary trends to set measurable goals.

Assessment Tools:

- Surveys to gauge attitudes toward restorative justice among staff and students.
- Focus groups with stakeholders to identify concerns and expectations.

Year One: Laying the Foundation

Establishing Roles

- Restorative Coordinator: Appoint a staff member to lead the initiative, oversee training, and monitor progress.

- Teacher Leaders: Identify educators passionate about restorative practices to serve as advocates.
- Student Ambassadors: Involve students in promoting restorative principles.

Timeline for Implementation

- Months 1–3: Conduct initial training for all staff and administrators.
- Months 4–6: Begin using restorative circles for community-building in classrooms.
- Months 7–12: Pilot restorative conferencing for addressing conflicts and discipline.

Year Two: Expanding and Embedding Practices

By the second year, restorative practices should become integral to the school culture.

Steps to Expand Implementation:

- Introduce restorative practices into extracurricular activities and parent-teacher conferences.
- Use student feedback to refine approaches.
- Develop mentorship programs pairing experienced staff with new teachers to sustain momentum.

Overcoming Common Challenges to Implementation

1. Resistance to Change:

- Solution: Provide evidence of success through data and case studies from similar schools.

2. Time Constraints:

- Solution: Integrate restorative practices into existing structures, such as advisory periods or staff meetings.

3. Equity Concerns:

- Solution: Use data to monitor disparities in discipline and ensure equitable application.

Importance of Community and Stakeholder Collaboration

Restorative schools thrive when they actively involve parents, community organizations, and students in the implementation process.

Collaborative Strategies:

- Host community forums to educate stakeholders about restorative practices.
- Partner with local restorative justice organizations for expertise and support.
- Encourage parent participation in restorative circles addressing school-wide issues.

Data Collection and Analysis

Tracking progress is essential to measure the impact of restorative practices and guide continuous improvement.

Key Metrics:

- Reduction in suspensions, expulsions, and referrals.
- Student and staff perceptions of school climate.
- Academic performance and attendance rates.

Data Tools:

- Surveys and focus groups for qualitative insights.
- Discipline dashboards for tracking quantitative outcomes.

Types of Professional Development for All Staff

Professional development ensures that staff are well-equipped to implement restorative practices effectively.

Training Topics:
- Restorative circle facilitation.
- Conflict resolution and de-escalation techniques.
- Implicit bias and cultural competency training.

Formats:
- Interactive workshops.
- Peer-to-peer coaching.
- Online modules for ongoing learning.

Tools for Implementation

Restorative Practice Frameworks:
- The Social Discipline Window: Balances high expectations with high support.
- The Restorative Justice Continuum: Guides schools from community-building to harm repair.

Classroom Tools:
- Talking pieces for restorative circles.
- Scripts for restorative dialogues and conferencing.
- Templates for individualized restorative action plans.

Interview Questions When Hiring for a Restorative Mindset

Hiring staff aligned with restorative principles strengthens the school's commitment to these practices.

Sample Questions:

1. How would you approach a conflict between students in your classroom?

2. Can you provide an example of how you've used relationships to manage behavior?

3. How do you address bias in discipline and classroom management?

4. What role do you believe empathy plays in fostering a positive school climate?

Expanding restorative practices in schools requires a comprehensive and collaborative approach. By focusing on readiness, professional development, and data-driven refinement, educational institutions can embed restorative principles into their culture, fostering safer and more inclusive environments where students thrive.

Key References

- Amstutz, L. S., & Mullet, J. H. (2005). The Little Book of Restorative Discipline for Schools.
- Evans, K., & Vaandering, D. (2016). The Little Book of Restorative Justice in Education.
- Gregory, A., Clawson, K., Davis, A., & Gerewitz, J. (2016). "The Promise of Restorative Practices to Transform Teacher-Student Relationships and Achieve Equity in School Discipline." Journal of Educational and Psychological Consultation.
- Wachtel, T. (2013). Defining Restorative. International Institute for Restorative Practices.
- Zehr, H. (2002). The Little Book of Restorative Justice. Good Books.

Implementing School-Wide Restorative Policies

The implementation of school-wide restorative justice policies requires a systemic approach that transforms the school's culture, focusing on fostering relationships, repairing harm, and reducing reliance on punitive measures. Successful implementation hinges on collaboration, consistent policy application, and professional development. Below is a scholarly examination of the steps, challenges, and benefits of implementing restorative policies at the school-wide level.

Key Components of School-Wide Restorative Practices

1. Vision and Leadership

- Establishing Restorative Goals: Define objectives for reducing exclusionary discipline, improving relationships, and fostering a positive climate.
- Leadership Buy-In: Principals and administrators must champion restorative practices, embedding them into the school's vision and strategic plan.

2. Whole-School Approach

- Incorporating Restorative Practices into Policy: Embed restorative justice in student handbooks, disciplinary policies, and staff codes of conduct.
- Cultural Change: Shift school culture from punitive to restorative by promoting inclusivity, collaboration, and accountability.

3. Professional Development

- Staff Training: Comprehensive training in restorative practices, including circle facilitation, conflict resolution, and implicit bias.
- Ongoing Coaching: Continuous support and feedback for educators to refine their practice.

4. Student and Family Involvement

- Student Voice: Engage students in designing and implementing restorative initiatives, such as peer mediation or student-led circles.

- Family Engagement: Host workshops and informational sessions for parents to foster community understanding and support.

Phases of Implementation

Phase 1: Preparation

- Conduct readiness assessments to determine the school's capacity for change.
- Form a restorative leadership team comprising administrators, teachers, and counselors.
- Develop an implementation timeline, starting with pilot programs before scaling school-wide.

Phase 2: Rollout

- Launch restorative circles in classrooms for community-building and conflict resolution.
- Introduce restorative conferencing for addressing harm and disciplinary issues.
- Establish data collection systems to track outcomes such as suspension rates, attendance, and student satisfaction.

Phase 3: Sustained Integration

- Incorporate restorative principles into everyday interactions, staff meetings, and curriculum development.
- Regularly review data and feedback to adjust practices and address challenges.
- Celebrate milestones and successes to maintain momentum and staff morale.

Challenges and Solutions in Implementation

1. Resistance to Change

- Challenge: Staff may view restorative practices as lenient or time-consuming.
- Solution: Provide evidence of restorative success in other schools, highlight alignment with equity goals, and involve staff in planning.

2. Resource Constraints
- Challenge: Limited funding and staffing may hinder implementation.
- Solution: Leverage community partnerships and prioritize cost-effective practices such as peer-led circles.

3. Consistency
- Challenge: Inconsistent application of restorative principles can undermine credibility.
- Solution: Train all staff uniformly and create clear restorative policies and procedures.

Benefits of School-Wide Restorative Policies

For Students

- Improved relationships with peers and teachers.
- Reduced suspensions, expulsions, and racial disparities in discipline.
- Enhanced social-emotional learning skills.

For Staff

- Greater job satisfaction due to reduced classroom disruptions and improved relationships.
- Tools for managing conflicts constructively.

For the School Community

- Stronger sense of trust and collaboration among students, staff, and families.

- Positive school climate conducive to academic achievement.

Case Studies and Evidence

1. Oakland Unified School District (California)

- Introduced restorative practices district-wide, reducing suspensions by 87% in restorative schools over five years.

- Improved student-teacher relationships and academic performance.

2. Denver Public Schools (Colorado)

- Implemented restorative policies to address racial disparities in discipline.

- Achieved a 40% reduction in suspension rates within the first year.

3. International Institute for Restorative Practices (IIRP)

- Schools partnered with IIRP to train staff, resulting in significant improvements in student behavior and school climate.

Key Resources and Tools

- Restorative Practices Whole-School Implementation Guide (IIRP): A step-by-step framework for introducing and sustaining restorative policies.

- Building a Positive School Climate Through Restorative Practices: Provides case studies and practical strategies for fostering inclusivity.

- Restorative Practices School Implementation Guidance (OSCE): A comprehensive guide for educators.

Implementing school-wide restorative policies requires a long-term commitment to cultural change, but the benefits for students, staff, and the broader school community are profound. By fostering relationships, addressing harm collaboratively, and prioritizing equity, schools can create environments where all students feel valued and supported.

References

- Amstutz, L. S., & Mullet, J. H. (2005). The Little Book of Restorative Discipline for Schools.
- Gregory, A., Clawson, K., Davis, A., & Gerewitz, J. (2016). "Restorative Practices in Schools: Reducing Disparities in Discipline." Educational Researcher.
- Oakland Unified School District. (2019). Restorative Justice Implementation Report.
- International Institute for Restorative Practices. (2018). Whole-School Restorative Practices Implementation Guide.
- Wachtel, T. (2016). Restorative Practices and School Transformation.

Case Examples of Schools Transitioning Fully to Restorative Models

The transition of schools to fully restorative models exemplifies the transformative potential of restorative justice (RJ) in education. Using methodologies like Participatory Action Research (PAR) and the Outcome Logic Model (OLM), case studies highlight the processes, successes, and challenges encountered during these transitions. This chapter examines a multi-site school-wide restorative justice (SWRJ) implementation program and explores lessons learned for educators, administrators, and RJ practitioners.

Overview of the Multi-Site SWRJ Implementation Program

The program involved five middle schools transitioning to restorative models, with university researchers and external RJ specialists collaboratively evaluating implementation.

Key Components of the Program:

1. Participatory Action Research (PAR):

- Engaged stakeholders in reflective practices to co-design and evaluate restorative strategies.

2. Outcome Logic Model (OLM):

- Framework for mapping resources, activities, outputs, and outcomes.

3. Evaluation Metrics:

- Focused on identifying gaps in practice, measuring outcomes, and refining implementation strategies.

Findings from the SWRJ Implementation

Success Factors

1. Administrator Buy-In:

- Leadership commitment was critical in fostering a culture supportive of RJ.

- Principals led efforts to align RJ practices with school policies and goals.

2. Focused Implementation Teams:

- Dedicated teams of teachers, counselors, and administrators drove the initiative.

- Cross-disciplinary teams ensured diverse perspectives and shared responsibility.

3. Strong Professional Development Systems:

- Comprehensive training equipped staff with skills for restorative circles, conferencing, and classroom management.
- Ongoing coaching reinforced confidence and consistency in practice.

4. Systematic Program Mapping Frameworks (OLM):

- OLM provided a structured way to identify and address gaps in resources, activities, and outcomes.
- Facilitated clear communication and goal alignment across stakeholders.

Challenges Identified

1. Leadership Turnover:

- Frequent changes in school leadership disrupted continuity and progress.
- Solution: Embedding RJ practices into school policies and culture to withstand personnel changes.

2. Overreliance on RJ Specialists:

- Schools leaned heavily on individual specialists, risking burnout and inconsistent implementation.
- Solution: Distributed leadership and training broader staff groups in RJ principles.

3. Imbalance Across Tiers:

- Focus was unevenly distributed, with disproportionate attention to Tier 1 practices (universal community-building) compared to Tier 2 and Tier 3 interventions (targeted and intensive supports).

- Solution: Comprehensive implementation plans that address all tiers equally.

Case Example Highlights

School A: Prioritizing Relationships over Discipline

- Location: Urban middle school.
- Focus: Replacing suspension-heavy policies with restorative circles for conflict resolution.
- Results:
  - Suspension rates dropped by 60% in three years.
  - Teachers reported improved classroom climates and reduced disruptions.

School B: Addressing Racial Disparities in Discipline

- Location: Suburban middle school with diverse demographics.
- Initiative: Targeted efforts to reduce racial disparities in disciplinary actions through restorative practices.
- Outcomes:
  - Equitable application of discipline increased student trust in the administration.
  - Racial disparities in suspensions decreased by 40%.

School C: Building Restorative Communities

- Location: Rural middle school.
- Key Efforts: Engaged parents and community members in restorative processes to support student success.
- Results:
  - Increased parent participation in school activities.
  - Strengthened relationships between the school and the broader community.

Key Learnings and Recommendations

1. Sustainable Leadership Structures:

- Develop policies embedding RJ principles into school culture to mitigate the impact of leadership changes.

2. Broad-Based Training:

- Avoid overdependence on RJ specialists by training all staff members, including non-teaching staff.

3. Balanced Tiers of Support:

- Ensure equal attention to universal, targeted, and intensive RJ practices to address the full spectrum of student needs.

4. Data-Driven Adjustments:

- Use OLM or similar frameworks to systematically monitor progress, identify gaps, and adjust strategies.

5. Community Engagement:

- Actively involve families and local organizations in restorative initiatives to strengthen community ties and increase accountability.

Implications for Educational Leaders and RJ Scholars

This case study underscores the transformative potential of RJ when implemented as a whole-school model. However, it also highlights the importance of sustained leadership, equitable resource allocation, and comprehensive evaluation frameworks to ensure long-term success. Researchers and practitioners should continue exploring the intersections of RJ with cultural competence, equity, and systemic change to enhance its impact.

References

- Morrison, B., Blood, P., & Thorsborne, M. (2005). Practicing Restorative Justice in School Communities: The Challenge of Culture Change.

- Gregory, A., & Evans, K. R. (2020). "Restorative Justice in Schools: Impacts and Challenges." Educational Leadership Journal.

- Wachtel, T. (2016). Restorative Practices: Building Relationships and Communities.

- Zehr, H. (2002). The Little Book of Restorative Justice.

- Outcome Logic Model Framework: Best Practices in Program Evaluation. University Research Publications.

CHAPTER 17
Family Group Conferencing Revisited – A Detailed Guide to Facilitating Successful Conferences

Family Group Conferencing (FGC) is a cornerstone of restorative justice, offering a collaborative, victim-centered process where families, victims, and offenders come together to address harm and collectively develop a plan for reparation. This chapter provides a detailed guide for facilitating effective FGCs, drawing insights from case studies such as the 1995 Bucks County firebombing and the extensive use of FGCs in Australia and New Zealand.

Key Phases of Family Group Conferencing

1. Preparation Phase

Preparation ensures that all participants understand the purpose, process, and expectations of the conference.

- Offender Admission of Guilt: Participation requires the offender's prior admission of guilt.
- Voluntary Participation: Both victims and offenders must agree to participate without coercion.
- Individual Meetings: Facilitators meet with victims, offenders, and their support networks to explain the process, address concerns, and prepare them emotionally.
- Logistics: Schedule the conference at a neutral and accessible location.

2. Opening Phase

The opening sets the tone for respectful and constructive dialogue.

- Facilitator's Role: The facilitator introduces the purpose of the conference, establishes ground rules, and creates a safe space for sharing.
- Introductions: Participants introduce themselves, stating their role and relationship to the incident.

3. Storytelling Phase

This phase allows participants to share their experiences and perspectives.

- Offender's Account: The offender explains their actions, what led to them, and how they feel about the harm caused.
- Victim's Perspective: Victims share the emotional, physical, and financial impact of the offense.

- Family and Community Input: Family members and community representatives discuss how the offense has affected them and the broader community.

4. Agreement Phase

Participants collaboratively develop a plan to address the harm and prevent future offenses.

- Victim's Needs: Victims articulate what they need for healing, such as an apology, restitution, or assurances of behavioral change.
- Restorative Plan: Participants agree on specific actions for the offender, such as community service, counseling, or restitution.
- Consensus Building: The plan is developed collectively, ensuring that all voices are heard and respected.

5. Closing Phase

The closing formalizes the agreement and reinforces the commitment to repair harm.

- Review of the Agreement: The facilitator reviews the agreed-upon plan, ensuring clarity and mutual understanding.
- Commitment Statements: Participants, including the offender, affirm their commitment to fulfilling the agreement.
- Follow-Up Plans: A timeline for monitoring and follow-up is established to ensure accountability.

Case Study: Bucks County Firebombing

Background

Two teenagers committed an arson offense that caused significant property damage and emotional harm to the victims. While the justice system processed the offenders, the victims' needs were not adequately addressed.

The Conference Process

- Participants: The offenders, their families, the victims, and community members attended the conference.
- Structure: The conference was led by an experienced Australian police officer using a structured script.
- Outcomes:
    - The offenders apologized and expressed genuine remorse.
    - Victims articulated their needs for assurances of non-repetition and a sense of community restoration.
    - The conference transformed two opposing groups into a unified community, fostering mutual understanding and healing.

Impact

- Victim Satisfaction: Victims reported feeling heard and supported.
- Reduced Recidivism: The structured, community-driven process led to significant reductions in repeat offenses.
- High Restitution Completion Rates: Over 90% of agreed restitution was completed without further intervention.

Key Considerations for Successful Family Group Conferencing

Facilitator Expertise

- Trained facilitators are critical to maintaining neutrality, guiding dialogue, and ensuring safety.
- Facilitators must be adept at managing emotions and power imbalances.

Building Trust

- Transparency in the process and respect for all participants build trust, fostering open communication.

Cultural Sensitivity

- Adapt the process to reflect cultural norms and values, ensuring inclusivity and relevance.

Monitoring and Follow-Up

- Regular check-ins with participants ensure accountability and support for fulfilling the agreement.

Benefits of Family Group Conferencing

- For Victims: Provides a platform to express their feelings, ask questions, and receive reparations.
- For Offenders: Encourages accountability, empathy, and reintegration into the community.
- For Communities: Strengthens social cohesion and reduces the likelihood of re-offending.

Lessons Learned

The case of the Bucks County firebombing and similar examples demonstrate the transformative potential of FGCs in addressing harm, promoting healing, and reducing recidivism. Success depends on careful preparation, skilled facilitation, and the active involvement of all stakeholders.

Key References

- Zehr, H. (2002). The Little Book of Restorative Justice. Good Books.

- Tauri, J. (1998). "Family Group Conferencing: A Restorative Justice Approach." Australasian Policing.

- Umbreit, M. S., & Coates, R. B. (2000). "Multisite Assessment of Victim-Offender Mediation and Restorative Conferencing." National Institute of Justice.

- Van Ness, D. W., & Strong, K. H. (2015). Restoring Justice: An Introduction to Restorative Justice. Routledge.

- Pranis, K., Stuart, B., & Wedge, M. (2003). Peacemaking Circles: From Crime to Community. Living Justice Press.

Addressing Challenges and Best Practices for Diverse Family Dynamics in Family Group Conferencing

Family Group Conferencing (FGC) is a powerful tool within restorative justice, offering an inclusive approach to repairing harm. However, diverse family dynamics pose unique challenges to the process, such as cultural differences, power imbalances, and emotional complexities. This chapter explores strategies and best practices to address these challenges, ensuring FGC remains effective and equitable across varied family structures.

Key Challenges in Diverse Family Dynamics

1. Cultural and Linguistic Differences

- Challenge: Families from diverse cultural backgrounds may hold differing views on justice, authority, and conflict resolution.

- Impact: Misunderstandings or resistance to restorative practices may arise if the process conflicts with cultural norms.

2. Power Imbalances

- Challenge: Unequal power dynamics, such as those between parents and children or genders, can inhibit open dialogue.
- Impact: Participants may feel silenced, leading to unbalanced agreements or unresolved harm.

3. Emotional Barriers

- Challenge: Strong emotions, such as anger, shame, or fear, can hinder constructive communication.
- Impact: Emotional overload may prevent participants from engaging meaningfully in the process.

4. Complex Family Structures

- Challenge: Blended families, estranged relationships, or extended kinship networks can complicate decision-making.
- Impact: Disagreements among family members may delay or derail the resolution process.

Best Practices for Addressing Challenges

1. Cultural Sensitivity and Inclusivity

- Adapt Practices: Tailor FGC processes to align with participants' cultural values and traditions.
- Culturally Competent Facilitators: Train facilitators in cultural awareness and employ interpreters when necessary.
- Inclusive Representation: Encourage participation from community elders or cultural leaders to bridge gaps in understanding.

2. Mitigating Power Imbalances

- Pre-Conference Preparation: Conduct individual meetings to address power dynamics and ensure equitable participation.
- Facilitator Neutrality: Facilitators should actively ensure all voices are heard, especially those of marginalized participants.

- Supportive Allies: Allow participants to bring advocates or support persons to provide emotional or logistical assistance.

3. Emotional Regulation

- Grounding Techniques: Use mindfulness exercises or structured opening statements to create a calm environment.
- Time Management: Allow for breaks during the conference to manage emotional intensity.
- Trauma-Informed Approach: Recognize and address past traumas that may influence participants' behavior and responses.

4. Navigating Complex Family Structures

- Clarify Roles: Clearly define the roles of each participant to streamline communication and decision-making.
- Flexible Agreements: Develop agreements that accommodate varying family circumstances and relationships.
- Follow-Up Plans: Implement robust follow-up mechanisms to address unresolved issues or changing dynamics.

Case Study: Addressing Diversity in FGC

Scenario

A restorative justice program in a multicultural urban setting faced challenges conducting FGC with a blended family from a refugee background. The family included two estranged parents, children from different marriages, and extended relatives.

Actions Taken

1. Cultural Mediation: Engaged a cultural liaison to explain the FGC process in alignment with the family's traditions.
2. Pre-Conference Meetings: Conducted separate sessions with each family subgroup to identify concerns and set expectations.

3. Inclusive Dialogue: Structured the conference to prioritize the children's voices, ensuring their needs remained central.

Outcomes

The family reached a consensus on co-parenting strategies, reestablished communication channels, and developed a shared understanding of their roles in supporting the children's well-being.

Theoretical Frameworks Supporting Best Practices

1. Intersectionality in Restorative Justice

- Emphasizes understanding the intersecting identities (e.g., race, gender, class) of participants to address systemic inequities effectively.

2. Family Systems Theory

- Highlights the interconnectedness of family members and the need to address relationships as part of the restorative process.

3. Trauma-Informed Care

- Focuses on creating a safe environment that acknowledges and mitigates the impact of trauma on participants' engagement.

Scholarly References

1. Zehr, H. (2002). The Little Book of Restorative Justice. Good Books.

2. Umbreit, M. S., & Coates, R. B. (2000). "Multisite Assessment of Victim-Offender Mediation and Restorative Conferencing." National Institute of Justice.

3. Van Ness, D. W., & Strong, K. H. (2015). Restoring Justice: An Introduction to Restorative Justice. Routledge.

4. Llewellyn, J. J., & Howse, R. (1999). "Restorative Justice: A Conceptual Framework." Law Commission of Canada.

5. Boyes-Watson, C. (2008). Peacemaking Circles and Urban Youth: Bringing Justice Home. Living Justice Press.

Addressing diverse family dynamics in Family Group Conferencing requires culturally sensitive facilitation, strategies to mitigate power imbalances, and frameworks to navigate complex relationships. By prioritizing inclusivity, emotional well-being, and flexibility, restorative justice practitioners can effectively support diverse families in achieving meaningful resolution and healing.

Chapter 17: Impact of Family Group Conferencing (FGCs) on Family Cohesion and Individual Growth

Scholarly Insights and Case Studies

Family Group Conferencing (FGC) has shown significant promise in strengthening family bonds and fostering personal growth for participants. These processes prioritize inclusive dialogue and collaborative decision-making, offering a restorative approach to addressing harm while enhancing relationships.

Key Impacts on Family Cohesion:

1. Improved Communication:

FGCs provide a structured and safe environment for families to openly discuss grievances and concerns, facilitating healthier communication patterns.

2. Shared Responsibility:

The process encourages collective problem-solving and accountability, reinforcing familial roles and shared goals.

3. Conflict Resolution Skills:

Families gain tools for managing future disputes constructively, reducing the risk of recurring conflicts.

4. Reconnection and Trust-Building:

By focusing on empathy and understanding, FGCs help rebuild trust among family members, which may have been eroded by the offense.

Individual Growth Benefits:

1. Empowerment for Victims and Offenders:

Victims feel heard and supported, while offenders take accountability for their actions, promoting self-awareness and responsibility.

2. Social Competency:

Participants, particularly youth, often report increased emotional regulation and problem-solving skills following FGC participation.

3. Emotional Healing:

The restorative environment aids in processing emotions constructively, reducing long-term psychological distress.

Evidence-Based Observations:

- Research highlights the success of FGCs in addressing youth offenses within Māori communities, where these practices align closely with cultural traditions, emphasizing collective well-being and respect for elders 【147】 【148】.
- Studies also show that involving extended family networks reduces reoffending and enhances the resilience of participants by fostering stronger support systems 【147】.

Recommendations for Effective Implementation:

1. Cultural Sensitivity:

Adapting the FGC framework to respect the cultural dynamics of participants ensures meaningful engagement.

2. Training for Facilitators:

Skilled mediators are essential to navigate complex family dynamics and maintain a constructive dialogue.

3. Systemic Support:

Integrating FGCs within larger social support structures, such as community services and legal frameworks, ensures sustainable outcomes.

These findings underscore the transformative potential of FGCs in promoting restorative justice while nurturing family cohesion and individual development. For further insights and methodologies, sources such as ResearchGate and other scholarly platforms on restorative justice provide a wealth of knowledge【147】【148】.

Chapter 18: Youth Conferencing in Restorative Justice

Unique Needs of Youth in Restorative Justice Settings

Youth conferencing in restorative justice settings is designed to meet the developmental, emotional, and social needs of young offenders while prioritizing accountability and repairing harm. Unlike traditional punitive systems, these restorative approaches integrate trauma-informed care, community engagement, and developmental support to address the unique vulnerabilities of youth.

Key Considerations for Youth in Restorative Justice:

1. Developmental Sensitivity:

Youth offenders often lack the emotional and cognitive maturity to fully grasp the consequences of their actions. Restorative conferencing incorporates methods to guide young individuals through understanding their actions, the harm caused, and how to make amends. This process is developmentally appropriate and often facilitated in supportive environments 【156】【157】.

2. Trauma-Informed Approaches:

Many young offenders have experienced adverse childhood experiences (ACEs) such as abuse, neglect, or exposure to violence. Restorative processes aim to minimize retraumatization by fostering safe spaces for dialogue, emphasizing healing for both victims and offenders, and addressing underlying factors contributing to the offense 【156】.

3. Family and Community Involvement:

Youth conferencing models often involve families and community members to provide support networks, build accountability, and foster reintegration. For example, Surrey Youth Restorative Intervention (YRI) in the UK integrates community-based support and has demonstrated a significant reduction in youth crime and recidivism 【157】【158】.

4. Skill Development and Rehabilitation:

Restorative justice programs focus on teaching conflict resolution, emotional regulation, and communication skills. These are vital for helping youth navigate their social environments more constructively and avoiding future offenses 【156】.

Evidence of Effectiveness:

- Reduced Recidivism: Youth conferencing programs consistently show lower reoffending rates compared to punitive systems. For example, evaluations of conferencing models in Northern

Ireland highlighted an 18% reduction in recidivism and high victim satisfaction rates【158】.

- Improved Outcomes for Victims and Offenders: Youth conferencing has been linked to high levels of victim engagement and satisfaction, with victims often valuing opportunities to participate in the justice process and support rehabilitation efforts【158】.
- Cost-Effectiveness: Restorative approaches, such as those implemented in Colorado and Surrey, are not only effective but also less costly compared to traditional justice systems【156】【157】.

Challenges and Recommendations:

- Consistency in Implementation: Ensuring quality facilitation and maintaining program fidelity across diverse settings is crucial.
- Cultural Relevance: Programs should account for cultural and community dynamics to resonate with participants.
- Support for Facilitators: Effective training and resources for facilitators are necessary to manage complex cases involving youth.

These findings underline the value of youth conferencing in restorative justice as a transformative approach to addressing juvenile offenses. Its focus on accountability, healing, and social reintegration highlights its potential to reshape how justice systems engage with young people.

Youth Conferencing in Restorative Justice (Continued)

Framework for Effective Youth Conferencing

To maximize the benefits of youth conferencing in restorative justice settings, a structured and supportive framework is essential. This section outlines the key components and principles that enhance the effectiveness of youth conferencing.

Key Components of Effective Youth Conferencing

1. Pre-Conference Preparation

- Individual Meetings: Facilitators meet with victims, offenders, and their families beforehand to set expectations, explain the process, and address concerns.
- Setting Ground Rules: Establishing norms for respectful communication ensures a constructive dialogue during the conference.

2. Facilitator Role

- Skilled facilitators guide the process neutrally, ensuring all participants feel heard and supported. Their ability to manage emotions and maintain focus is critical for successful outcomes.
- Facilitators also encourage active engagement from youth, helping them articulate their feelings and take ownership of their actions【156】【158】.

3. Participant Engagement

- Victim Involvement: Victims play a crucial role in expressing the harm caused and contributing to solutions. In Northern Ireland's youth conferencing programs, 69% of conferences included victim participation, significantly enhancing accountability and healing【158】.
- Family and Community Support: Families provide emotional backing, while community representatives bring broader perspectives on social responsibility.

4. Outcome Agreement

- Agreements typically include reparative actions like community service, apologies, or educational initiatives tailored to the offender's circumstances and the victim's needs.

- Programs such as New Zealand's Family Group Conferencing integrate culturally relevant outcomes to ensure meaningful reparations【156】【157】.

Principles of Youth Conferencing

1. Restorative Focus

- The process emphasizes repairing harm over punishing wrongdoing, creating opportunities for learning and growth.

2. Trauma-Informed Practice

- Recognizing and addressing the trauma that often underlies youth offending is essential for fostering empathy and emotional healing.

3. Accountability and Empowerment

- By actively participating in the resolution process, young offenders gain a sense of responsibility while victims feel empowered through their involvement.

4. Cultural Competence

- Conferences must respect the cultural backgrounds of all participants, integrating traditional practices where appropriate【157】.

Case Study: Northern Ireland Youth Conferencing Model

Overview

Northern Ireland's youth conferencing program integrates restorative principles within its justice system, aiming to reduce youth crime and reoffending.

Process

- Victims and offenders meet in structured conferences facilitated by trained professionals.
- Conferences result in agreements tailored to repairing harm, such as community service or education programs.

Outcomes

- Victim Satisfaction: Over 88% of victims who participated expressed satisfaction with the process and its outcomes.
- Recidivism Reduction: Youth conferencing participants demonstrated a significantly lower likelihood of reoffending compared to those processed through traditional juvenile justice methods.
- Community Involvement: The model actively involves communities, fostering collective accountability【158】.

Challenges in Youth Conferencing

1. Engaging All Stakeholders

- Ensuring voluntary participation from victims and offenders can be challenging, particularly in serious cases.

2. Resource Intensity

- Youth conferencing requires significant time and resources for preparation, facilitation, and follow-up.

3. Cultural and Social Barriers

- In diverse communities, navigating cultural differences requires tailored approaches and additional facilitator training 【157】【158】.

Recommendations for Improvement

1. Enhanced Training

- Providing facilitators with specialized training in trauma-informed care, cultural competence, and conflict resolution.

2. Data-Driven Approaches

- Regular monitoring and evaluation of youth conferencing programs to refine methods and improve outcomes.

3. Cross-Sector Collaboration

- Integrating restorative justice within schools, social services, and law enforcement to provide holistic support for youth.

4. Scalable Models

- Adapting successful programs like those in Northern Ireland and New Zealand for implementation in diverse contexts.

Youth conferencing in restorative justice holds transformative potential for addressing juvenile offenses by fostering accountability, empathy, and healing. Tailored frameworks that account for developmental, cultural, and emotional factors are critical for maximizing the impact of these programs on youth, victims, and communities 【156】【158】.

Chapter 18: Guidelines for Youth-Focused Conferences and Community Engagement

Youth-focused conferences in restorative justice prioritize developmental appropriateness, emotional support, and community involvement. Below are key guidelines for implementing such conferences effectively, along with practical examples.

1. Preparation and Readiness

Guideline: Conduct thorough pre-conference preparation with youth participants and stakeholders to ensure readiness.

Example:

In New Zealand's Family Group Conferencing model, facilitators meet individually with the young offender, their family, and the victim to explain the process, clarify expectations, and identify goals. This builds trust and ensures all parties feel emotionally prepared.

2. Create a Safe and Inclusive Space

Guideline: Ensure the conference environment is safe, neutral, and welcoming for all participants.

Example:

In Northern Ireland's Youth Conferencing Program, meetings are held in community centers or neutral spaces to avoid triggering environments such as police stations or courts. Facilitators also set ground rules emphasizing respectful dialogue.

3. Developmentally Appropriate Facilitation

Guideline: Use age-appropriate language and techniques to engage youth.

Example:

During youth restorative sessions in Colorado's Restorative Justice Council, facilitators use storytelling and role-playing to help young offenders understand the impact of their actions. This method caters to their developmental stage and builds empathy.

4. Victim-Centered Approaches

Guideline: Prioritize the needs of the victim, allowing them to express the impact of the harm and participate in determining reparative actions.

Example:

In the Surrey Youth Restorative Intervention program, victims are asked open-ended questions about their experiences, such as, "How has this incident affected you?" Victims are then empowered to propose reparative measures, such as written apologies or community service projects.

5. Encourage Accountability and Ownership

Guideline: Facilitate youth in taking responsibility for their actions and engaging in meaningful reparations.

Example:

In Minnesota's Restorative Conferencing Initiative, youth offenders work with victims to draft a restitution plan, which might include repairing damaged property or participating in community service directly related to the offense.

6. Family and Community Involvement

Guideline: Actively involve families and community members to provide support and reinforce accountability.

Example:

In Hawaii's Pono Kaulike program, family members participate in the conferencing process, offering insights into the young offender's background and collaborating on a reintegration plan that leverages family strengths.

7. Holistic Follow-Up

Guideline: Develop a plan for monitoring progress and providing ongoing support.

Example:

In New Zealand, Family Group Conferencing includes a post-conference follow-up to ensure agreements are honored. Facilitators and community mentors regularly check in with youth and families to provide additional resources, such as counseling or educational support.

8. Focus on Community Engagement

Guideline: Collaborate with local organizations to provide restorative opportunities and reintegration support.

Example:

In Roca, Inc.'s program in Massachusetts, youth are connected with local businesses for job training and mentorship as part of their restorative agreements, fostering long-term community ties.

9. Tailor Interventions to Cultural Contexts

Guideline: Adapt conferencing processes to reflect the cultural backgrounds and values of participants.

Example:

Māori Family Group Conferencing integrates tikanga Māori (cultural protocols) and the guidance of kaumatua (elders) to ensure the process aligns with the cultural values of the participants and their communities.

10. Professional Training for Facilitators

Guideline: Ensure facilitators receive ongoing training in trauma-informed care, youth psychology, and conflict resolution.

Example:
In Canada's Restorative Practices in Schools program, facilitators undergo annual training focused on developmental psychology and cultural competence to better address the needs of young offenders and victims.

Implementing these guidelines fosters accountability, healing, and reintegration for youth offenders, while also addressing the needs of victims and strengthening community relationships. Real-world examples, such as those in New Zealand and Northern Ireland, demonstrate the transformative potential of youth-focused restorative justice practices when implemented thoughtfully and inclusively.

Outcomes of Youth Conferencing in Various Justice Systems

Youth conferencing in restorative justice systems has demonstrated significant outcomes in various contexts, contributing to reduced recidivism, improved victim satisfaction, and positive social reintegration of young offenders. Research has underscored its effectiveness as a diversion strategy that emphasizes accountability and community engagement.

Key Findings from Studies:

1. Reduction in Recidivism:

- Studies, such as the work by Sherman et al. (2000), highlight that restorative youth conferencing can reduce recidivism rates. For instance, a comparison of youth participating in Family Group Conferencing (FGC) versus traditional criminal justice processes showed recidivism rates dropping by approximately 20-38% in various jurisdictions 【169】 【171】 .

- Research by Nugent et al. (2001) on victim-offender mediation (VOM) further noted a 32% reduction in reoffending rates among youth participants, emphasizing the restorative process's effectiveness 【170】 【171】 .

2. Victim Satisfaction and Empowerment:

- Victims involved in youth conferencing reported higher satisfaction rates (79% compared to 57% in traditional justice processes). They also expressed reduced fear of re-victimization after participating in restorative dialogues 【171】 .

3. Behavioral and Social Improvements:

- Programs like those evaluated in Minnesota showed offenders becoming more likely to comply with restitution agreements, reflecting an increased sense of responsibility and engagement with community values 【171】 .

4. Context-Specific Applications:

- In regions like Australia, conferencing models tailored for property crimes and violent offenses have provided nuanced insights. While outcomes for property crimes were mixed, significant reductions in recidivism for violent offenses demonstrated the model's flexibility and adaptability 【170】.

Examples of Effective Programs:

- Vermont Reparative Boards: These panels involve trained community members working with juvenile offenders to create reparation plans, achieving compliance rates above 80% and fostering community trust 【171】.
- New Zealand Youth Court Conferences: These conferences integrate Māori cultural practices, focusing on offender accountability, victim empowerment, and community restoration. They are recognized globally as a model for incorporating cultural elements into youth justice systems.

Challenges and Future Directions:

- Ensuring equal participation from victims and offenders, particularly in cases with power imbalances, remains a challenge.
- Scaling these programs requires addressing logistical issues like facilitator training and community buy-in.
- Long-term studies are needed to evaluate sustained impacts and integrate evidence-based improvements.

Overall, youth conferencing provides a promising alternative to traditional punitive systems by fostering meaningful engagement between victims, offenders, and communities, leading to measurable improvements in justice outcomes and social harmony.

CHAPTER 19

Adaptation of Restorative Practices in Virtual Formats

Virtual restorative justice practices have gained traction across Europe, especially during the COVID-19 pandemic, necessitating adaptations for online platforms. Four European countries—Finland, Belgium, Northern Ireland, and Estonia—offer diverse case studies showcasing the integration of virtual formats in restorative justice. These practices range from online victim-offender mediation to virtual restorative circles, highlighting innovative approaches to maintain restorative principles in digital environments.

Key Adaptations and Evidence:

1. Remote Mediation and Circles:

- In Finland and Estonia, virtual restorative circles addressed community conflicts exacerbated by isolation during the pandemic.

Sessions preserved key restorative elements like active listening and mutual accountability through structured online facilitation 【176】【177】.

- Belgium successfully implemented video conferencing for victim-offender mediations, allowing victims to voice their experiences while ensuring safety and accessibility.

2. Community Engagement and Accessibility:

- Northern Ireland piloted virtual family group conferences, focusing on youth offenders. These sessions demonstrated enhanced accessibility for participants unable to meet physically while preserving the restorative focus on accountability and dialogue.

3. Benefits:

- Reduced logistical barriers improved participation rates, especially for victims and communities in remote areas.
- Studies indicated increased flexibility and inclusivity, promoting diverse participation across socio-economic groups.

4. Challenges:

- Maintaining emotional engagement and trust in a virtual space was complex, particularly for sensitive cases.
- Technological issues, such as internet access, presented barriers for participants in rural or underprivileged regions 【176】【177】.

Lessons Learned:

- Training and Tools: Facilitators required specialized training in digital platforms and maintaining emotional sensitivity online.

- Hybrid Models: A combination of in-person and virtual sessions offered a balanced approach, addressing technological and emotional challenges.
- Policy and Frameworks: Aligning virtual practices with established restorative justice policies ensured credibility and effectiveness.

These case studies underscore the potential of virtual restorative justice formats to extend access and uphold restorative principles while navigating the challenges of digital adaptation.

Chapter 19: Analysis of Virtual Restorative Justice in Germany, France, Spain, and the UK

Virtual Restorative Justice (VRJ) has emerged as a versatile tool in European justice systems, with each country showcasing unique adaptations and challenges. A comparative analysis reveals the following:

Germany:
- Advanced Integration: VRJ, particularly "außergerichtlicher Tatausgleich" (ATA), is well-established for mediations in less serious crimes.
- Legal Clarity: Strong legal frameworks support VRJ, ensuring consistency in practice.
- Broad Access: Programs are accessible nationwide, bolstered by public funding and institutional support.

France:
- Victim-Centered Focus: VRJ emphasizes victim empowerment and is closely integrated with victim assistance services.

- Specific Application: Utilized mainly in cases of juvenile delinquency and minor offenses.

- Implementation Gaps: Broader systemic adoption remains inconsistent.

Spain:

- Emerging Use: Pilot VRJ programs are gaining traction, particularly in regions with targeted restorative efforts.

- Accessibility Issues: Digital and socio-economic barriers limit participation, especially in underserved communities.

- Localized Progress: Programs thrive in specific regions but lack a cohesive national strategy.

United Kingdom:

- Experimental Programs: Several pilot VRJ initiatives were launched during pandemic restrictions.

- Focus on Rehabilitation: UK models often integrate VRJ with offender reintegration efforts.

- Future Potential: Evaluations of pilot programs may pave the way for nationwide VRJ expansion.

Common Challenges and Opportunities:

1. Technology Access: Reliable technology and training are prerequisites for effective VRJ participation.

2. Legal Guidelines: Clear frameworks are necessary to ensure procedural integrity.

3. Victim Safety and Support: Mechanisms must prioritize victim welfare and agency.

4. Cultural Adaptation: Tailoring VRJ to local cultural contexts ensures inclusivity.

This analysis highlights the growing importance of VRJ in enhancing restorative outcomes across diverse justice systems in Europe. With sustained innovation and policy alignment, VRJ has the potential to significantly improve access to justice while maintaining restorative principles.

Insights and Challenges in Implementing Online Restorative Processes

Challenges and Solutions:

1. Technological Access and Literacy:

- Challenge: Participants may lack reliable internet or digital literacy skills.
- Solution: Offer pre-session technical support and provide devices or internet subsidies for those in need. Simplify platforms for ease of use.

2. Virtual Presence and Engagement:

- Challenge: Maintaining participant focus and ensuring active dialogue can be difficult in virtual settings.
- Solution: Train facilitators in virtual engagement techniques and use interactive tools like breakout rooms or polling.

3. Privacy and Security Concerns:

- Challenge: Risk of data breaches or privacy violations during virtual sessions.
- Solution: Use secure, encrypted platforms and establish confidentiality agreements with all participants.

4. Non-Verbal Communication:

- Challenge: Limited body language cues in virtual spaces may lead to misunderstandings.

- Solution: Encourage participants to verbalize emotions and train facilitators to identify and address misinterpretations.

5. Power Dynamics:

- Challenge: Existing inequalities may be amplified in online formats.

- Solution: Skilled facilitators should ensure balanced participation by addressing imbalances proactively and creating equitable speaking opportunities.

6. Legal and Ethical Considerations:

- Challenge: Variations in jurisdictional laws and ethical concerns about admissibility of online processes.

- Solution: Work with legal advisors to ensure compliance and develop ethical guidelines specific to online restorative practices.

Potential to Expand Restorative Justice Access:

- Broader Reach: Online formats eliminate geographical barriers, allowing participants in remote areas to access restorative justice.

- Flexible Scheduling: Virtual meetings accommodate diverse time zones and individual schedules, improving attendance and inclusivity.

- Cost-Efficiency: Online processes reduce costs associated with travel and physical venues, making restorative justice more accessible to underfunded communities.

- Anonymity for Safety: Digital settings can provide a buffer for participants who feel unsafe meeting in person, fostering open and honest discussions.

While challenges exist, online restorative processes offer significant opportunities to expand access, adapt to diverse needs, and uphold the principles of healing and accountability in a digital age.

CONCLUSION

The Future of Restorative Justice

Emerging Trends:

1. Integration with Technology: Virtual platforms are transforming restorative justice by expanding access, especially for remote or underserved communities. Innovations in secure and user-friendly technology will further enhance participation and inclusivity.

2. Data-Driven Practices: Increasing use of data collection and analysis to evaluate effectiveness, reduce recidivism, and identify best practices tailored to specific cultural or community needs.

3. Systemic Applications: Broader adoption in institutions beyond criminal justice, such as schools, workplaces, and community organizations, to address conflict holistically.

Future Directions:

- Global Collaboration: Sharing knowledge and frameworks internationally to adapt restorative justice to diverse cultural and legal contexts.
- Policy Integration: Strengthening support through legal frameworks and government-backed initiatives for sustainability and equity.
- Cultural Sensitivity: Expanding programs that honor Indigenous traditions and integrate restorative principles with cultural relevance.

Restorative justice is poised to evolve as a critical tool for building harmonious communities, addressing harm through healing, and fostering accountability across various sectors.

Supporting and Expanding Restorative Practices in Communities and Societies

1. Awareness and Education:

Promote restorative justice (RJ) through workshops, community forums, and educational programs in schools to build awareness and understanding.

2. Policy and Funding:

Governments and organizations can establish supportive policies and allocate funding for RJ initiatives in criminal justice, education, and community settings.

3. Training for Facilitators:

Develop certification programs for facilitators to ensure high-quality implementation across various sectors.

4. Community Engagement:

Encourage grassroots involvement by integrating RJ principles into local conflict resolution programs and neighborhood initiatives.

5. Research and Evaluation:

Invest in longitudinal studies to measure RJ's impact, identify best practices, and ensure continuous improvement.

6. Cross-Sector Collaboration:

Foster partnerships among justice systems, schools, businesses, and non-profits to create comprehensive RJ frameworks.

Expanding restorative practices requires a commitment to inclusivity, resource allocation, and cultural adaptability, ensuring that RJ principles are integrated into the fabric of societal interactions.

Final Reflections on the Transformative Impact of Restorative Justice

Restorative justice (RJ) transforms lives by fostering accountability, healing, and reconciliation. It empowers victims, allowing them to voice their experiences and feel validated, while encouraging offenders to take responsibility and actively work to repair harm. For communities, RJ strengthens social cohesion and promotes understanding by addressing the root causes of conflict. Across justice systems, schools, and societies, RJ demonstrates the power to reduce recidivism, rebuild relationships, and restore dignity. Its holistic approach offers a hopeful path forward, emphasizing humanity over retribution.

www.ingramcontent.com/pod-product-compliance
Lightning Source LLC
LaVergne TN
LVHW052225200926
848481LV00001B/214